Towards a full life:

Researching policy innovation for people with learning disabilities

David Felce, Gordon Grant, Stuart Todd, Paul
Ramcharan, Stephen Beyer, Morag McGrath,
Jonathan Perry, Julia Shearn, Mark Kilsby and
Kathy Lowe

OXFORD   BOSTON   JOHANNESBURG   MELBOURNE   NEW DELHI   SINGAPORE

Butterworth-Heinemann
Linacre House, Jordan Hill, Oxford OX2 8DP
225 Wildwood Avenue, Woburn, MA 01801-2041
A division of Reed Educational and Professional Publishing Ltd

 A member of the Reed Elsevier plc group

First published 1998

© Reed Educational and Professional Publishing Ltd 1998

British Library Cataloguing in Publication Data
A catalogue record for this book is available from the British Library

Library of Congress Cataloguing in Publication Data
A catalogue record for this book is available from the Library of Congress

ISBN 0 7506 3196 1   1002852464

Composition by Scribe Design, Gillingham, Kent, UK
Printed and bound in Great Britain by Biddles Ltd, Guildford and King's Lynn

Towards a full life

Contents

About the authors

David Felce BSc, MSc, PhD
Professor of Research in Learning Difficulties, Director, Welsh Centre for Learning Disabilities Applied Research Unit, University of Wales College of Medicine, Cardiff

Gordon Grant BSc, MSc, PhD
Professor of Cognitive Disability, School of Nursing and Midwifery, University of Sheffield, Sheffield

Stuart Todd BSc, PhD
Research Fellow, Welsh Centre for Learning Disabilities Applied Research Unit, University of Wales College of Medicine, Cardiff

Paul Ramcharan BSc, PhD
Research Fellow, Centre for Social Policy Research and Development, University of Wales, Bangor

Stephen Beyer PhD
Deputy Director, Welsh Centre for Learning Disabilities Applied Research Unit, University of Wales College of Medicine, Cardiff

Morag McGrath BSc, PhD
Research Fellow, Centre for Social Policy Research and Development, University of Wales, Bangor

Jonathan Perry BSc, MSc
Research Fellow, Welsh Centre for Learning Disabilities Applied Research Unit, University of Wales College of Medicine, Cardiff

Julia Shearn BSc
Research Officer, Welsh Centre for Learning Disabilities Applied Research Unit, University of Wales College of Medicine, Cardiff

Mark Kilsby BA
Research Officer, Welsh Centre for Learning Disabilities Applied Research Unit, University of Wales College of Medicine, Cardiff

Kathy Lowe BA, PhD
Research Fellow, Welsh Centre for Learning Disabilities Applied Research Unit, University of Wales College of Medicine, Cardiff

Foreword

Every once in a while, a book comes along which offers the potential for major development in social policies and, more importantly, renewal of our collective energy to improve the wellbeing of fellow citizens who are the focus of such policies. This is such a book.

The last twenty years in Britain have hardly been characterized by much government inspired effort to strengthen communities and ensure the inclusion of people most at risk of disadvantage: rather the reverse. Perhaps the single most notable exception has been the All Wales Strategy (AWS) for people with learning disabilities. Launched by the Secretary of State for Wales in 1983, the AWS was a visionary initiative to secure for people with learning disabilities in Wales a full life in the community – growing, living and working with their mostly non-disabled family, friends and associates. Moreover, unlike many other well-intentioned policies, this initiative was led from the centre, backed by significant extra public resources, sustained over more than a decade and made the subject of a major research evaluation – the basis for this book.

Published now, as the new government's transformational intent is beginning to take shape, the detailed assessment of the AWS which follows is important for three main reasons. First, whatever the progress in Wales since 1983, there is clearly still a long way to travel 'Towards a full life' for people with learning disabilities and their families. Indeed, as a more general review of the UK situation expressed (Mental Health Foundation, 1996):

Although people with learning disabilities are increasingly living in ordinary communities, many live in poverty, have little meaningful activity during the day, few friends and no real hope for change in the future.

This book offers an informed and persuasive agenda for a wide variety of people in Wales and beyond to re-engage with the challenges highlighted by this seemingly depressing diagnosis.

Second, people with learning disabilities are only a small part of the larger range of people who need the opportunities and support associated with what we call 'community care', itself the focus of recent major reform (the NHS and Community Care Act, 1990), and reflecting some of the same goals as the AWS. However, the evidence of this research is that these wider policies have been partly responsible for undermining the AWS and are themselves in need of serious reappraisal if their principled rhetoric is to be made more meaningful in practice.

Third, the new government has made tackling exclusion and inequality more generally a key element in its contract with the British people, as part of (re-)building a society based on interdependence and mutual responsibility. It requires new approaches to policy implementation which are outcome-oriented, holistic and delivered with the participation of all the people affected. Arguably the AWS was a modest forerunner of such ambition; it will be vital to learn from its strengths and weaknesses if wider disappointment is to be minimized. Again, this book is illuminating on the requirements for social changes which go beyond reshaping services to strengthening communities.

The genesis of policy promise

To understand the significance of the AWS, it is necessary to start further back. It was in the late 1960s, when many of us were enjoying growing affluence and new opportunities, that public attention was drawn to the very different experiences of some of our fellow citizens by the first of what was to become a series of institutional scandals: the mistreatment and exploitation of patients at Ely Hospital, Cardiff. It is a sad commentary on the concern of the rest of us that it took these scandals to highlight what with hindsight is only common sense: if large numbers of very vulnerable people are segregated for life in isolated and underfunded institutions, they are likely to be denied key aspects of the human rights others take for granted. However, the scandals of a generation ago did open up the possibilities for reform, even if far too slowly delivered.

As one example, the King's Fund itself decided in 1970 to make raising professional awareness and improving standards in learning disability services a major focus of its work. This was one of several such endeavours, but by 1978, when I joined the Fund as Community Care Director, it was already clear that something more radical was needed. The scandals had not stopped; indeed the Inquiry at Normansfield where my sister Pat was living had just reported. Significant investment, particularly through the NHS (but also in Social Services and later through Social Security funding of residential care) was being allocated but often to establish new building-based services which seemed likely to replicate some of the weaknesses in those they were replacing, even if in nicer physical environments. At Normansfield, the 'price' of the Inquiry was extra revenue and two million pounds of capital – at late 'seventies prices – to build 24-place 'bungalows' and a day centre in the hospital grounds. They stand now as empty monuments to inadequate imagination, following the hospital's closure in 1997. And throughout all this, the majority of adults with learning disabilities continued to have no option except to live in the parental home for most of their lives.

The King's Fund response to this situation, again allied with many other progressive interests, was to launch – and indeed sustain throughout the 1980s – the *An Ordinary Life* (AOL) initiative, as a focus for rethinking the opportunities and support which should be available to people with learning disabilities, producing evidence-based design guidance for the necessary supports to community living, mobilizing and assisting local change strategies and learning from experience (King's Fund, 1980). You might think that the goals of this initiative as expressed in its title were modest enough, but then, as now, really delivering on its core principles was a substantial challenge.

The initial focus for this work, partly because of the availability (and waste) of capital was ensuring the access of people, irrespective of the severity of their disabilities, to ordinary housing and support in the community (i.e. in your street and mine). This was followed by similarly detailed attention to family support, employment, leisure and the strategies required to achieve comprehensive patterns of opportunities and support to all the people in defined populations (Towell, 1987; Towell and Beardshaw, 1991).

In our early conferences to share this thinking and learn from local experiences across Britain, we had to look to Scandinavia and North America for practical demonstrations of well-developed supports to community living for people with severe disabilities (the achievements in Eastern Nebraska being a particular source of inspiration). We also regularly invited contributions (for example on person-centred planning) from leaders of the NIMROD project then taking shape in Cardiff (and itself one delayed response to the Ely Inquiry) which promised to be the first demonstration of comprehensive provision for a small population of precisely the kind we were advocating.

It was because of the AOL initiative and the NIMROD connection that I found myself, probably in 1981, invited to Cardiff to meet Tony Pengelly, a senior official in the Welsh Office, to discuss the prospects for an AWS based on the same philosophy. This began what has become a long-term interest in Welsh progress. A little later, as a member of the Department of Health's Research Liaison Group, I was involved in considering the proposals for AWS evaluation and became a member of the group which linked the Welsh Office to the research teams. From this I graduated to become a member of the Secretary of State's Advisory Panel for the Strategy (AWAP), serving for seven years through the period of 'high tide' and after.

Mr. Pengelly had recently transferred from defence procurement to health. This was fortunate in that he was probably both used to ordering and cancelling battleships and not weighed down by too much knowledge of conventional thinking in the field of learning disabilities. He was sure he could persuade Ministers to make the 'financial space' for a major initiative (surprising though it may seem now, from savings in acute hospital spending) and had himself been convinced of the importance of radical change in the lives of people with learning disabilities. He was, however, understandably concerned about feasibility. I was enthusiastic about the proposed direction of travel (and the model of value-based government leadership it would offer elsewhere in the United Kingdom!), but I also remember emphasizing the need to complement the central policy framework with real investment in strengthening the capacity of local agencies to deliver on the strategy, including its commitment to fully involving people with learning disabilities themselves. (Both these issues were to become recurrent themes of later discussions in the AWAP: AWAP, 1989; AWAP, 1991.)

Ministers were duly persuaded and indeed the Secretary of State himself identified with the launch of the Strategy in 1983 with its explicit commitment to the three AOL principles (Welsh Office, 1983):

- people with a mental handicap have a right to ordinary patterns of life within the community;
- people with a mental handicap have a right to be treated as individuals; and
- people with a mental handicap have a right to additional help from the communities in which they live and from professional services in order to enable them to develop their maximum potential as individuals.

Lessons from experience

So much is history. The book takes up the story of what happened to the AWS over the following 13 years, the evolving arrangements for local implementation and its impact in the lives of Welsh people with learning disabilities, their families and communities.

For what is probably the most sustained research programme ever mounted on a single social policy issue, the Department of Health had the good sense to commission two research teams, not just one in the North and one in the South, but also bringing different perspectives to this work. The Cardiff team works broadly within the 'applied behavioural science' paradigm, illuminating the relationships between structure, process and outcome in service development. The Bangor team consists mainly of sociologists, with a keen insight into the place of services in family and community life. Brought together here, these two perspectives offer a unique appreciation of what has been a complex undertaking. The book as a whole provides a mine of evidence, ideas and as yet unresolved questions for all those concerned, to do better in securing a full life for people with learning disabilities and their families.

In every area of the Strategy there are important findings. The AWS has achieved a major expansion in support to families, but have these new domiciliary supports been flexible enough to respond to the families' own views of what would be most helpful? It has spread through Wales a strong commitment to offering small homes to people in ordinary houses but have staff been sufficiently prepared to offer effective support to the tenants with more severe disabilities (and has policy still left untouched the question of when adults with learning disabilities should be given the opportunity to move out from their parents' homes)? The AWS has greatly widened the opportunities for day-time activities but have real jobs been too small a part of this and what can be done about the 'benefits trap' which continues to make employment a risky option for most people? There has been a related expansion in leisure activities but have these given too little attention to the requirements for people really to join in with other members of the community? It has taken a long time to build the significant consumer involvement in shaping and reviewing local services (for example there has been major growth in self advocacy groups) but how fragile are these arrangements to changing circumstances like the disruption engendered by local government reorganization? And so on.

In turn these detailed findings raise some fundamental questions. By the standards of British public administration, the AWS has been a bold and well-formulated initiative, pursued with considerable energy and persistence. Even so, it can still be asked whether it really has been a *strategy* in the specific sense of seeking to plan for the whole of the eligible population in each locality within some plausible resource envelope, bringing in all the relevant parties (for example, those responsible for the people and resources still in the traditional hospitals). Similarly, while the local agencies and their community partners have undoubtedly achieved a great deal, it can still be asked whether, notwithstanding the very clear statement of principles with which the AWS began, too much attention has been given to the role of *services* in securing the presence of people with learning disabilities in their communities and not enough to 'opening up' the opportunities and mobilizing the *natural supports* required for their more meaningful community participation.

Looking forward

Of course, in the words of Sheryl Crow, 'No-one said it would be easy.' Indeed the AWS architects envisaged from the outset that after the first decade we would still be travelling hopefully, rather than having arrived. Nevertheless, if an optimist is someone who sees the glass as being half-full, readers may conclude that the research teams are more inclined to a 'half-empty' assessment. The central importance of this book is that it offers all those involved the material for a review of what has been achieved and the ideas required to reinvigorate pursuit of the original AWS aspirations.

A key lesson from Wales, as elsewhere, is that fundamental change in the position of people with learning disabilities in our society cannot be achieved by government on its own, by local agencies and paid staff on their own, by people and their families on their own, or by communities on their own. Rather progress requires all to become partners in informed action.

One contribution now would be for the Secretary of State, perhaps in the context of the government's wider commitment to tackling social exclusion, to ask his officials and others involved to produce and publish a Welsh Office review of the implications of this research for future policy and strategy. For a long time in the research liaison group and AWAP, I encouraged officials to produce a regular account, not just of what research was being done and its findings, but also what impact these had on Welsh Office policies. It would be timely now to do this for the whole research programme so well summarized in this book.

Whether or not government takes the initiative, a second contribution would be for all the new unitary local authorities, with assistance from their professional staff and local partners, to review local performance against the findings here on the requirements for technical competence in service development. The expectation from this research must be that they will be able to identify ways of improving significantly the quality of life for people with learning disabilities and their families even within existing resources. At the same time there would be merit in scanning the government's wider policy agenda, for example on Welfare to Work, Lifelong Learning, the expansion of Social Housing, etc. to ensure, in the words of the title of another AWAP publication (1996) that these policies *Include me in!*

Third, people with learning disabilities, their friends and advocates may take heart from their achievements in recent years while keeping up the struggle to be properly heard and fully involved.

Fourth, all of us as citizens need to recognize our collective responsibility for building communities which welcome, and indeed benefit from the involvement of everyone – translating this practically into support for inclusive policies, in school, in work, at leisure, and our personal efforts to open up opportunities for people who are missing out.

Even better, if people in Wales are able to link these four contributions together, we should see not so much the dissipation of the AWS anticipated by the research teams but rather, in their words, a 'phoenix rising from the ashes'. Reading and reflecting on this book will be a good starting point for making it happen!

David Towell
King's Fund

References

All Wales Advisory Panel (1989). *Proposals for the Independent Review of Services for People with Mental Handicaps in Wales.* Cardiff: Welsh Office.

All Wales Advisory Panel (1991). *Consumer Involvement and the All Wales Strategy.* Cardiff: Welsh Office.

All Wales Advisory Panel (1996). *Include Me In!* Cardiff: Welsh Office.

King's Fund (1980). *An Ordinary Life.* London: King's Fund.

Mental Health Foundation (1996). *Building Expectations.* London: Mental Health Foundation.

Towell, D. (1987). *An Ordinary Life in Practice.* London: King's Fund.

Towell, D. and Beardshaw, V. (1991). *Enabling Community Integration.* London: King's Fund.

Welsh Office (1983). *All Wales Strategy for the Development of Services for Mentally Handicapped People.* Cardiff: Welsh Office.

Preface

This book represents the results of a sustained effort to evaluate the implementation and impact of a national policy to improve the quality of life and social standing of people with learning disabilities. It has kept a number of social scientists busy for about a dozen years. Most are represented among the authors to this book, but others such as Roger Blunden, Gerry Evans and Stuart Humphreys have moved on to other pursuits during the period. They made a significant contribution to the work which we report here.

Our research was funded by the Welsh Office and we are grateful for the support of the many individuals who have steered the All Wales Mental Handicap Strategy over the years and helped us specify our research brief and keep on task. In particular, we are grateful to Bob Woodward and Jane Jenkins who between them acted as research liaison officers throughout the period. The commitment shown by the Welsh Office to have its own policy and actions independently evaluated is worthy of special notice.

Our research would not have been possible without the collaboration of many hundreds of people in what were the eight counties of Wales; people involved in planning, managing, delivering and using the services which we have studied. We are grateful to them all. Staff have opened up their working lives to our scrutiny. People with learning disabilities and their families have given us access to almost every aspect of their lives. In return, we have sought to represent their experience accurately. Clearly, any errors are our own responsibility. We hope that the collaboration which this book represents helps to sustain the improvement in the circumstances and lifestyles of people with learning disabilities and their families which have occurred in recent years.

David Felce
Welsh Centre for Learning Disabilities Applied Research Unit
University of Wales College of Medicine, Cardiff

Gordon Grant
School of Nursing and Midwifery,
University of Sheffield, Sheffield

Chapter 1

Researching the All Wales Strategy

Most children and about one-half of all adults with learning disabilities in Wales, as in Britain, live in the community with their families (DHSS, 1971; Todd *et al.*, 1993). The All Wales Strategy for the Development of Services for Mentally Handicapped People (AWS) was launched in 1983 to 'correct the historic anomaly . . . which has left the bulk of public service provision in large and, for many, remote hospitals whilst the great majority of mentally handicapped people and their families receive little or no support in their homes where it is most needed' (Welsh Office, 1983, p. i). In adopting the principles first stated in the model of care chapter of the Report of the Committee of Inquiry into Mental Handicap Nursing and Care (DHSS, 1979), the AWS was the first national policy in the UK to make the commitment that people with learning disabilities have a right to experience normal patterns of life within the community, however severe their disabilities. The AWS was, therefore, widely seen as an important acceptance and legitimation by national policy makers of the views of those who had been advocating community-oriented reform for some time. Matched by a commitment to significant resource investment, this new alliance of policy makers and reformers was greeted as a major opportunity to develop a pattern of local services and support arrangements that would enable people with learning disabilities to 'receive the respect and equal opportunities that are their due' (Welsh Office, 1983, p. ii) and 'to blend with confidence in their communities' (Welsh Office, 1983, p. 6, para. 4.2vi).

The AWS signalled a wholesale restructuring of service provision and the development of new service processes at planning, management and operational levels. The Welsh Office, therefore, saw the need to evaluate its implementation. As a national experiment driven by a detailed central policy, centrally-dictated administrative arrangements and central finance, tracing how the recommendations of the AWS were translated into the development of services for people with learning disabilities and their families locally was important to evaluate. Moreover, many of the new arrangements advocated by the AWS were relatively untested. Evaluating whether new patterns of services resulted in new ways of working and improvements in the quality of life experienced by service recipients was equally important. The Welsh Office commissioned a broad and sustained programme of research into the AWS, mainly from two research centres, the Welsh Centre for Learning Disabilities Applied Research Unit and the Centre for Social Policy Research and Development.

This book summarizes the research undertaken by these two centres. It provides a stocktake of the service changes engendered, the effect the AWS had on service culture and its impact on the balance between new and traditional services. It addresses the question of what was achieved under the AWS both quantitatively and qualitatively. The major changes in service availability are described numerically at an all Wales level alongside further research which has depicted the processes within key service elements – the assessment of individual need and individualized service planning, the provision of residential services, the development of day services and the growth of support to families – and the quality of outcome achieved. In addition, the perspectives of various stakeholder groups throughout Wales are given, including providers or commissioners from health, social services, education and the independent sector, people with learning disabilities and their carers. Overall, the research provides an analysis of the achievements and missed opportunities of the AWS, its prospects for the future and the lessons which can be learned about the widespread implementation of policy-driven reform. It is in the light of these lessons that we set directions for practice and policy in the last two chapters.

Constructing a programme of research that could capture the potentially wide-ranging effect of the AWS across a country of just under three million people over a ten-year term presented a number of complexities, particularly as the research was funded through a series of short fixed-term grants. The issue of research perspective was at least partially solved by commissioning work from two teams who brought different approaches to the task. In addition, a strategy of mixing discrete studies of particular services with more global investigations of change was adopted to create a picture of changing service coverage and quality within the context of longitudinal development. Figure 1.1 illustrates the research conducted classified according to five broad themes.

One component of the combined research programmes has involved the implementation of the AWS as a policy initiative. Studies were conducted at the beginning and end of the research period, talking to service agencies and other stakeholders such as service user and parent representatives in the eight former Welsh counties. These parties were invited to comment on the introduction and evolution of administrative arrangements and planning mechanisms, the generation of priorities for action at different stages of implementation and the changing Welsh Office leadership and monitoring role.

A second strand of research has involved quantifying service change at a national level and reporting general trends in service development over the course of the AWS. Particular attention has been given to the development of multidisciplinary teams, family aide services, respite services, day services, supported employment and residential services. Linked to this effort was a four-year longitudinal study of the impact of service change on a random sample of individuals and their families in four demographically different, but collectively representative, districts. A further longitu-

Research Focus and Timing	Date 83 84 85 86 87 88 89 90 91 92 93 94 95	Policy Implemen-tation	Service Develop-ment	Service Organiza-tion	Participa-tion of users and families	Outcomes for users and families
Initial county response to the AWS	••••••••	Δ			Δ	
Planning and service development at a national level	••••••••••••••• •••	Δ	Δ			
Sample survey of AWS impact on users and families	••••••••••••		Δ		Δ	Δ
Survey of multidisciplinary community teams	•••••••		Δ	Δ		
Family carers: needs and perspectives	••••• ••••••••••••			Δ	Δ	Δ
Assessment of service packages	••••••••••••			Δ	Δ	Δ
Family aide services	•••••••••		Δ	Δ		Δ
Respite services	••••••		Δ	Δ		Δ
Housing services	••••••••			Δ		Δ
Traditional day services	••••••••			Δ		Δ
Alternative day services	•••••••		Δ	Δ		Δ
Supported employment	•••••••••••••••••		Δ	Δ		Δ
Advocacy	••••••••••		Δ	Δ	Δ	
Community care assessment	••••••	Δ		Δ	Δ	
Retrospective interviews in 8 counties	••••••	Δ	Δ		Δ	

Figure 1.1 The focus and timing of studies of policy implementation, service development, service organization, user or family participation and outcomes

dinal perspective has been gained by obtaining detailed accounts from parents who have looked after their adult sons and daughters with learning disabilities throughout the period and experienced whatever changes have occurred first hand. Research on consumer involvement has also attempted to track the emergence and impact of self-advocacy by people with learning disabilities and the participation of advocate and parent representatives in planning.

A third focus for the research has been the evaluation of service organization – the internal processes and working of particular service elements. Studies have been conducted on multidisciplinary community teams, individual planning and community care assessment, advocacy, family aide services, respite care services, staffed housing, traditional day services for adults and more recent day service alternatives, and the development of supported employment. An analysis of the combinations of services which people with learning disabilities and their families received (individual service packages) has attempted to examine how service development reflected assessed need and provided the basis of improved outcome.

Fourthly, the participation of users and their families in planning at county, local and individual levels has been a specific theme within several research areas. It has been a central focus of the research on advocacy and it has been an important facet of the four major surveys undertaken on the implementation and impact of the AWS. Finally, the fifth focus has been on the quality of outcome achieved within different types of service: family support services, staffed housing, traditional and alternative day services, supported employment and supported housing. This has been supplemented by case studies of people and the quality of their service support arrangements.

At one level, the research clearly refers to a specific policy initiative in the field of learning disabilities relevant to Wales. At another, viewed within the context which we summarize in Chapter 2, the AWS is but one example of a wider reform movement which has affected the developed countries in the world remarkably similarly (Hatton, Emerson and Kiernan, 1995; Mansell and Ericsson, 1996). The ideological and applied developments upon which the direction of reform encapsulated in the AWS were predicated were neither exclusive to Wales nor necessarily better represented in Wales. The direction of reform was also not unique to Wales but rather paralleled reform or, at least, aspirations for reform elsewhere. As a concerted statement of intent to achieve such reform, the AWS provides a case study of widespread relevance.

Finally, although the AWS has been a distinctive policy, Wales is not isolated from other policy developments which affect England and Wales or Britain as a whole. Most significant in recent years have been the global changes in the organization of health and social care embodied in the NHS and Community Care Act 1990 (NHSCCA). The AWS was to some extent seen as a forerunner of the arrangements put forward in the White Paper, *Caring for People* (Secretaries of State, 1989) which predated the Act. *Caring for People* and the AWS share the rhetoric of promoting individual choice and independence. Both sought to clarify responsibilities, giving local authorities lead agency status for social care provision. Both advocated the assessment of need and coordination of service arrangements on an individualized basis and both sought to change service culture away from a focus on congregate residential provision. Also, both implied a more varied and responsive range of service supports. The lessons from the AWS have clear relevance for the further pursuit and implementation of the Care in the Community policy in Britain. Analysis of the effect that the implementation of the NHSCCA has had on the progress of the AWS is also of general relevance. The NHSCCA introduced a variety of new arrangements such as the purchaser-provider split and systems of care management. Whether such developments have reinforced or cut across organizational and planning mechanisms originally set in place under the AWS – such as joint agency strategic planning, multidisciplinary person-centred service planning at the local level, and the involvement of service users and their families as equal partners – has considerable implications for the welfare of people with learning disabilities both within and outside of Wales.

The scope and style of this book

Our research has generated many research reports over the years. Articles have been submitted to scientific journals and have been published following peer review. Our intention has been to give a scientific account of the implementation and impact of the AWS and science requires many methodological details to be addressed. Although this book is about our research, it is not about our science. Details of the characteristics of research participants, research designs, measurement and the like have been omitted. Our purpose here is to bring the results of our research together in a single summary of main findings and to discuss their implications for policy and service development in Britain. Our intention has been to tell the story of the AWS and of our research without constantly interrupting it to describe research methods or related research findings. What is lost in detail we hope is made up for in readability.

Finally, a number of our studies have recorded the views of service users, parents or service staff about particular services, service processes or the AWS in general. We have incorporated some of these to illustrate points we have developed in the book. They often possess a directness of expression which captures and adds life to the general point we have been making. However, they should not be viewed as finely weighted qualitative evidence. Many are derived from Todd *et al.* (1997) but, for similar reasons to those we have explained above, we do not interrupt the flow of the text by repeated citation.

We begin by setting the AWS in the context of changing ideas over the course of the twentieth century.

References

Department of Health and Social Security (DHSS) (1971). *Better Services for the Mentally Handicapped*. London: HMSO.

Department of Health and Social Security (DHSS) (1979). *Report of the Committee of Inquiry into Mental Handicap Nursing and Care*. London: HMSO.

Hatton, C., Emerson, E. and Kiernan, C. (1995). People in institutions in Europe. *Mental Retardation*, **33**, 132.

Mansell, J. and Ericsson, K. (1996). Deinstitutionalisation in Britain, Scandinavia and the USA. *Tizard Learning Disability Review*, **1**, 1, 44–46.

Secretaries of State for Health, Social Security, Wales and Scotland (1989). *Caring for People: Community Care in the Next Decade and Beyond*. London: HMSO.

Todd, S., Felce, D., Beyer, S. *et al.* (1997). *Stakeholder Perspectives on the Course of the All Wales Strategy*. Cardiff: Welsh Centre for Learning Disabilities Applied Research Unit, University of Wales College of Medicine.

Todd, S., Shearn, J., Beyer, S. and Felce, D. (1993). Careers in caring: the changing situations of parents caring for an offspring with learning difficulties. *Irish Journal of Psychology*, **14**, 130–153.

Welsh Office (1983). *All Wales Strategy for the Development of Services for Mentally Handicapped People*. Cardiff: Welsh Office.

Chapter 2

The AWS in the context of developing post-war policy

The roots of any reform lie in the prevailing circumstances which precede it. The overwhelming emphasis during the three-quarters of a century leading up to the All Wales Strategy (AWS) was on institutional provision. The scale of such provision in England and Wales trebled in the 20 years between 1924 and 1944, from about 17 100 to about 51 200 places, and continued to increase subsequently to a peak of about 60 000 to 65 000 places, a level which persisted through the first three post-war decades (DHSS, 1971a, 1972; Ayer and Alaszewski, 1984). The 1971 White Paper *Better Services for the Mentally Handicapped* (DHSS, 1971a) introduced a number of targets for the development of alternative services but, as was recognized by the Secretary of State for Wales in his Foreword to the AWS, too little tangible progress was made in the decade which followed (Welsh Office, 1983). The imbalance in service investment and the inadequacy of care in the community due to the institutional legacy of past policy were seen as central problems for the AWS to address.

Changes in ideology

A rationale for the restriction of people with learning disabilities had emerged around the turn of the century with fears of contamination of the national genotype if people with 'low intelligence' were allowed to breed unhindered. In addition to other social grounds for admission, institutional provision at that time became a purveyor of segregation as an explicit and highly visible form of social control, irrespective of what might originally have been its more charitable or humanitarian aims (Scull, 1977). The tendency to build large institutions in isolated country areas resulted from a definite policy (Malin, Race and Jones, 1980). Exclusion from normal life was imposed and typical opportunities denied as a direct result of the concern to prevent procreation. Unsurprisingly, the extent to which institutional admission has been prevented and reversed has become a strong symbol of changed thinking about the place of people with learning disabilities in our society.

The movement towards reform derived from a variety of factors which were felt in various ways in much of the developed world. Changes in ideology underpinning provision for people with learning disabilities can be seen as part of a more generalized concern for social justice and equality of opportunity for many disadvantaged sections of society in the immediate post-war period. Promotion of social equality implied the right to developmental opportunity and the right to live in the least restricted way possible. The unacceptable standards of institutional care were exposed and normalization (Wolfensberger, 1972; Nirje, 1980), as described later in this chapter, emerged as a new guiding principle. Research provided a more accurate understanding about the abilities and potential of people with learning disabilities and a rationale of scientific enquiry permitted the first steps to be taken to providing alternative forms of care.

The fears of the eugenics period had moderated by the 1950s and earlier claims about the inevitable hereditability of low intelligence, the decline in the intellectual quality of the population and the link between low intelligence and criminality had been overturned (Sutherland and Cressey, 1960; Maxwell, 1961). The enforced separation of people with mild or borderline learning disabilities on the grounds of preventing genetic pollution became redundant. At the same time, research on the prevalence of learning disabilities and on social definitions of disability and labelling underlined the gross restriction of civil liberties which had been imposed on a group of people who, like so many of their peers not so labelled, could have lived ordinary independent lives in the community had they not been institutionalized. Protection of people from institutionalization without receipt of treatment in their own best interests and the safeguarding of access to life in the community were established as rights issues. In the USA, protection was pursued in the courts and through amendments to the constitution, establishing the rights to habilitation and to treatment in the least restrictive environment (Wyatt v. Stickney, 1972; O'Connor v. Donaldson, 1975; Haldeman v. Pennhurst State School and Hospital, 1977, 1985). In Sweden and Denmark, normalization was enacted as the guiding principle for the development of services for people with learning disabilities.

In Britain, the ideology which informed the foundation of the welfare state set a new context for defining the function of institutions for those people who clearly required service support and help (Scull, 1977). Incarcerating and segregating settings were now to be defended in terms of the benefits they brought to their users. Pragmatic concern for the economic burden to society of the rapid expansion of institutional provision between the wars had already surfaced and led to the adoption of a model of self-sufficient, economic community. The productive use of land and associated craft activities which stemmed from this emphasis created an account of constructive purpose to institutional life and a genuine asylum based on the evocation of village life from a supposedly more benign and caring era. The incorporation of the local authority colonies into the National Health Service, with its association of treatment and cure, completed the metamorphosis of the institutions from places of restriction of individual liberty and rights in the interests of society to places of treatment, protection and care for the benefit of their inmates.

Such a change in the image of the institutions was achieved against a backdrop which allowed their internal workings to be a closed arena.

However, gradually their functions and the realities of their organization became open to detailed scrutiny. Scandalous events and conditions in the institutions came to public attention and prompted a series of official inquiries, beginning with that into accusations of ill-treatment at Ely Hospital, Cardiff (DHSS, 1969, 1971b, 1978; House of Commons, 1974). These highlighted the significance of academic critique and journalistic coverage in developing an accurate description of institutional life (Goffman, 1961; Blatt and Kaplan, 1966; Morris, 1969; Oswin, 1971). The attention of politicians, service providers, the research community and the public was brought to the fact that institutions were often places of profound humiliation, which stripped individuals of human worth and dignity. This multiple exposure brought the basic issue of the duty of care owed to vulnerable members of society into the public domain. It also established the lack of legitimacy of the institutions which, despite vested interests and natural conservatism, they could never regain.

Open to such scrutiny, little was found to be defensible on therapeutic, habilitative or humanitarian grounds. The conditions for people with learning disabilities in institutional care were poor: the buildings were old, the settings impoverished, and the staffing insufficient and ill-qualified. Documented benefits for residents were few or non-existent. Despite being accorded the status of hospital after 1948, the long-standing involvement of medical personnel, and the specific registration in mental handicap nursing, the claim to being an appropriate treatment environment could not be sustained and other occupational groupings emerged to make claims of professional competency (Scull, 1977). The frame of reference for defining the underlying problem was shifting from medical to educational and for defining the nature of ongoing care from nursing to social support. Even at a simple level, the ability to represent mental handicap hospitals as centres of treatment excellence was undermined by their unfavourable comparison to hospitals for other client groups. Per capita revenue expenditure per person was lower. Professional staff were fewer and generally viewed as being of lower calibre and of lesser status than their colleagues in other services.

In support of the evolving definition of a condition which is now seen primarily as a learning disability, educational research was producing a new view about what could positively be achieved. Early post-war work demonstrated that a large proportion of adolescents and adults living in institutions were capable of employment in the community (O'Connor and Tizard, 1951, 1956) and that people with more severe disabilities could learn functional skills (Clarke and Hermelin, 1955). The application and dissemination of teaching expertise, stemming from the development of behavioural psychology in the USA, had a major impact in demonstrating the habilitation potential of people with severe or profound learning disabilities (Berkson and Landesman-Dwyer, 1977). The debate as to whether all people are educable, to the extent to which it still exists at all, is now centred only on a small proportion of those rare individuals who have the most profound and multiple impairments (Bailey, 1981; Kauffman and Krouse, 1981; Martin, 1981).

The new concern for the potential of people with severe learning disabilities, coupled with Bowlby's (1951) findings on the negative effects of institutional care on children, directed attention to whether the normal opportunities and conditions for development existed within institutions. Again, institutions were exposed for their barrenness, their lack of stimulation and normal social milieu and their detrimental effect on development (Lyle, 1959, 1960; Oswin, 1971). Moreover, their deficiencies were seen as inherent in their size, remoteness and professionalized structures (Jones, 1953; Rapoport, 1960; Goffman, 1961). In the 'small is beautiful' climate emerging in the late 1960s (Schumacher, 1973), the more radical analysis suggested that improvement would only come from a reinvestment of resources in a new pattern of services; it could not be achieved by reform within existing provision.

Early demonstration of possibilities: alternatives to institutions in the 1950s and 1960s

Although ideas were changing fast, the style and distribution of services remained fairly constant in the immediate post-war decades. The period was mainly significant for a number of research findings and service developments which began to question the monopoly claims of the institutional system as the only feasible mode of service delivery. Tizard (1960, 1964) responded to his own research on the educability of people with learning disabilities and to the growing criticisms of institutional care by moving a group of children from a hospital ward to a smaller, more homely setting, run on educational principles, and comparing their development to a similar group who remained in the hospital. The success of this early experiment was followed by further developments in Wessex, in which all children (and subsequently all of the more disabled adults) needing residential services from certain areas were accommodated in what were then considered to be small domestic settings in the community (Kushlick, 1967). Although soon to lose any significance in terms of the precise design of the services provided – they were an intermediate stage on the way to genuinely small homes – such reforms had an enduring importance in demonstrating that community care for those people with the most severe disabilities and difficulties then in institutions was possible. Evaluation showed that such services also brought benefits: in increased development, family contact and participation in everyday activity (Felce, Kushlick and Smith, 1980).

The proposition that a new pattern of community-based services was possible and desirable also drew support from research on the balance of institutional and family home care. Despite the emphasis on institutionalization in the early half of the century, epidemiological survey data from the early 1960s (Kushlick, 1970; DHSS, 1971a) when institutional provision was at its peak, showed that community residence was still the reality for the majority of children and a large proportion of adults being looked after by their parents or other relatives. In relation to children, it could not even be said that institutional care outweighed home care for those with the greatest disabilities or additional difficulties. Not all of such individuals were institutionalized; at least as many with similar characteristics remained in the family home (Kushlick, 1970). Tizard and Grad

(1961) showed the heavy price paid by families who maintained their child with learning disabilities in the family home: they were, on average, economically worse off, had fewer social contacts and were more prone to severe family problems than families who had placed their child in an institution. The basis for policy concerned with developing support services in the community was becoming established in parallel to the concerns surrounding residential provision. Policy in the shape of *Better Services for the Mentally Handicapped* (DHSS, 1971a) had discussed a range of ways of providing practical assistance in the home, but had set no explicit targets, focusing instead in setting norms for the built environment – day centres and residential services. However, by the time of the launch of the AWS, it was acknowledged that the 'inadequacy of care in the community creates a cycle of dependence on institutional care because this is often the only option open to families who can no longer cope on their own' (Welsh Office, 1983, p. i).

Developing ideas in the 1970s

The themes emerging in the post-war decades were further consolidated during the 1970s as a result of a continuing international critique and reappraisal of the status of people with disabilities in society and the role and function of services. The principle of normalization was incorporated in Denmark's 1959 Mental Retardation Act and expressed the aim of services as 'to create an existence for the mentally retarded as close to normal living conditions as possible' (Bank-Mikkelson, 1980, p. 56). Later, the definition was elaborated to include 'making normal, mentally retarded people's housing, education, working, and leisure conditions . . . bringing them the legal and human rights of all other citizens' (Bank-Mikkelson, 1980, p. 56). In similar vein, Nirje (1980, p. 33) defined normalization with regard to services in Sweden as 'making available to all mentally retarded people patterns of life and conditions of everyday living which are as close as possible to the regular circumstances and ways of life'. In both countries, these statements highlighted access to normal patterns of living for all, irrespective of level of disability: a commitment which was not found in Britain until stated as one of the determining principles of the AWS.

Although policy in Britain throughout the 1970s remained equivocal, couched in terms of maintaining 'as normal a life as . . . handicap or handicaps permit' (DHSS, 1971a, p. 10), developments in Scandinavia, particularly the use of ordinary housing for providing residential services, illustrated and added a further impetus to the extent of reform which would have to be undertaken if the large institutions were to be replaced. More radical reform messages were also coming from the USA. Wolfensberger (1972) had developed normalization as a more general social theory. Normative standards and equality on such issues as rights, individuality, development, social integration, culture-appropriateness, age-appropriateness, access to generic services and typical patterns of living were explicit benchmarks within this framework by which the impact of services on people's lives could be judged (Wolfensberger and Glenn,

1975). The spread in the UK of training based on Wolfensberger's conceptualization of normalization and, later, social role valorization (Wolfensberger, 1983) from the late 1970s onwards consolidated its influence on service reform in Britain (Brown and Smith, 1992).

Deinstitutionalization as a movement had gathered pace in the USA from the mid-1960s onwards (Lakin, Bruininks and Larson, 1992). Wolfensberger's work on the implications of normalization for the design of services had a direct influence on the Eastern Nebraska Community Office of Retardation (ENCOR). The ENCOR service attracted particular attention in Britain in the late 1970s as a model which provided residential services in genuinely small settings in ordinary housing (Thomas, Kendall and Firth, 1978). As in Scandinavia, the separation of specialist services from the medical model consolidated an alternative formulation of social care. The Wessex developments, proclaimed at the beginning of the decade as examples of domestic-style accommodation, were being criticized by its end as not going far enough (King's Fund, 1980a). The expanded remit for social services departments in *Better Services for the Mentally Handicapped* (DHSS, 1971a), which still only established them as equal provision partners with health, was deemed insufficient. Adoption of a new model of care and the transfer of agency responsibilities for provision and the training of staff were advocated (DHSS, 1979; King's Fund, 1980a). The King's Fund Centre's 'An Ordinary Life' initiative acted as a focus for the conceptualization, design and implementation of community services throughout the 1980s.

One component of this conceptualization was the notion of comprehensiveness. As used, for example in the first Wessex developments, the term 'comprehensive' referred to the fact that a service element, such as a residential service system, would cater comprehensively for all people needing that service without excluding people with particular levels of disability or additional difficulties. As ideas developed, the notion of comprehensiveness also came to stand for the range of service elements which might be developed to provide support to individuals and their families at various ages and stages of their lives: early counselling, pre-school provision, schooling, further education, day services, support for recreation, support during retirement, generic and specialist professional input, respite services, home support services, advice services and toy/resource libraries. Development of thinking about comprehensiveness in both senses can be seen in the 'Ordinary Life' initiative (King's Fund, 1980a) and in publications produced by the Independent Development Council for People with Mental Handicap (IDC, 1982).

The growing diversity of service elements reflected a variety of research and service developments occurring at that time. Attention to the developmental potential of the person with learning disability and the support needs of families complemented the theme of deinstitutionalization. The new optimism that development could be enhanced by more intense and well-targeted education saw expression in work on early intervention. Giving parents accurate information and constructive advice was emphasized. So, too, was gaining parental involvement to work in partnership with services. Approaches to enhancing the child's development and promoting effective parenting varied and included early counselling

(Cunningham, 1979), workshops for parents (Cunningham and Jeffree, 1975; Callias, 1976; Pugh, 1981), home teaching services (Cunningham and Sloper, 1977; Revill and Blunden, 1979), support for other family problems (e.g. Davis, 1985; Davis and Rushton, 1991), the organization of self-help and parent support groups (Pugh and Russell, 1977; Holland and Hattersley, 1980) and parent-to-parent support schemes (Hornby, Murray and Cunningham, 1987).

Special schools had come under the control of local education authorities in 1971 and begun the process of adaptation to mainstream educational principles and practices. Schooling for all and equality of opportunity was part of that agenda, including compensatory pre-school provision for children with profound and multiple disabilities (Sebba, 1980). Opportunity groups, based on the playgroup model but catering deliberately for a mixture of children with and without disabilities, provided normal developmental and social experiences (Lovell, 1973). Multipurpose resource centres provided activities for the child, opportunities for professional assessment and a source of multidisciplinary advice for parents (Brimblecombe, 1974). Moreover, the initial steps were being taken which enabled children with disabilities to attend local mainstream nursery schools and primary classes (Mittler, 1979).

Greater recognition was also being given to the need to support families. Some forms of support – counselling, assessment of the child and the availability of a spectrum of professional advice, and the support of other parents – have already been mentioned. A strongly voiced demand from parents over many years was the need for regular periods of respite (Grant and McGrath, 1990). This was seen as essential to renew parental energies, to develop other aspects of family life which might not find a place in the usual daily round, and to devote more time to other children in the family. Family-based respite schemes developed in the mid-1970s diversified the options available so as to avoid the confusing state of constant change highlighted by Oswin (1984) in her study of residentially provided short-term care. For example, other local families were recruited to offer temporary stays to the child with disabilities so that reciprocal long-term relationships between those providing respite and the child and their family could be encouraged. Providing help in the home was another form of family support which was also beginning to emerge. Domiciliary workers could offer an extra pair of hands at busy times, an escort service for the child going to school or to an activity in the community or a sitting-in service so as to allow the parents to go out during the day or in the evening (Shearer, 1978; King's Fund, 1980b).

NIMROD: a comprehensive local service in the community for people with learning disabilities

NIMROD – New Ideas for the care of Mentally Retarded people in Ordinary Dwellings – was one of the first attempts in the UK to bring together a number of elements of a comprehensive local service under one administrative entity, and to offer them to all people with learning disabilities in a defined geographical area (Welsh Office, 1978). It was provided between 1981 and 1986 to serve an area of about 60 000 total population in a part of Cardiff. Eligibility for the service was based on residence in that area, or previous residence if institutionalized. No-one was considered to be too severely disabled or behaviourally problematic to be extended the services offered by NIMROD.

The elements of the NIMROD service were to include intensively and minimally staffed residential accommodation in ordinary housing, individual and family support services, professional services, a volunteer service and an administrative base which also housed an information and resource library. Deinstitutionalization was not the sole aim of the NIMROD service, although it was envisaged that people from the area living in existing hospitals would have the opportunity to move to an appropriately staffed housing service. Such housing would also serve those in need living in the local community. In this, NIMROD was the first service to make the commitment to meet residential needs comprehensively in local ordinary housing. It was also the first service to offer a multiple set of supports to individuals and their families. This included the provision of Community Care Workers who could fulfil a number of functions: individual teaching in an extension of the Portage model (Revill and Blunden, 1979), support for parents in the home, support for individuals to do community activities outside of the home, or visiting supervision and support for people living alone or in unstaffed group homes. Family-based respite care was also to be arranged. The NIMROD Centre provided a base for the administrative and professional staff of the service, a meeting place for individuals and families, a resource library and a source of information.

Some services were outside the scope of NIMROD. Although the NIMROD professional team included social workers, a psychologist and a speech therapist, other specialist professionals, including doctors, physiotherapists and community nurses were provided by the pre-existing services in the usual way. So, too, were early childhood services, education services and day care for adults. Despite these limitations, NIMROD represented a significant practical attempt to respond to the new agenda of providing a comprehensive local service and to establish an infrastructure of complementary resources in one locality. Moreover, it recognized the need to coordinate service input for individuals and families by adopting and developing a system of regular Individual Planning (Blunden, 1980), which would act as a source of review for all service users in the area.

The NIMROD development received national attention as a pilot study in the implementation of community care throughout the early 1980s. It was also the subject of an extensive longitudinal evaluation, the results of which are summarized in Lowe and de Paiva (1991) and referred to here in later chapters. NIMROD had considerable influence on the development of the AWS, as it was based in Cardiff, part funded by the Welsh Office and had the involvement of researchers who were also funded by the Welsh Office and based in Cardiff. The work of the Working Party which led to the AWS began in December, 1981, the year NIMROD became operational. It reported in 1982 and the AWS was launched in March, 1983, by which time NIMROD was becoming an established service.

The All Wales Strategy

The AWS was introduced in 1983 and comprised 'bold and imaginative proposals for a radical new service in Wales' (Audit Commission, 1987, p. 8). It set out three guiding principles and emphasized that these applied to all people with learning disabilities, however severe their disability. People were to have rights to normal patterns of life within the community, to be treated as individuals, and to receive additional help from the communities in which they lived and from professional services in order to develop their maximum potential as individuals. The AWS set a direction for the development of a range of local services and gave explicit guidance on the form of some of the needed services. It was given an initial life of ten years, a period which was hoped to be 'long enough for a substantial impact on the volume and quality of services to be made' (Welsh Office, 1983, p. 38). It was envisaged that additional recurring resources totalling approximately £26 million per annum at 1983 prices would be committed to the development of services by the end of the first ten-year period. However, neither the initial term nor the additional funding on offer were sufficient to make the pattern of services envisaged by the Working Party comprehensively available throughout Wales (see Chapter 3). Evaluation of initial progress made under the AWS was integral to decisions about its future extension.

The AWS reflected the conceptualization of a comprehensive local service of its time; it was clearer in some areas than in others. However, it stated that 'the concept of new patterns of comprehensive services lies at the heart of the Strategy' (Welsh Office, 1983, p. 4, para. 4.1). Fundamental change in the nature of residential provision was central to its implementation and symbolic of the move from institutional to community services. The AWS was very clear: 'support staff should be available to help run a range of accommodation ... which caters for individual preference and ability ... in ordinary houses ... made available from local ... housing stock. This means that new purpose built hostels, hospitals or units should not form part of the new patterns' (Welsh Office, 1983, p. 6, para. 4.2v). The implications for existing hospital services were also recognized. Their role was to 'continue to care for ... mentally handicapped people until such time as community services have been successfully developed to take on the whole job' (Welsh Office, 1983, p. 8, para. 4.2xi).

Development of other community services stemmed from 'the preeminent importance of the family ... and the heavy burden on the family that is caused by stress and lack of help' (Welsh Office, 1983, p. 5, para. 4.2ii). For each person and family, the AWS sought 'full access without question to the same services, including health services, that are available to the rest of the community' (Welsh Office, 1983, p. 5, para. 4.2i). It wanted to help generic service providers to be more open to serving people who had traditionally been marginalized, a task it saw primarily as educational. It also sought to promote professional input and a greater network of community support: the availability of 'advice, support and teaching from social workers, community nurses, care assistants, other parents and voluntary organisations ... as and when required' (Welsh Office, 1983, p. 5, para. 4.2ii). In addition, 'short-term relief should be

readily available ... (and) locally based, flexible and capable of responding to emergencies, e.g. the illness of a parent' (Welsh Office, 1983, p. 5,
para. 4.2iii). Help to families was also to include 'a range of domiciliary
support ...(such as) family aid (sic) services' (Welsh Office, 1983, p. 7,
para. 4.2vii).

The AWS was less specific on education and day services. It endorsed
section two of the 1981 Education Act and sought 'the maximum possible access and integration with ordinary education facilities' (Welsh
Office, 1983, p. 7, para. 4.2ix) but without giving any guidance on
minimum targets or reasonable achievement. In keeping with the times,
it did not set a clear vision for day services for adults. Existing segregated
and centralized day services (adult training centres, social education
centres and the like) were seen as the primary source of day provision,
a situation which would continue into the future for many service users.
The AWS recognized some of the inherent problems in the model: such
centres 'provide an all-purpose service which is not conducive to the
promotion of independence or responsive to individual needs' (Welsh
Office, 1983, p. 7, para. 4.2viii). It therefore sought a broadening of the
range of options available: 'more appropriate forms of constructive activity need to be developed, (and) there needs to be imaginative developments ... to create employment opportunities and ... better career
guidance and work preparation courses' (Welsh Office, 1983, p. 7, para.
4.2viii). The AWS, therefore, called for innovation and the development
of diversity; it did not provide a clear direction towards a new pattern of
local day services.

Ultimately, the AWS sought to affect the place which people with learning disabilities had within society, substituting a life apart or on the
margins for one of full involvement. 'Provision for recreational and social
opportunities' was urged 'in parallel with dwellings' and success was seen
as dependent 'on the involvement of the general public ... (which) service
providers should place special emphasis on sensitive and imaginative
efforts to develop' (Welsh Office, 1983, p. 6, para. 4.2vi). Establishing
neighbourhood networks of voluntary help was also seen as desirable.

Finally, consistent with its individual focus and with the emerging
notion that effective support required the concerted mustering of a
variety of complementary services and community resources, the AWS
advocated the widespread introduction of individual planning. 'Staff
should work together with mentally handicapped people and their
families in the preparation, implementation and regular review of individual programme plans for the development of the mentally handicapped
person' (Welsh Office, 1983, p. 7, para. 4.2x). Coordination of the individual planning system was to be done by multidisciplinary professional
teams established locally. Each person with a learning disability was to
have a nominated keyworker. In addition to providing specialist professional input, the multidisciplinary team was to act as a single point of
contact for individuals, families and generic services alike, and be a focus
for local planning and the collation of information on individual need
which could be fed into the county planning system. Involvement of the
consumer – the individual with a learning disability and the family – in
the decisions surrounding the provision and review of services was an

avowed commitment. Such involvement was mirrored by a similar commitment to representation in local and county planning forums. Both commitments were an attempt to establish a radical mechanism to make needs-led and individually focused service provision a reality.

The AWS, therefore, set a framework for the administrative arrangements to be followed. It put forward a model planning system in which representatives of consumers and all relevant agencies met at county level to produce plans. It was made plain that the Welsh Office would expect people with learning disabilities, their families and voluntary sector representatives to be widely consulted about the content of plans and have a permanent place in the planning and monitoring of services. Local authority social services were given 'lead agency' status in recognition of the shift from the medical model to a social care definition of the prime task to be achieved. This clearly signalled the eventual disposition of resource investment in the area. The AWS envisaged that the expenditure tied up in traditional services would be liberated as new and better services were developed and that this would be available for reinvestment. Increased revenue could also come from local authorities. However, the allocation of additional funding as part of the AWS recognized that the redevelopment and growth in the scope of services was of such a scale that it would need to be largely funded by the Welsh Office. This funding was not allocated through the Rate, subsequently Revenue, Support Grant. Legislation enabled it to be allocated via 'ring fenced' grants to local authorities for the development of specific agreed proposals. The financial control vested in the Welsh Office gave the officers overseeing the implementation of the AWS the ability to vet plans and ensure that AWS allocations were spent in developing services consistent with AWS principles. A particular intention was to invest a third of the available revenue in two 'Vanguard Areas' which were to achieve more rapid progress. The selected areas would spearhead change, test service models and processes and generate experience which could be disseminated to the rest of Wales.

Finally, in addition to the thrust of fundamental reform, the AWS contained recommendations to improve existing services. It called for operational policies and working practices in local authority hostels and adult training centres to be reviewed so as to reduce institutional and overprotective patterns of care and promote a greater attention to individual need. Staff were seen as an important resource. Counties were asked to review the training needs of staff and arrange multidisciplinary courses on a joint agency basis, bringing staff together to equip them with the skills and attitudes for the new tasks ahead. Staff ratios in day services were to be increased to allow more time for staff training. Recruitment policies were to be revised to reflect AWS objectives. The future of the hospitals was not stated explicitly, although it was clear that their role would reduce as community services were developed to take their place. The Welsh Office did ask for an end to hospital admissions as soon as development in any area permitted this to occur. The AWS also saw the need to improve levels of nursing staff and conditions in hospitals generally out of concern for the quality of life of those who would inevitably continue to live in the hospitals for some time.

The context and scope of the AWS

The reputation of services for people with learning disabilities had been severely dented by the occurrences at Ely Hospital which led to the first official inquiry in Britain into conditions and treatment experienced by people with learning disabilities in institutional care (DHSS, 1969). Even though other inquiries were soon to follow, the Ely scandal had a profound effect and it is possible to trace a chain of events throughout the next decade which stemmed from it. It is also important to realize that forward thinking on learning disability services was a contested arena; there was not a consensus on the direction or content of what was needed. The hospital scandals underscored a certainty that something was needed to improve service standards but agreement over what was required was lacking.

Arguments about the extent of fundamental reform tended to divide on agency lines. For example, as is described in greater detail in Chapter 6, South Glamorgan Health Authority issued alternative, less radical proposals prior to the NIMROD development. The decision to locate operational and management responsibilities for NIMROD with the local authority social services department was probably related to continuing health service resistance to relinquishing the hospital model. Further health service initiated proposals at the turn of the decade to redevelop hospital sites throughout Wales similarly did not find sufficient support in the Welsh Office. The AWS was thus launched against an agreed backdrop that change was essential but without unanimity of view. In particular, health services appeared reluctant to embrace fundamental reform. It is understandable, therefore, that the Welsh Office looked to put the developmental emphasis in the community and backed social services departments as the primary implementation arm.

The service models advocated by the AWS were relatively untried. So, too, were planning processes which apparently gave parents and service users greater power. While resistance may have been greater on the health side, traditional attitudes and support of the status quo were also to be found in local authorities and their staff and representative groups. In addition, some relatives of people with learning disabilities advocated retention and improvement of existing services rather than their replacement by what could be seen as unrealistic proposals. Recognition of this atmosphere of claim and counterclaim and of debate rather than certainty is important to the understanding of the AWS as an experiment.

References

Audit Commission (1987). *Community Care: Developing Services for People with a Mental Handicap. Occasional Papers No. 4.* London: HMSO.

Ayer, S. and Alaszewski, A. (1984). *Community Care and the Mentally Handicapped.* London: Croom-Helm.

Bailey, J. S. (1981). Wanted: a rational search for the limiting conditions of habilitation. *Analysis and Intervention in Developmental Disabilities,* **1**, 45–52.

Bank-Mikkelson, N. E. (1980). Denmark. In: *Normalisation, social integration and community services.* (R. J. Flynn and K. E. Nitsch, eds) pp. 51–70. Baltimore: University Park Press.

Berkson, G. and Landesman-Dwyer, S. (1977). Behavioral research on severe and profound mental retardation (1955–1974). *American Journal of Mental Deficiency*, **81**, 428–454.

Blatt, B. and Kaplan, F. (1966). *Christmas in Purgatory*. Boston: Allyn and Bacon.

Blunden, R. (1980). *Individual Plans for Mentally Handicapped People: A Draft Procedural Guide*. Cardiff: Mental Handicap in Wales Applied Research Unit, University of Wales College of Medicine.

Bowlby, E. J. M. (1951). *Child Care and the Growth of Love*. Geneva: WHO.

Brimblecombe, F. (1974). Exeter project for handicapped children. *British Medical Journal*, **4**, 706–709.

Brown, H. and Smith, H. (1992). *Normalisation: A Reader for the Nineties*. London: Routledge.

Callias, M. (1976). Parent group training: An NSMHC experiment. *Parents' Voice*, **26**, 5–7.

Clarke, A. D. B. and Hermelin, B. F. (1955). Adult imbeciles: their abilities and trainability. *Lancet*, **ii**, 337–339.

Cunningham, C. (1979). Parent counselling. In: *Tredgold's Mental Retardation*, 12th edn. (M. Craft, ed.) pp. 313–318. London: Balliere Tindall.

Cunningham, C. C. and Jeffree, D. M. (1975). The organisation and structure of workshops for mentally handicapped children. *Bulletin of the British Psychological Society*, **28**, 405–411.

Cunningham, C. and Sloper, P. (1977). Down's syndrome infants: a positive approach to parent and professional collaboration. *Health Visitor*, **50**, 2, 32–37.

Davis, H. (1985). Counselling parents of children who have intellectual disabilities. *Early Child Development and Care*, **22**, 19–35.

Davis, H. and Rushton, R. (1991). Counselling and supporting parents of children with developmental delay: a research evaluation. *Journal of Mental Deficiency Research*, **35**, 89–112.

Department of Health and Social Security (DHSS) (1969). *Report of the Committee of Inquiry into the Allegations of Ill-treatment of Patients and Other Irregularities at the Ely Hospital, Cardiff*. London: HMSO.

Department of Health and Social Security (DHSS) (1971a). *Better Services for the Mentally Handicapped*. London: HMSO.

Department of Health and Social Security (DHSS) (1971b). *Report of the Farleigh Hospital Committee of Enquiry*. London: HMSO.

Department of Health and Social Security (DHSS) (1972). *Census of Mentally Handicapped Patients in Hospital in England and Wales at the End of 1970*. London: HMSO.

Department of Health and Social Security (DHSS) (1978). *Report of the Committee of Inquiry into Normansfield Hospital*. London: HMSO.

Department of Health and Social Security (DHSS) (1979). *Report of the Committee of Inquiry into Mental Handicap Nursing and Care*. London: HMSO.

Felce, D., Kushlick, A. and Smith, J. (1980). An overview of the research on alternative residential facilities for the severely mentally handicapped in Wessex. *Advances in Behaviour Research and Therapy*, **3**, 1–4.

Goffman, E. (1961). *Asylums*. New York: Doubleday.

Grant, G. and McGrath, M. (1990). Need for respite-care services for caregivers of persons with mental retardation. *American Journal on Mental Retardation*, **94**, 638–648.

Haldeman v. Pennhurst State School and Hospital, 446 F. Supp. 1925 (E. D. Pa. 1977).

Haldeman v. Pennhurst State School and Hospital, Civil Action No. 74–1345. Final settlement agreement (E. D. Pa. 1985).

Holland, J. M. and Hattersley, J. (1980). Parent support groups for the families of mentally handicapped children. *Child: Care, Health and Development*, **6**, 165–173.

Hornby, G., Murray, R. and Cunningham, C. (1987). *Parent to Parent: Leaders Training Manual*. Manchester: Hester Adrian Research Centre, University of Manchester.

House of Commons (1974). *Report of the Committee of Inquiry into South Ockenden Hospital*. London: HMSO.

Independent Development Council for People with Mental Handicap (IDC) (1982). *Elements of a Comprehensive Local Service for People with Mental Handicap*. London: King's Fund Centre.

Jones, M. (1953). *The Therapeutic Community*. New York: Basic Books.

Kauffman, J. M. and Krouse, J. (1981). The cult of educability: searching for the substance of things hoped for; the evidence of things not seen. *Analysis and Intervention in Developmental Disabilities*, **1**, 53–60.

King's Fund (1980a). *An Ordinary Life: Comprehensive Locally-based Residential Services for Mentally Handicapped People*. London: King's Fund Centre.

King's Fund (1980b). *Stress and the Caring Relative. Crossroads Schemes for Mentally Handicapped People*. London: King's Fund Centre.

Kushlick, A. (1967). A method of evaluating the effectiveness of a community health service. *Social and Economic Administration*, **1**, 29–48.

Kushlick, A. (1970). Residential care for the mentally subnormal. *Royal Society of Health Journal*, **90**, 255–261.

Lakin, K. C., Bruininks, R. H. and Larson, S. A. (1992). The changing face of residential services. In: *Mental retardation in the Year 2000*. (L. Rowitz, ed.) pp. 197–247. Berlin: Springer-Verlag.

Lovell, L. (1973). The Yeovil Opportunity Group: a playgroup for multiply handicapped children. *Physiotherapy*, **59**, 8, 251–253.

Lowe, K. and de Paiva, S. (1991). *NIMROD: an overview*. London: HMSO.

Lyle, J. G. (1959). The effect of an institution environment upon the verbal development of imbecile children: I Verbal intelligence. *Journal of Mental Deficiency Research*, **3**, 122–128.

Lyle, J. G. (1960). The effect of an institution environment upon the verbal development of imbecile children: III The Brooklands residential unit. *Journal of Mental Deficiency Research*, **4**, 14–22.

Malin, N., Race, D. and Jones, G. (1980). *Services for the Mentally Handicapped in Britain*. London: Croom Helm.

Martin, R. (1981). All handicapped children are educable. *Analysis and Intervention in Developmental Disabilities*, **1**, 5–11.

Maxwell, J. (1961). *The Level and Trend of National Intelligence*. London: University of London Press.

Mittler, P. (1979). *People Not Patients: Problems and Policies in Mental Handicap*. London: Methuen.

Morris, P. (1969). *Put Away*. London: Routledge and Kegan Paul.

Nirje, B. (1980). The normalization principle. In: *Normalization, Social Integration and Community Services*. (R. J. Flynn and K. E. Nitsch, eds) pp. 31–49. Baltimore: University Park Press.

O'Connor, N. and Tizard, J. (1951). Predicting the occupational adequacy of certified mental defectives. *Occupational Psychology*, **25**, 205–211.

O'Connor, N. and Tizard, J. (1956). *The Social Problem of Mental Deficiency*. London: Pergamon.

O'Connor v. Donaldson, 422 U. S. 563 (1975).

Oswin, M. (1971). *The Empty Hours*. London: Allen Lane.

Oswin, M. (1984). *They Keep Going Away*. London: King's Fund Publishing Office.

Pugh, G. (1981). *Parents as Partners*. London: National Children's Bureau.

Pugh, G. and Russell, P. (1977). *Shared Care*. London: National Children's Bureau.

Rapoport, N. N. (1960). *Community as Doctor*. London: Tavistock.

Revill, S. and Blunden, R. (1979). A home training service for pre-school developmentally handicapped children. *Behaviour Research and Therapy*, **17**, 207–214.

Schumacher, E. F. (1973). *Small is Beautiful: a Study of Economics as if People Mattered*. London: Blond and Briggs.

Scull, A. T. (1977). *Decarceration: Community Treatment and the Deviant*. London: Prentice-Hall.

Sebba, J. (1980). *A System for Assessment and Intervention for Preschool Profoundly Retarded Multiply Handicapped Children*. Manchester: Hester Adrian Research Centre, University of Manchester.

Shearer, A. (1978). *A Community Service for Mentally Handicapped Children: Barnardo's Chorley Project*. Barnardo Social Work Papers No. 4. London: Barnardo's.

Sutherland, E. H. and Cressey, D. R. (1960). *Principles of Criminology*. Chicago: Lippincott.

Thomas, D., Kendall, A. and Firth, H. (1978). *ENCOR – a Way Ahead*. London: Campaign for Mentally Handicapped People.

Tizard, J. (1960). Residential care of mentally handicapped children. *British Medical Journal*, **1**, 1041–1043.

Tizard, J. (1964). *Community Services for the Mentally Handicapped*. London: Oxford University Press.

Tizard, J. and Grad, J. C. (1961). *The Mentally Handicapped and their Families*. London: Oxford University Press.

Welsh Office (1978). *NIMROD: Report of a Joint Working Party on the Provision of a Community Based Mental Handicap Service in South Glamorgan*. Cardiff: Welsh Office.

Welsh Office (1983). *All Wales Strategy for the Development of Services for Mentally Handicapped People*. Cardiff: Welsh Office.

Wolfensberger, W. (1972). *Normalisation: the Principle of Normalisation in Human Services*. Toronto: National Institute on Mental Retardation.

Wolfensberger, W. (1983). Social role valorization: a proposed new term for the principle of normalisation. *Mental Retardation*, **21**, 234–239.

Wolfensberger, W. and Glenn, L. (1975). *Programme Analysis of Service Systems: Handbook and Manual (3rd edn)*. Toronto: National Institute on Mental Retardation.

Wyatt v. Stickney, 344 F. Supp. 387 (M. D. Ala. 1972).

Chapter 3

Analysis of the policy and its implementation

The AWS received an enthusiastic welcome on its launch from those seeking community-oriented reform and it has maintained a high public reputation since. For the first time in Britain, contemporary service philosophy and broad service development aims were combined in a single national policy and backed by the promise of significant additional resources. The comprehensive scope of reform, although challenging, was seen as a necessary prelude to the changes in lifestyle envisaged for people with learning disabilities. Recognized as a radical policy, it provided a reference point and was seen as a testbed for the wider community care reforms which followed. For example, the Association of County Councils took the AWS as a model in responding to Sir Roy Griffiths' (1988) proposals on community care by suggesting that . . . 'more progress would, however, be possible within a fully planned, cost-effective community care framework. Such a framework is being developed and applied in Wales through the All Wales Strategies for mental handicap and mental illness. The major elements of Sir Roy Griffiths' recommendations have effectively been pilot tested in Wales' (Association of County Councils, 1989, pp. 1–2). This chapter reviews the factors which underpinned the reputation of the AWS as a well-formulated policy. It examines the extent to which that reputation was justified and explores problems which were encountered during its implementation. It begins by setting the context in which the AWS was launched by briefly summarizing prior policy and seeking to explain why an emerging focus on community care had not been pursued more vigorously.

Problems in policy prior to the AWS

As was shown in Chapter 2, the AWS incorporated a principled approach to service provision and based its prescription of needed service supports on ideas and practices emerging at that time. In this way, it signalled a clear departure from the past. The transition from institutional to community-oriented thinking was not new, but British policy had previously been reluctant to relinquish institutional service models, a step which was only finally taken after the succession of scandal enquiries between 1969 and

1978 had removed their last vestiges of legitimacy. In 1988, Griffiths observed that 'at the centre, community care has been talked of for thirty years and in few areas can the gaps between political rhetoric and policy on the one hand, or between policy and reality in the field on the other hand have been so great' (Griffiths, 1988, p. iv). Webb and Wistow (1982) had reached a similar conclusion, pointing to the government's primary failings in 'bridging the gaps between broad statements of policy and the detailed guidance of production processes and the work of practitioners, and between services, or output policies, and resource policies' (p. 28).

Such criticisms are justified by a failure in policy to relate the nature of service delivery to desired outcomes and to develop a commitment to the necessity of wholesale change. Commentators have pointed to the inadequate exposition of the values underlying the concept of community care and to insufficient clarity in the outcomes which the government wished to deliver for disadvantaged people through such a policy (e.g. Walker, 1984). Although there is merit in such an analysis, the earlier national policy *Better Services for the Mentally Handicapped* (DHSS, 1971, Chapter 3) did contain a detailed specification of general principles. Therefore, it was not necessarily a lack of clarity in or agreement over the goals to be achieved which was the problem, but the failure to face the inconsistency between the existing nature of service provision and desired outcome. *Better Services* continued to focus on physical settings – hospital, hostel and day centre provision – and maintained the idea that a service network based on such provision, albeit with improvements in practice, could be of high quality and deliver outcomes consistent with its stated principles. In this respect, policy continued to echo the past. The 1957 Royal Commission on the Law Relating to Mental Illness and Mental Deficiency had concluded that 'it is not now generally considered in the best interests of patients who are fit to live in the general community that they should be in large or remote institutions such as the present mental and mental deficiency hospitals' (Ministry of Health, 1957, p. 17, para. 46). However, the Commission's vision of community care was founded on provision of a range of centres offering training, occupation or social activity and residential accommodation in private, voluntary and local authority homes and hostels.

Those who advocated more fundamental change were viewed as the radical fringe (e.g. Campaign for the Mentally Handicapped (CMH), 1972). Policy for people with learning disabilities and other client groups recognized a range of ways of helping people live in the community, but the notion of progressive patient care, whereby those with the greatest disabilities entered a more specialist world, provided a generic defence of institutional provision. *Better Services*, itself, mentioned the need of families for practical assistance including home helps, domiciliary nursing, laundry services, sitters-in, play centres, day nurseries, youth clubs and respite during emergencies or holidays, but no targets were set in these areas. Neither were such services highlighted in planning exercises held with local authorities in 1972 (DHSS, 1972). *Health and Welfare* (Ministry of Health, 1963) provided a list of services to promote care in the community for elderly people including: provision of suitably adapted ordinary housing, warden supervised housing, home helps, laundry services, provision of cooked meals, chiropody at home, friendly visiting and the availability of additional transport to help people attend social events. Many of these ideas were also taken up for younger people with disabilities in the Chronically Sick and Disabled Persons Act, 1970. However, policy throughout the 1970s was not incisive and continued to straddle community-oriented and institutional positions.

The blurring of distinctions which was to be found in policy in this period echoed the Seebohm Report (1968) which addressed the organization of personal social services. Seebohm recognized the importance of seeking a definition of community which was based on networks of social support between people. Hence, the report stated that, 'although traditionally the idea of community has rested upon geographical locality, and this remains an important aspect of many communities, today different members of a family may belong to different communities of interest as well as the same neighbourhood. The notion of community implies the existence of a network of social relationships, which amongst other things ensure mutual aid and give those who experience it a sense of well-being' (para. 476). However, at the same time, it promoted a definition of community that included segregated provision which would continue to cut people off from communities of interest: 'community care has come to mean treatment and care outside hospitals or residential homes. This limitation of the term is unfortunate, for such institutions are part of the community' (p. 107). Such thinking continued to resonate. For example, the policy, *The Way Forward,* suggested that the term 'community' covered a range of provision including community hospitals, hostels, day hospitals, residential homes, day centres and domiciliary support (DHSS, 1977, p. 9).

Confusion in the conceptualization of required service change made it difficult for the government to be specific about the quality of provision and its links to outcome. The reluctance to generate a sufficiently radical reform agenda consistent with the articulated principles removed the ability of government to establish effective control over policy implementation (Webb and Wistow, 1982). *Better Services* had set clear service provision norms which indicated an expansion of local authority residential and day services and a reduction in hospital places. It called for joint local and health authority ten-year plans to be drawn up for each health region to specify how progress towards the provision targets would be made and to set a date when further admission to hospital for residential care ('social care' in today's terminology) as opposed to treatment would cease. Subsequently, such plans were formulated by less than one-third of health regions and their constituent local authorities. Moreover, projected local authority service expansion was curtailed by the worsening resource climate of the mid-1970s. A permissive policy stance meant that there was divergence between local authorities in levels of service provision (Webb and Wistow, 1982). Slow progress was recognized in 1976 by the then Secretary of State, Barbara Castle, who sought to generate momentum to reform by establishing the National Development Group as a body to advise on good practice and the Development Team, with its associated panel of experts, to stimulate change in local areas. However, consistent with the tradition of British central government and a non-specialist civil service, policy continued to be specified in broad terms only (DHSS, 1981a, 1981b, 1985).

The National Development Group and Development Team made de facto policy, for example, in their recommendation of Community Mental Handicap Teams and their promotion of community units linked to a base hospital 'centre of excellence'. However, their guidance was piecemeal, sometimes contentious as in the latter example and not backed by a coherent central government resource policy. Such constrained policy formulation has been criticized by Walker (1984, p.7) as insufficiently comprehensive: 'Although planning objectives may be established within the framework of bureau-incrementalism, as for example in the case of DHSS guidelines for the growth of day care and domiciliary services (DHSS, 1976, 1977), these are more properly regarded as incremental or programming targets. The distinction is important, because these planning targets are modifications to the existing pattern of services, and do not rest necessarily on an assessment of needs and objectives. In this framework, the fundamental reappraisal of the welfare services necessary to overcome the problems of widespread poverty, deprivation and deep-seated inequalities is never considered as a realistic option.'

The way that joint planning and financing mechanisms between statutory agencies was promoted prior to the AWS provides a good example of incrementalism and stands in contrast to the more radical reforming agenda of the AWS. In 1974, legislation imposed a statutory duty on local authorities and health authorities (later incorporated in section 22 of the NHS Act 1977) to cooperate with each other in planning and operating health and related social services and to establish Joint Consultative Committees (JCCs). Each JCC was to comprise elected members from health and local authorities and was to be aided and advised by Joint Care Planning Teams comprising senior officers. Joint funding arrangements were introduced allowing health authorities to fund local authority social services projects for up to three years before local authorities had to meet the longer term revenue consequences. Further changes in the early 1980s included voluntary agency representation on JCCs, the extension of joint funding to education departments, district council housing departments and voluntary service providers, the extension of joint funding to cover capital expenditure, and the extension of the period before local authorities had to fund projects from their own resources to ten years. Although providing a mechanism for change at a time when general economic stringency was becoming a growing problem, the difficulties faced by joint planning teams in negotiating the new relationships between unfamiliar partners, the limited amount of money available through joint funding compared to the size of the task and the obstacle of the longer term financial liability of the local authorities served to limit their impact.

In summary, policy throughout the 1970s and early 1980s may have had a direction set by the principles of *Better Services*, but lacked the organizational and funding mechanisms which were required to engender significant reform. Joint funding was a minor palliative. Central government exhorted but did not require action. It devolved responsibility and avoided the wholesale financial implications of a centrally promoted initiative, opting instead to back a number of pilot schemes (Renshaw *et al.*, 1988;

Knapp *et al.*, 1992). As a result, the Audit Commission's (1986) review of community care provision was deeply scathing about the twenty-year legacy of ineffective policy implementation. Progress to shift resources from institutional care to support people in the community had been decidedly slow despite the professed intentions of policy. One reason was that there was an inevitable inertia in the absence of a central investment strategy in liberating expenditure tied up in existing services. Finance to bridge the double funding of community and hospital services as the transition proceeded was inadequate. In addition, other resource policies were having a detrimental effect. Although local authorities were being exhorted to improve community care provision, they were being financially restricted.

Without resources for service development, change could only be incremental and skewed in favour of existing resource investment patterns. The expenditure tied up in the long-stay hospitals was the most significant single element by far. A reform agenda led by deinstitutionalization was inevitable, particularly as the discharge of people from hospital allowed access to social security payments to help meet rising costs. Such a policy was consistent with the idea that the negative consequences of the scale and remoteness of residential care was the problem to be tackled – the size, architectural design and location of services were commonly seen as their important determining features. As Bean and Mouncer (1993) have argued in relation to psychiatric hospital closure, it was a policy 'legitimised not by careful demonstration of its merits . . . but by rendering the alternative simply unacceptable' (p. 11). Hospital resettlement, therefore, emerged as the major policy of the 1980s in England. As a study of Regional Health Authority planning for people with learning disabilities in 1987 found: 'regional estimates of need tended to focus heavily on people currently living in long-stay hospitals and much less work had been done on trying to estimate and plan for meeting the needs of people already living in community settings. . . . Central government pressure on health authorities to run down the large long-stay hospitals is undoubtedly one reason why the needs of people in the community are being largely ignored. . . . Only two regions make it quite clear that their plans serve all those with learning difficulties – regardless of where they are living at present' (IDC, 1988, p. 19).

The All-Wales Strategy as a community care policy

The AWS both permitted and established a different path for service reform in Wales. Investment in the community to meet the needs of people living in the community was not only possible through the availability of new resources, but also made a policy priority. The incrementalism of joint financing was swept away by designating local authority social services as the lead agency and by projecting revenue investment at such a rate that authorities needed to be well organized to respond to the proffered opportunity. The scale of the resources to be made available was more than enough to pump prime change to existing services; innovation and the development of previously unavailable services was also possible. A reduction in the demand for hospital and other traditional forms of care was predicted as a result of building up community services. The transfer of resources from such outmoded services was anticipated to reinforce the direction of development. The transfer of such resources from health to local authorities was clearly signalled by the social care model adopted. However, the expenditure tied up in the hospitals was not the vehicle of change and resettlement not an express policy focus.

Although the AWS is widely seen as a community care policy, such a label is not confirmed by academic analysis. Arising from notions of community which emphasize interpersonal relationships, Abrams (1978) argued that the decisive context of care is not the community as defined territorially. His position derives in part from the changing nature of community in contemporary Britain and the idea that a simple policy of providing resources locally as a way of facilitating the community to care appeals to types of community which do not exist or are disappearing. Early studies contributed to the view that urban and rural communities were based on social relations which reflected cohesiveness, stability, continuity and reciprocity (Rees, 1950; Young and Willmott, 1962). However, subsequent critique has suggested that the self-help and solidarity described were responses to survival needs rather than expressions of altruism (Stacey, 1960; Pahl, 1965; Bell and Newby, 1971). As survival needs have become less urgent concerns, at least for the more affluent majority, and commonality of interest and altruism have become less likely as communities have become more fragmented and geographically mobile, a closer analysis of specific communities of interest has become more vital for a community care policy to be effective.

Abrams (1978) drew distinctions between professional or specialist services and lay or non-specialist support within closed or open settings (Figure 3.1). Community care according to this matrix would be predicated upon a community development approach which would establish, 'the provision of help, support and protection to others by lay members of societies acting in everyday domestic settings' (Abrams, 1978, p. 78). Such an emphasis would be geared towards the development of neighbourhood groups, good neighbour schemes, more vigorous citizen participation in the affairs of the locality and innovative voluntary organizations. While the AWS hinted at aspects of this approach, its proposals remained firmly rooted in the reform of deficient services, reform which would be likely to decrease segregation and promote community participation for those served, but would leave the nature of communities relatively unaffected. The AWS, therefore, represented a move from institutional treatment to community treatment in Abrams' terms. As it stated, 'the services which are provided are in many cases inadequate; facilities are too large, too impersonal and insufficiently localised to provide for the integration of mentally handicapped people into their communities and to offer them the chance to develop a variety of personal relationships' (Welsh Office, 1983, para. 3.8). In short, changed service support was seen as a springboard to typical community lifestyles. (We will return to the distinction between community treatment and community care in later chapters.)

We will appraise the AWS and its subsequent success, therefore, as a policy to reform the nature of services and promote a network of

		Setting	
		Closed	Open
Personnel	Professional/ specialist	Institutional treatment	Community treatment
	Lay/Non- specialist	Institutional care	Community care

Figure 3.1 Conceptualizations of support (Abrams, 1978). Permission to reprint this figure has been kindly granted by the National Council for Voluntary Organisations

specialist, locally-available support throughout Wales, sufficient for all people with learning disability to maintain or regain community residence and the ties, associations and opportunities which that brings.

Webb and Wistow (1982) have argued that there are six key components for effecting change through policy. First, a policy must have a sound theoretical or empirical base which provides a credible link between the recommended action and the outcome to be achieved. Second, specific organizational and administrative structures need to be established to carry through the policy. Existing mechanisms are often inappropriate even though they may be expected to have general utility. Third, support for the policy must reach a critical level among those who need to put it into action. Fourth, effective communication of the policy to those key actors is an important step in securing their support. Fifth, appropriate levels and types of resources to put the policy into effect need to be secured. Pressures to determine resource policy separately from service delivery policy at central government level often result in resource policy driving and distorting service policy to the detriment of desired outcome. Sixth, having control over the process of service delivery is crucial if the envisaged outcomes are to be achieved.

In the remainder of this chapter, we will explore the strengths of the AWS against the six Webb and Wistow (1982) criteria and examine its weaknesses and the problems encountered in its implementation. We will then go on to report the progress achieved with respect to its central service development aims: multidisciplinary teamworking and individual planning (Chapter 4), consumer involvement and advocacy (Chapter 5), residential services (Chapter 6), family support services (Chapter 7) and day services (Chapter 8).

The strengths of the AWS

A sound theoretical or empirical basis?

The AWS was distinctive for embracing the logic that a progressive redefinition of the outcomes to be achieved for people with learning disabilities in society implied wholesale reform of services. Its vision, that people with a learning disability should have the rights to ordinary patterns of life within the community, to be treated as individuals and to receive additional help from their communities and from professional services so as to develop their maximum potential, reflected a growing advocacy of a social rather than pathological model of handicap (United Nations General Assembly, 1972; DHSS, 1979). The experience, social situation and quality of life of people with learning disabilities were seen as resulting primarily from societal reaction and imposed marginalization rather than being inherent in their intellectual impairment. The AWS was consistent with its principles in stating that services which segregated people, albeit to deliver specialist expertise related to their disabilities, had no place in the future pattern of provision. Neither had services which were so large that people's individual character, needs and aspirations were unlikely to be differentiated.

That the service developments recommended by the AWS were compatible with its principles was an undoubted strength of the policy. As has already been described in Chapter 2, the architects of the AWS reflected many of the ideas which had emerged in the previous decade in their suggestions for service development. Despite pilot examples of the types of services that the AWS advocated, the empirical basis of many of their recommendations was weak, as it was almost bound to be given the rapid development of thinking and the genesis of many of the proposals in other countries such as the USA and Scandinavia. Although the NIMROD scheme provided experience in Britain of multidisciplinary team working, individual planning, supported community housing and domiciliary support as an integrated service package, the results from the research commissioned by the Welsh Office were not reported until many years after the AWS had come into being. There was some pre-existing evidence to support the advantage of community residential services over traditional hospitals, but there had been very little evaluation of the changing state of day services, the impact of respite and family support services, the working of multidisciplinary community teams or individual planning. Policy was being pursued mainly on the basis of a mixture of ideological belief and logical analysis and the Welsh Office showed a strong commitment to funding independent research on the AWS because of this. In addition, they proposed that service development in two Vanguard Areas (Ynys Mon and Arfon districts in Gwynedd and the Rhondda Valleys in Mid Glamorgan) should be accelerated so that early experience could be disseminated prior to more extensive reform elsewhere (see below).

Specific organizational and administrative arrangements

An internal Welsh Office Working Group with representation from Health, Social Work, Housing and Education, under the chairmanship of the Chief Social Work Services Officer, was set up to oversee the progress of the AWS. The preference for this kind of ad hoc multidisciplinary working group by the Welsh Office has been noted elsewhere (Hunter and Wistow, 1987; pp. 40–42). Officers from the group, along with officers from the Health and Social Services Policy Division, were responsible for scrutinizing plans from counties and for the funding strategies recommended to ministers. In addition, an All Wales Mental Handicap Advisory Panel, modelled on the National Development Group, was established to recommend good practice and advise the Secretary of State and the Welsh Office on the suitability of county development plans.

The social services lead responsibility for implementing the AWS squarely placed the ultimate responsibility for domiciliary, day and residential services with local authorities and explicitly signposted the end of the dominant role of the National Health Service with this client group. Control over the additional finance to be invested was maintained by the Welsh Office by making special arrangements for its payment. Rather than adding it to the Revenue Support Grant, legislation was enacted so that the Welsh Office could make ring-fenced allocations to support agreed projects. The Welsh Office, therefore, retained an effective financial sanction by which to ensure compliance with the overall service philosophy being promoted.

However, although driving the AWS centrally, the Welsh Office also wanted to shift ownership of the policy to the local level. The additional funds to be invested were approximately equal to the total existing expenditure tied up in traditional services. Together, these sources constituted about half of the resources thought to be required for comprehensive implementation of the pattern of service set out by the Working Party (Welsh Office, 1982; Felce, Beyer and Todd, 1995). The AWS would reach its halfway point after its first ten-year period only if the new investment had acted as a catalyst to change the nature of existing services and the disposition of existing revenues. The Welsh Office needed to gain widespread support for the AWS. Its central leadership had to be complemented by local commitment and a balance found between central and local determination of service development.

In support of gaining local commitment and in recognition of the multi-agency breadth of the AWS reform, the Welsh Office issued guidance on the way plans were to be formulated under the stewardship of social services departments. They sought the creation of County Joint Planning Teams which would bring together all relevant interests and be capable of preparing a jointly agreed plan for each county. Guidance was firm on the nature of planning relationships and the importance of consultation. Plans were to be prepared jointly and in full consultation with health authorities, relevant voluntary organizations and other service providers as well as representatives of people with learning disabilities and their families (Welsh Office, 1983). The emphasis on consumer representation in planning was a distinctive feature of the AWS and, presumably, reflected a belief that these mechanisms would produce a service which was underpinned by consumer need. The identification of need was to be localized, with professionals and consumers meeting to consider the requirements of individuals and families. This information was to be collated and fed into area and county planning.

At the outset, counties were asked to submit ten-year development plans. These were to be detailed for the first three years, in outline for the next four, and contain a statement of intent for the final three. Such plans were to be submitted by the end of October 1983, except for the two Vanguard Areas which were to formulate more considered plans to be submitted in 1984 in order to maximize their potential as pilot demonstration projects. The intended emphasis was represented in a pro forma issued by the Welsh Office as part of the guidance to counties on how plans were to be formulated. It consisted of a series of headings to be covered, with detailed questions that should be answered within each section. Each plan was to include: (1) statements of philosophy and objectives that accorded with those of the AWS; (2) a description of discussions which had been carried out between statutory agencies and with people with learning disabilities, their parents, and voluntary organizations; (3) some estimation of numbers of people with a learning disability and their need for services; (4) the pattern of services to be developed; (5) an assessment of staffing levels and staff training likely to be required; (6) clear estimates of costs for the first three years; (7) arrangements for monitoring new provision and arrangements for managing services, within which there were to be roles for the representatives of people with learning disabilities and their families.

Engendering support locally

Although the AWS found a natural constituency of support among those advocating progressive reform, it was launched in a complex arena. Support or opposition did not necessarily divide on occupational or agency lines. Much of the reform and change in thinking of earlier decades could be characterized as a professional movement peopled by representatives from service, research and campaigning bodies. By and large, reform was not consumer driven. The views of people with learning disabilities remained largely untapped. Moreover, although the development of particular services, such as family respite, commanded broad parental support and sections of the parent voice supported a more wholesale community emphasis, the parental position was too divided to constitute a strong pressure group. Community-oriented reform was not strongly advocated by those professional groups most closely associated with hospital provision, the specialist psychiatrists and nurses, although there were, of course, exceptions and members of other health service disciplines, such as clinical psychology, were generally in favour of reform. Paradoxically, while social services were to be made responsible for leading change, many of the alternatives to institutional provision seen in the 1970s and early 1980s had been health service initiatives. Social services, although deriving a certain reflected kudos from their lack of responsibility for the long-stay hospitals, did not have a reputation for running high quality services. Indeed, they continued to provide large centralized hostels and day services. Overall, experience of providing the services which the AWS outlined was not widespread. Those responsible for the AWS had a complex task to broaden the basis of support for its policy and equip constituent authorities with the competence to develop and manage leading-edge services.

There was a big learning curve to go through between the organization and the staff coming together and understanding their joint values – getting the AWS into people's heads!

Choosing to nominate local authorities as lead agencies was, arguably, as much a result of needing to gain local support for the AWS as a reflection of changing service philosophy. The fact that social services departments were not responsible for the strongest symbol of institutional thinking, the hospitals, made them less threatened by the direction of reform. In contrast, the health authorities had a much greater vested interest in maintaining the status quo. The plans for change that they had brought forward in the years just prior to the AWS were conservative. It is likely that this apparent intransigence of the health authorities would have been viewed as an obstacle by officers taking policy forward centrally. A policy launch needs to be met by a certain degree of support. Targeting the most supportive agency to lead change certainly created a context in which local commitment could grow. In addition, the fact that the AWS was vague about the future of the long-stay hospitals allowed controversial issues such as the future role of the health service, the responsibility of the specialist consultant psychiatrist and the future employment of nurses to be left aside. Deinstitutionalization did not need to be faced in the short-term because the resources needed for service redevelopment did not depend on it. It was possible to launch the AWS without inflaming opposition or tackling some of the most difficult issues to be addressed.

It was recognized that social services departments were starting from a low base in terms of experience of strategic planning for people with learning disabilities, much of this work previously having fallen to health authorities. Social services also had relatively little experience of people with the most severe learning disabilities, multiple impairments or challenging behaviour. Cross-fertilization of experience from health would be necessary. Initial bids were requested from local authorities to facilitate the joint planning process at county level and to help fill some of the identified gaps. Grants were made to establish the planning and professional infrastructure in local areas. Most counties appointed development officers, although not all took the opportunity to bring in new experience, and a rapid and widespread introduction of multidisciplinary community teams was achieved.

The Welsh Office also helped to promote a constructive dialogue by issuing detailed guidance to counties to help them respond to the challenge of planning for the AWS. The quality of this guidance is generally regarded as better than any that had been issued in the past. Members of the Welsh Office's Working Group spent considerable time in working with counties in the plan formulation period, and the extent of personal interest and commitment contributed by these officers was acknowledged and welcomed. Despite the emphasis placed on the importance of local decision-making, which is often a justification for a lack of central prescription, local agencies and personnel frequently tend to see clear guidance as simplifying the nature of the task ahead and indicative of central government commitment to an area. Comments made in a recent survey reveal the first years of the AWS to be a golden period of Welsh Office direction of the AWS.

In the early days, they (the Welsh Office) were very much hands on, not only in the sense of dealing with the central resource but also in a detailed involvement in why one wanted the resource, how one was going to use it, to monitor it.

I think it was positive, particularly in the early years, that there was some kind of overall monitoring even though it crucified everybody.

Communicating the policy

The AWS started life as a high profile policy and to that extent its message was broadcast not only within Wales but also throughout the rest of Britain. The Welsh Office reinforced its normal communication processes by funding a series of workshops in each county, organized by the British Institute of Mental Handicap (now British Institute of Learning Disabilities). Members of fledgling County Joint Planning Teams were brought together, received an induction to the AWS and were helped to lay down a broad framework for their future planning. More generally, training was seen as a crucial element in promoting change in line with the AWS. Multidisciplinary training teams at county level were promoted to develop in-service courses which could be shared by the staff of statutory and voluntary agencies and parents alike. The early years saw the appointment of specialist training officers and significant expenditure on training courses, particularly in the re-orientation of existing staff to the demands of the AWS. Subsequently, the Welsh Office established a centralized Training Support Unit to facilitate the cross-fertilization of learning and experience, an initiative which was soundly based even though it did not fulfil its promise.

In the early days it was to do with reorientation, it was all to do with values and principles, lots of training, lots of discussion and some early services like social care workers, respite care and the development of accommodation. It was very much focused on changing attitudes.

Resource policy

Willingness to back policy with additional funding is often interpreted as evidence of commitment to change. The AWS advocated both the provision of new services that had not previously been available and the replacement of poor quality, poorly resourced services by better ones. The expenditure implied by the AWS was considerably greater than that currently invested. The Working Party which initiated the AWS calculated that the pattern of services it envisaged would ultimately cost four times the 1983 level of expenditure without allowing for inflation. The AWS did not commit central government to this level of expenditure, but it did not rule it out either. Rather, in view of the untried nature of much of what was proposed, together with the uncertain abilities of field authorities to manage the process of change, an interim goal was set for a first ten-year phase. By 1993, funding was set to increase to half the level of that eventually required; £26 million recurring revenue at 1983 prices would be invested to complement an approximately equivalent amount which was already being spent. There was an expectation of slower growth in expenditure in the first years and an acceleration towards the end of the decade as implementation became more certain. For example, £1.6 million was expected to be invested in 1983/84 compared to the average annual growth of £2.6 million. This injection of new resources was regarded as one of the strongest elements of the AWS. In providing a credible resource policy to match service reform, the AWS overcame a central failing noted in earlier policies (Webb and Wistow, 1982).

In addition, the AWS identified a shortfall in specialist staff resources. Wales was seen to have inadequate numbers of nurses, psychologists and other professionals such as occupational therapists, speech therapists and physiotherapists specializing in working with people with learning disabilities. Even if funding had been available, scarcity of trained personnel would have been a barrier to appointment. The Welsh Office, therefore, identified an additional coordination role for itself and sought to ensure an increased throughput of trained professional staff.

Retaining or gaining control over the process of service delivery

Relative to many other statements of policy, the AWS was specific about the types of service change needed to fulfil its aims. The Welsh Office also chose to exert a more significant level of control over its policy than central government had typically done in the past, moving away from a traditionally permissive posture. The AWS was a centrally generated policy and was very much associated with the Welsh Office. Its initial success or failure would be interpreted as a success or failure of Welsh Office management. The principal vehicle for retaining managerial control was the Welsh Office's role in the planning process and the influence it derived from the power to give or withhold funding. This power was exercised through the creation and refinement of a system for monitoring plans. The Welsh Office issued guidance on monitoring in November 1983 and a more comprehensive guide on basic principles in March 1984. Following the early experience of vetting plans, the Welsh Office organized a two-day workshop with relevant planners from counties in January 1986. This led to the adoption of a standard method of reporting progress on all funded projects under five headings:

1 Objectives of each initiative
2 Means of achieving objectives
3 Achievements
4 Lessons learnt
5 New objectives arising.

In the early years they (Welsh Office) were very much involved and obviously the county plans had to go in. The annual reviews ... used to be quite a daunting occasion. ... At one time you had to account for how you were spending the money and what services you were providing and there were a number of issues that were all laid out. They were very formal agendas. At one stage you couldn't do anything without their say so.

In the early years, the Welsh Office closely scrutinized the plans submitted by County Joint Planning Teams to ensure that they met the principles set out in the AWS. Unacceptable plans were not funded. As county plans were approved, an annual cycle of progress review meetings was established based on the formal submission of monitoring reports from counties. Meetings between members of the Welsh Office Working Group and the County Joint Planning Team would then follow with an agenda to review progress and future funding arrangements. Initially, review was carried out on a project by project basis, with Welsh Office agreement required for each project in turn or else funding would be withheld. This degree of control was then moderated for those counties which had made a better start to service development under the AWS. They were given 'programme' status whereby funding was matched to a set of proposals while the county retained control over specific project priorities within the overall agreement. Meanwhile, other counties continued on the pre-existing 'project' status.

In summary, the AWS had considerable merit in the attention given to the six elements outlined by Wistow and Webb (1982). However, inherent difficulties emerged during the first stages of implementation and beyond.

Problems in implementation

Delay in formulating joint plans

As in many other parts of Britain, experience of cooperation between agencies prior to the AWS was limited. Joint planning was not perceived as successful. In some parts of Wales, motives were viewed with suspicion and relationships were tense. Some of these feelings were exacerbated by granting social services lead agency status. Health authorities, the dominant provision partner, felt that their long track record in the area had been devalued. There was also a widespread view that social services lacked competence in the area. Such attitudes were a clear challenge to conducive and productive joint working.

There were rivalries and jealousies. There was a feeling in the health authorities that they were the poor relations in the early stages. The whole of the money seemed to be going on voluntary sector or social services schemes that were not necessarily the more appropriately aligned to the principles of the Strategy. It was seen that health couldn't be regarded as an appropriate body to take forward new ideas. There were schemes put forward that didn't receive approval because they were from health.

In the beginning, there was a feeling of prejudice against Health: (1) the health authority was the heaviest investor in revenue terms; (2) we knew full well that local authorities were doing virtually nothing; (3) the health service had made considerable strides since the likes of the Ely Inquiry; (4) the local authorities did not have the professional expertise to handle leadership; (5) local government, through its elective processes, was far slower and could be frustrated by the parochial views of councillors; and (6) there was a feeling at the time that the senior social services officers were not up to it.

Unfortunately, much depended on establishing effective joint planning quickly, as the County Joint Planning Teams were the pivot of strategic planning. The extent of change that was embodied in the organizational and administrative processes involved in joint-agency working and consumer consultation and the lead time required to adjust to their demands was severely underestimated. Tangible results from the AWS in terms of service development were expected over too short a period (Beyer *et al.*, 1986).

No-one in 1983 was totally prepared, there was so much that needed to be done. God knows what had been going on in the previous fifty years. There was a very low baseline on both sides (health and social services) and we spent the first four to five years working out what we needed.

The biggest pitfall of the AWS was that expectations were blown sky-high. I think since then it's been about trying to dampen expectations and to make them more realistic. Anyone with a modicum of common sense should've known that the AWS would never be realized in such a short space of time.

The original intention had been to agree draft development plans by April 1984, subject to detailed discussions and amendments. Health and social services had discussed each other's plans in the past and carried out planning for joint financed projects, but they were not used to creating comprehensive joint plans. There was relatively little experience of involving consumers at all, let alone involving them in long-term planning and management structures. The result was that the new planning system took much longer to bed down than was expected. Moreover, virtually no allowance was made for the time required to input any assessment of need into the planning system.

The emphasis on consumer representation also caused initial difficulties. It was to be operationalized by giving parents, voluntary organizations and people with learning disabilities a place at the planning table. The AWS understandably generated heightened expectations of change. Many consumer representatives report that they initially interpreted the AWS as a charter for them to tell professionals what they required both through individual planning meetings and their involvement in county planning. However, in the first instance, parents often argued for a greater availability of existing services rather than for reformed services and this generated a tension between principled and consumer-driven development.

We were all caught up in trying to make sense of all these new ideas. Not that there was a lot of resistance, except from parents. Parents thought the services we had then were good but that we didn't have enough of them. So in the early days it was about trying to convince parents of the need for change and that change didn't mean taking services away but replacing them with something better.

'Close the special schools, shut down residential schools'. That was the message we were picking up from social services. But most parents with children in special schools were their champions. If anything there's a greater demand from parents now for special schools than there was ten years ago.

It soon became apparent that senior officers retained an independent perspective on what was required and were also responsive to Welsh Office expectations that proposals would reflect the direction set by the

AWS. County Joint Planning Groups continued to be the official mechanism for planning, but a suspicion grew that the real planning went on elsewhere, in the corridors of County Hall or the Welsh Office.

They (parents) can't step back from it (the immediate demands of caring) as can officers. They expected to see things delivered much more quickly. They came so often with their vast experience and knowledge of their individual situations, but found it difficult to use that as an exemplar for a broader strategic view. That's understandable. I think they started to get frustrated as they expected plans to be tailored to their individual need.

To a considerable extent, it was very much guided by the principles of the AWS. Without the Strategy, something else would have happened. There is an issue. People say that they want something and then they are told that it is not available because it is not in line with AWS principles. You have a choice but you only have a choice if it is in line with Strategy principles.

Ultimately, the process of discussing and developing agreed plans over many years helped forge a mutual understanding and effective working relationships between different groups. Compared to the earlier difficulties, the final level of collaboration was seen as an important and abiding success of the AWS and a tribute to the measures that had been taken centrally and locally to promulgate its principles. However, at the beginning, the change in practice and attitudes required in joint working contributed to delay.

So the first phase was about putting people together, getting people to work for a common aim, one goal. The strengths of the AWS were that it has brought people together, health, social services, education, parents. I suppose it was about changing peoples' perspectives on the possible.

As a result of these related strands, the production and approval of the initial AWS plans fell behind the intended timetable. The Welsh Office refused to sanction the majority of plans because they included ideas for services at odds with the AWS philosophy, or they contained an inadequate attention to detail, or they lacked clear evidence of consultation with consumers and their representatives. Plans put forward by only three of the eight counties were approved between May and July 1984. Those of the other five received approval, often subject to further discussion or development work, between February 1985 and February 1986. Significantly, proposals for development in the two Vanguard Areas were approved at least a year after approval was given to the first three county plans. The Vanguard Area idea to create accelerated development so that those following could learn from the experience gained never fulfilled its function and the special status of both districts was withdrawn three years later. The two areas were perhaps not wisely chosen as they had no conspicuous advantages in terms of any pre-existing claim to the quality of their services or competence of the local agencies to provide and manage the type of services which the AWS espoused. (It is possible that they were chosen because of a completely different set of political considerations.) The strategic thinking and project management required to be successful in transforming them into areas of national leadership was insufficient.

The Vanguard Area proposal was not the only idea which missed the mark in practice despite its merit in principle. The general hope that common cause would result in inter-county collaboration and cross-boundary learning was not fulfilled despite the efforts of the Welsh Office to stimulate sharing of experience and common interests. Such concern is illustrated by its promotion of the Training and Development Officers Forum, through which those centrally involved in taking the AWS forward in the eight counties had the opportunity to meet quarterly and focus on defined issues. Competition between counties in their ability to secure AWS finance and a traditional reluctance to air difficulties in public meant that common interests were rarely met by collaborative initiatives. Moreover, problems in the constitution of the All Wales Advisory Panel also limited its effectiveness. Its role was to recommend good practice to field authorities and advise the Welsh Office on the suitability of county plans. Those involved in planning at county level reported that this dual role made it difficult for the Panel to be seen as impartial advisors. This problem was particularly acute at first because its initial membership was exclusively drawn from Wales, a fact which meant that appointees to the Panel who held office in one authority had influence over the proposals of neighbouring authorities. This concern generally hampered the effect the Panel had on local development and planning (Beyer *et al.*, 1986).

Lack of a model for strategic planning

Although the Working Party report had set out a pattern of services to be developed and made assumptions about final levels of provision sufficient for deriving cost estimates, the AWS did not set targets or describe norms for service development. Rather, it fostered a culture of local determination of need, based on individual assessment. In this respect, the AWS was only a loose service prescription. There was no blueprint for the AWS, no standard picture of service coverage to be put in place. A common straightforward approach to strategic planning, namely devising and costing a series of provision steps between what was currently available and the desired endstate was, therefore, not available. Rather, a more complex and organic process was attempted whereby plans would reflect local priorities ascertained through discussion between consumers and professionals. Individual planning was put forward as a fundamental mechanism for establishing what support individuals and families required consistent with AWS principles. However, inadequate thought was given to the complexity and resource implications of developing a needs-led, bottom-up system of strategic planning. Moreover, as we will see in Chapter 4, the notion of county planning being the embodiment of locally assessed needs was disabled by the low coverage and fragile implementation of individualized planning.

By rejecting a more traditional form of strategic planning, but failing to establish the alternative, the AWS had a gap at the centre of its machinery for developing and reviewing strategic plans. As we have described above, considerable efforts were taken by the Welsh Office to develop specific monitoring arrangements for the AWS. Those responsible were able to judge proposals against the principles of the AWS and also according to whether criteria set for their production had been met. However, service development proposals coming forward to the Welsh Office were generally not

related to an eventual mapping of services, nor was proposed revenue investment part of a costed final picture or total expenditure framework. Planning
was typified by the production of new discrete service elements rather than
a fundamental reappraisal of the needed distribution of resources for an area
or population. The Welsh Office was unable to judge how any particular
proposed service development would fit within the eventual overall pattern,
whether it was consistent with a final equitable distribution of services in
relation to population and whether its proposed costings were within the
resource investment assumptions embodied within the AWS.

The AWS has been consistent in being unable to provide an overview of development or strategic thinking about how all these new services were fitting
together. It's always encouraged ad hoc planning. As we've moved through the
AWS, it became more and more 'add-ons'.

It was ... every year deciding what are we going to do. Planning ... was ...
very much a shopping list ... as the money continued to roll in.

I suppose there was an initial phase which was about philosophy attitude and
bidding for schemes. A lot of people took existing schemes off the shelf ... some
... good ... some less good. It did actually prove more difficult later on to weave
them into a coherent pattern of service in terms of the principles of the strategy.
... There was no proper needs assessment.

What we seem to have is a patchwork of uncoordinated schemes – nobody has
done an appropriate assessment of need.

The result of this inability to relate proposals to interim goals can be
seen in recent events. First, services continued to be maldistributed.
Service catchment areas continued to be larger than necessary or, in other
words, the potential for developing local services was not fully realized.
The continued inequality in provision has been pointed up by the differences in the service levels inherited by the twenty-two new unitary authorities created under the 1996 local government reorganization in Wales
which, in general, are considerably smaller than the previous eight
counties. Secondly, the escalation of service costings during the first phase
of the AWS was unconstrained. It set a trajectory which finally caused the
Welsh Office to impose severe financial limits to the final stages of hospital resettlement. Since this change, proposals for alternative provision in
the community have had to be kept within a total budget set by existing
hospital expenditure. This has meant that the last residents to move,
typically those with more severe learning disabilities and challenging
behaviour, have less resource intensive services than some which had been
provided in the immediately preceding years.

The money's run out in terms of offering a good service to people ... maybe
because people were extravagant initially and spent too much on the first wave.

The last phase has been frustrating. We've had to deal with a lack of funds for
the things we want to do. We've put down the structures, built up a vision, worked
out detailed plans. But now it's about rationing.

Confusion about community development and hospital resettlement

Some of the problems in strategic planning can be attributed to a lack of
clarity over hospital provision and the health service role. Although the
AWS has been widely seen as appropriate in prioritizing community

development, there has been a major failure to recognize the importance of also making alternative provision to replace the hospitals. One direct consequence of nominating the local authorities as lead agencies while avoiding being explicit about hospital resettlement was that the AWS tended to be seen as predominantly a strategy for investment in social services.

The initial reaction was that the AWS was something to do with social services and nothing to do with health. Health stayed out of it.

As the future of the long-stay hospitals was to be the subject of separate negotiations between the Welsh Office and health authorities at a later date, health authorities could reasonably accept being a junior partner. Lead agency status could be viewed merely as an indicator that the primary focus for new investment was to be on those service elements which were traditionally the responsibility of social services to provide. The more challenging perspective, namely that social services had a lead responsibility for developing comprehensive plans for all social care irrespective of the current disposition of expenditure or agency management of services, was not necessarily promoted or understood. Even ten years later, social services departments saw themselves as secondary to health where planning for people in hospital was concerned. Whether lead agency status had any functional meaning remained a moot point. Neither was it clear whether lead agency status entitled social services to plan how to reinvest the money currently administered by health to fund the hospitals. Nor was the funding tied up in the hospitals redesignated by the Welsh Office to end the prevailing perceptions of agency ownership (Felce, 1994).

It was something we all had at the back of our minds but never admitted. I think for years there was a hidden tension that we weren't really tackling the issue of resettlement from hospitals. They had to close, but politically they had to stay open.

Although such blurring of issues provided a basis for transacting business, ultimately, it contributed to the undermining of the comprehensive scope of the AWS. Until replacing hospital provision was recognized as being encompassed by the orbit of the AWS, the impact which AWS finance could have on pump-priming change in health authority expenditure was limited. As we have already stated, the AWS was not driven by deinstitutionalization. However, there was never more than a global assumption that priority was rightly placed on the needs of people living in the community. Those already admitted to residential services had clearly demonstrable needs for accommodation and support. They also experienced a particularly poor quality of life, far removed from the principles of the AWS. Thus, their needs for alternative accommodation were clearly salient to the implementation of the AWS. A policy on resettlement needed to be developed at an early stage; criticism of deinstitutionalization being more concerned with the manner by which hospital reduction is achieved rather than in the intended goal.

The proposition that some adults living with their parents in the community had unmet accommodation needs was well founded given the low level of provision outside of the hospital institutions. Despite enthusiasm for developing better informal or formal domiciliary support, there is a limit to its generalizability to obviate the need for alternative accommodation. A policy of increasing support to people in their own homes may be the most effective option for people who have their own homes. However, most people with learning disabilities living in private households live in the parental home or that of another close relative. Domiciliary support in this context is by no means equivalent. Principles concerned with achieving a typical lifestyle and pattern of existence promote the need for alternative supported accommodation when individuals reach adulthood.

Thus there were two distinct sources of residential need to be served. The AWS provided the opportunity for a service development approach led by the local authorities whereby suitable community arrangements could be developed to serve both hospital and community constituencies. Such an approach, with an emphasis on the local neighbourhood, can be seen as a 'community-pull' model of achieving hospital resettlement. The focus of planning and service development is located within the community and the resulting service provision not only meets latent local demand but allows those with local ties to leave hospital. This approach can be contrasted with a 'hospital-push' model in which planning is exclusively concentrated on hospital residents, led by health staff, located within the hospitals and poorly integrated with the community developments being pursued by social services (Felce, 1994).

However, this opportunity was missed. The integration of hospital resettlement within a wider community development strategy was not achieved. Whether or not there was a deliberate attempt to launch the AWS without triggering opposition from the hospital lobby and to reintroduce the issue of the replacement of hospital services a little later is a matter of conjecture. However, when the Welsh Office asked for plans to be formulated in 1985, the request was directed only to the health authorities (Welsh Office, 1985), confirming any initial impression that planning reform of the hospital sector was not part of the AWS.

There was an anxiety among health people that they ought to be involved, especially following the document on the specialist hospitals. We responded to it by saying 'Aha, this is our bite of the cherry; we can actually do something on the health side now!'

Guidance two to three years later asked for resettlement plans to be annexed to county plans. Although meant as a correction of the earlier single agency approach, it served to reinforce the idea that planning in relation to the hospitals was not an integral part of the county plan and not led by social services. The distinction introduced at the same time between AWS programme funds and special allocations to speed resettlement reinforced the idea that agency responsibilities remained divided on traditional lines. Subsequent to the mid-term review of the first phase of the AWS, resettlement was designated as one of a number of core areas (see below) and 'hospital-push' resettlement became a reality. In this respect, development in Wales proceeded as it had done in England, a story to which we will return in Chapter 6.

It seems that nothing else matters at the moment except getting people out of hospitals. ... The push towards resettlement has hijacked the AWS. ... It's all resettlement now.

The loss of the ability to vet plans and withhold funding

A review of the progress of the AWS was published by the Welsh Office in 1987. This hinted at disquiet over lack of progress in service development in some parts of Wales (Welsh Office, 1987a, b, c). The high degree of central control had helped to maintain consistency between plans and AWS policy, but there had been practical difficulties on both sides. The Welsh Office was criticized by those involved at county level for consistently modifying their demands for data in search of consistent good quality monitoring information. Counties often found it difficult to cope with the changes in requirements and to respond in the timescale required within the Welsh Office annual planning cycle. These problems were compounded by difficulties on the part of the Welsh Office in carrying through the review process and announcing allocations in good time. In the early years of the AWS, counties had been unable to spend all allocated finance as they encountered difficulty in recruiting staff and getting projects up and running. This compounded the underutilization of earmarked funds arising from the delays in agreeing initial plans.

Although AWS spending had been predicted to begin slowly and increase over the ten-year period, there was still a considerable discrepancy between the allocation and take up of funds. Pressure from the Treasury began to grow either to use or scale down projected expenditure. The financial basis of the AWS was in jeopardy and there were considerable risks attached to continuing to scrutinize county proposals. After the initial planning round where funds were withheld while counties revised their proposals, the Welsh Office hand was weakened. Counties which could generate proposals in keeping with AWS principles found a central government keen to spend up to allocated levels. Subsequently, those which made the greater progress were accorded 'programme status' and given freer reign to switch funding between projects.

A further constraint on the Welsh Office's ability to monitor progress was the lack of data on outcome. The authors of the AWS recognized that the application of its principles implied that the ultimate benchmark by which its success should be judged was the extent to which people were enabled to live lives similar to other people without disabilities. Traditional performance indicators such as the levels of services provided or resources invested do not reflect outcome. A working group considered the statistical information required early in the life of the AWS and came forward with proposals which, at least in part, addressed this difficulty. However, they were not followed up and the Welsh Office was destined to monitor the progress of the AWS in terms of service change coupled with a nose for the soundness of innovation.

Failure to engage education

The AWS was launched as a multiagency strategy and local education authorities were, in principle, equal partners in County Joint Planning

Teams. However, the AWS did not add to or change the existing policy thrust on the education of school children with learning disabilities and, therefore, did not change the perception of local education officers as to the source or content of educational policy. Leadership of the AWS itself was vested in the Health and Social Services Policy Division. It has been widely recognized that coordination between relevant central government departments in response to the AWS has been inadequate. In education, the AWS was seen as mainly a strategy for health and social services and as one primarily concerned with adults. Such perceptions were held centrally and in local authorities. Despite the issue of their low involvement in the AWS periodically coming to the surface, education authorities remained peripheral.

Education was a major failure of the AWS. . . .
   The Welsh Office should really have put more thought in coordinating its AWS work across its own divisions. . . . It was as if one hand of the Welsh Office didn't know what the other hand was doing. . . . There was one set of advice coming from the AWS and another . . . (from) the education division. We thought the AWS wasn't our ball park and that there was no real money to attract us into it. The main emphasis went on adults. . . . So it was a chance lost in terms of the AWS being a comprehensive strategy.
   . . . the AWS was seen by us as a chance to get something for a group of children who were really being left out. However, it seemed that the AWS had left us out too. It's never really helped education and over time it's become even more remote.

Changes in the light of experience

A review of progress in the first five years recognized that tangible changes had been less great than had been expected and that parents, in particular, were critical of what had been achieved. A major new initiative was announced in December 1988 to respond to the problems highlighted; its aims being to accelerate the development of a central 'core' of services across all counties and enable growth to take place where counties were most prepared for it. The initiative had three elements. The first was a change to the way plans and progress would be reviewed and financial allocations timetabled, replacing the original ten-year plans developed between 1983 and 1985 with a system of rolling three-year plans. A report was to be placed before the Welsh Office in April of each year giving detailed information on current levels of service provision and registered populations, reviewing progress made in the prior three years and setting out whether previously specified targets had been met, and providing proposals for the next three years with financial estimates. Reports would be the subject of detailed discussions from May to July. Counties would then submit definitive bids for funding in the next financial year, with outline estimates for the subsequent two years. Allocations would be made in January. The Welsh Office also sought to 'invest in success' and initiated 'programme status' as already described for those counties which had shown a capacity to develop services successfully.

   The second element was revised guidance on the content of plans. Details were required for the first time of how plans for reduction in the

size of the hospitals related to developments in the community. There w
also a stronger emphasis on estimating the needs of the population beii ₃
served. The original hope that proposals should be underpinned by data
from individual planning was deflated by evidence that only 16% of multidisciplinary community teams had carried out such planning with respect
to more than 25% of their clients (McGrath, 1991). The new planning
guidelines, therefore, suggested that the extent to which plans were based
on demonstrable needs would be taken into account in deciding central
funding. Plans were to include quantitative and qualitative targets against
which progress could be measured and there would be a requirement to
show how and when money and staff resources from existing inappropriate facilities such as long-stay hospitals would be transferred to other
services.

Thirdly, the initiative established a set of core priorities for service
development in order that ... 'those with handicaps and their families
receive during the period of the strategy, significant and visible improvements in continuous support, respite care and day care which will enable
them to live fulfilled lives'. Having failed to achieve all round progress,
the Welsh Office (1988) relinquished the comprehensive scope of the
AWS in order to make more significant progress in a number of key areas
more likely. The core services were: (1) respite care in non-institutional
settings; (2) family-based care for children currently in hospital, hostels
and other institutional settings; (3) accommodation in ordinary housing
for adults (with a range of support from unstaffed to intensively staffed);
(4) support for families and other informal carers in their own homes; (5)
services for people with behavioural problems; (6) innovative day-care
opportunities, for example, in colleges of further education; and, (7) the
development of the role of ATCs.

Related to the above, £1.5 million was specially designated to support
schemes to resettle residents from selected hospitals and hostels into the
community. The monies would have to be spent on the people concerned
and would not be carried over into the next financial year if not spent.
A recurring allocation would be added to the county budget in subsequent years. There was an explicit objective to focus minds on accelerat-
ing the yearly movement out of hospital which up until 1989 had been
relatively insignificant (Welsh Office, 1989). As time progressed, resettlement was to become the major source of development resources within
counties.

The initiatives of 1988/9 were among the last before the AWS was
overtaken by the more general community care policy. Although first seen
as building on the AWS, the wider Community Care legislation introduced
new requirements which were unrelated to the AWS and weakened what
were thought to be important, if yet to be realized, commitments to a
consumer driven needs-led approach backed by explicit values. Community care policy appeared to represent a shift back to determining service
eligibility in crude terms via a professionally dominated system of care
management instead of a real concern with individual need and individually-tailored services. The language of consumer choice was apparently
central to the new policy but it was less explicit than the AWS about the
outcomes to which services should be directed.

Community care sounded very similar to the Strategy, but of course it wasn't. What I think we failed to do most was get across the basic principles of working to the (Social Services) Department so that they have great difficulty in understanding the difference between a community care assessment and an individual plan.

The IP (Individual Planning) system did make a difference to that individual focus but I think that the community care process is very much resource-led and the individual does not get anything like the focus now.

Moreover, in the purchaser/provider split, it introduced a major reorganization to which authorities had to devote time and effort. The separate introduction of this change in health and local authorities tended to upset the joint planning relationships that had been built up over time. Parents and voluntary organizations were distanced, the emphasis now being on social services consulting over their plans rather than creating joint plans with all parties.

The purchaser-provider split has lessened the input from the parents due to the purchasing power of agencies.

One of the issues ... has been the purchaser-provider split. More and more voluntaries are seen as providers and that partnership element that we worked on quite strongly five years ago has not truly survived that change.

The Welsh Office re-stated their commitment to the AWS in launching a second phase from 1993. Revised guidance was circulated in 1994, but not officially issued until 1996. The funding strategy of the first ten years was not to be sustained and the central role of the Welsh Office in leading and reviewing policy was lessened. Although re-stating the original AWS principles and wording guidance on service models permissively so that those services previously viewed as consistent with the principles could still be developed, a non-prescriptive stance was being taken, consistent with a non-interventionist political lead. Autonomy of local decision-making, consumer choice and the availability of a range of provision options were emphasized accordingly. Resettlement became the prime commitment for new money. Ring-fencing of money already allocated was to remain, but would be reviewed in 1997. Some interest groups saw the shift in priorities as the hijacking of the AWS, and few now saw the completion of a comprehensive set of community services as being likely.

The power (exercised by the Welsh Office) has receded and with it some of the responsibility.

There are lots of subtle changes, e.g. qualifying statements such as 'where appropriate' and 'where necessary'. You have to read between the lines.

Finally, local government reorganization has introduced a new set of challenges. An increased number of smaller unitary authorities has directly affected the breadth of remit of senior social services officers and development and planning personnel. Coupled with the broader thrust of community care policy and the lower profile of the AWS, there is considerable concern that the distinctiveness of learning disability policy, which has been a feature of the last dozen years, has all but disappeared. We will return to discuss policy in the current context in the concluding chapters. We will now move on to look at the service development achieved in the AWS years in more detail, starting with the introduction of multidisciplinary community teams and individual planning and the extent to which these promoted individually-tailored service delivery. Following chapters look at the development of advocacy and changes in residential, day and family support services. It is not surprising that such a complex strategy for organizational change has encountered difficulties along the way. Many of the recommendations made by the architects of the AWS were relatively untried. The AWS built up a strong commitment to its aims and principles within Wales and support for its strategic direction and processes. The next five chapters assess its achievements in areas central to its agenda.

References

Abrams, P. (1978). Community care: some research problems and priorities. In: *Social Care Research*. (J. Barnes and N. Connelly, eds.) pp. 78–99. London: Bedford Square Press.

Association of County Councils (1989). *Caring for People: Making a Reality of Community Care*. London: Association of County Councils.

Audit Commission (1986). *Making a Reality of Community Care*. London: HMSO.

Bean, P. and Mouncer, P. (1993). *Discharged from Mental Hospitals*. London: Macmillan and MIND.

Bell, C. and Newby, H. (1971). *Community Studies*. London: Allen and Unwin.

Beyer, S., Evans, G., Todd, S. and Blunden, R. (1986). *Planning for the All-Wales Strategy: a Review of Issues Arising in Welsh Counties*. Cardiff: Mental Handicap in Wales Applied Research Unit, University of Wales College of Medicine.

Campaign for the Mentally Handicapped (CMH) (1972). *Even Better Services?* London: CMH.

Department of Health and Social Security (DHSS) (1971). *Better Services for the Mentally Handicapped*. London: HMSO.

Department of Health and Social Security (DHSS) (1972). *Circular (72) 35*.

Department of Health and Social Security (DHSS) (1976). *Priorities for Health and Personal Social Services in England*. London: HMSO.

Department of Health and Social Security (DHSS) (1977). *Priorities in the Health and Social Services: the Way Forward*. London: HMSO.

Department of Health and Social Security (DHSS) (1979). *Report of the Committee of Enquiry into Mental Handicap Nursing and Care*. London: HMSO.

Department of Health and Social Security (DHSS) (1981a). *Care in Action: a Handbook of Policies and Priorities for the Health and Personal Social Services in England*. London: HMSO.

Department of Health and Social Security (DHSS) (1981b). *Care in the Community: a Consultation Document on Moving Resources for Care in England*. London: HMSO.

Department of Health and Social Security (DHSS) (1985). *Government Response to the Second Report from the Social Services Committee, 1984–85 Session: Community Care with Special Reference to Adult Mentally Ill and Mentally Handicapped People*. London: HMSO.

Felce, D. (1994). *Planning for High Quality: Providing Housing for People with Severe or Profound Learning Disabilities*. Cardiff: Welsh Centre for Learning Disabilities Applied Research Unit, University of Wales College of Medicine and also available from the Welsh Office.

Felce, D., Beyer, S. and Todd, S. (1995) A strategy for all seasons. *Community Care*, 3–9 August, 22–23.

Griffiths, R. (1988). *Community Care: Agenda for Action*. London: HMSO.

Hunter, D. J. and Wistow, G. (1987). *Community Care in Britain: Variations on a Theme.* London: King's Fund.

Independent Development Council for People with Mental Handicap (IDC) (1988). *Frameworks for Change.* London: King's Fund Centre.

Knapp, M., Cambridge, P., Thomason, C. *et al.* (1992). *Care in the Community: Challenge and Demonstration.* Aldershot: Ashgate.

McGrath, M. (1991). *Multi-disciplinary Teamwork: Community Mental Handicap Teams.* Aldershot: Avebury.

Ministry of Health (1957). *Royal Commission on the Law Relating to Mental Illness and Mental Deficiency.* London: HMSO.

Ministry of Health (1963). *Health and Welfare: the Development of Community Care.* London: HMSO.

Pahl, R. (1965). *Urbs in Rure.* London: Weidenfield and Nicolson.

Rees, A. (1950). *Life in a Welsh Countryside.* Cardiff: University of Wales Press.

Renshaw, J., Hampson, R., Thomason, C. *et al.* (1988). *Care in the Community: the First Steps.* Aldershot: Gower.

Seebohm Report (1968). *Report of the Committee on Local Authority and Allied Personal Social Services.* London: HMSO.

Stacey, M. (1960). *Tradition and Change: a Study of Banbury.* Oxford: Oxford University Press.

United Nations General Assembly (1972). *Declaration on the Rights of Mentally Retarded Persons*, Resolution 2856, 26th Session, 1972.

Walker, A. (1984). *Social Planning: a Strategy for Socialist Welfare.* Oxford: Basil Blackwell.

Webb, A. and Wistow, G. (1982). *Whither State Welfare? Policy Implementation in Personal Social Services, 1979–80.* London: Royal Institute of Public Administration.

Welsh Office (1982). *Report of the All Wales Working Party on Services for Mentally Handicapped People.* Cardiff: Welsh Office.

Welsh Office (1983). *All Wales Strategy for the Development of Services for Mentally Handicapped People.* Cardiff: Welsh Office.

Welsh Office (1985). *Circular HC (85) 46.*

Welsh Office (1987a). *All Wales Strategy for the Development of Services for Mentally Handicapped People: Review of Progress Since March 1983.* Cardiff: Welsh Office.

Welsh Office (1987b). *Community Care: an Efficiency Scrutiny.* Cardiff: Welsh Office.

Welsh Office (1987c). *Community Care and Efficiency Scrutiny: Action Plan.* Cardiff: Welsh Office.

Welsh Office (1988). *All Wales Mental Handicap Strategy: Planning and Progress Review and Financial Allocation Timetable for 1988/89 Onwards.* Cardiff: Welsh Office.

Welsh Office (1989). *The All Wales Strategy: Annual Report 1987/88.* Cardiff: Welsh Office.

Young, M. and Willmott, P. (1962). *Family and Kinship in East London.* Harmondsworth: Penguin Books.

Chapter 4

Responses to need at the local level: multidisciplinary community teams, individual plans and service packages

As Chapter 2 illustrated, the period before the launch of the AWS in 1983 was characterized by a strong, historically rooted commitment to long-stay hospital provision and centralized community services, this despite the gradual development of thinking which went beyond a 'bricks and mortar' response towards the difficulties of people with learning disabilities. Like the other countries of the UK, Wales had failed to invest in an adequate community infrastructure for people with learning disabilities. As many studies had shown, community services were typically unplanned, fragmented, poorly coordinated, and without adequate mechanisms to involve individuals and their families in decision-making (Bayley, 1973; Wilkin, 1979; Glendinning, 1983; Ayer and Alaszewski, 1984). The critique of a buildings-based service model was bringing considerable pressure to create alternative provision. But how might arrangements for delivering coordinated, needs-led services be designed? And what were the impacts of the new arrangements on individuals and their families? The proposals in the AWS were based on ideas and practice which had developed in the five years before its launch.

Before the AWS

Two interrelated and eminently logical solutions were proposed to provide mechanisms for local service coordination based on a close understanding of individual needs. The first was the establishment of multidisciplinary community teams (MCTs), originally termed community mental handicap teams, but now mostly renamed community learning disability teams. But MCTs could only ensure coordinated service delivery if they had access to an effective means of addressing the needs and wants of individual service users and families. The second solution was, therefore, the development of an individual planning system, initially promulgated by the Jay Committee (DHSS, 1979).

Prior to the AWS, MCTs in Britain had had a relatively short history, so short in fact that a considerable amount of organizational learning was yet to accumulate about their processes and effects. The Court Report (DHSS, 1976) had urged the establishment of multidisciplinary district handicap teams (DHTs) to serve children with physical or mental handicaps. Mansell (1990), in a short history of the MCT in Britain, credits the National Development Group and Development Team as being responsible for promoting the idea of MCTs within the field of learning disability. Teams were seen as fulfilling some central key roles, especially the coordination of service delivery, provision of direct services, and gate-keeping to other services. Importantly, they were to provide a single point of access for individuals and families to local services. Apart from assisting families and liaising with the range of local health and social services, MCTs were also seen as a vital link to hospitals and to health authority 'community units' providing residential and day care (Simon, 1981). This additional emphasis was a source of confusion which undoubtedly led to variability in the structure and function of MCTs. By 1981, two-thirds of health districts in England were found to have DHTs and MCTs either fully operational or planned (Plank, 1982). MCTs in Wales appear to have developed subsequent to their active promotion by the AWS.

Reviewed by McGrath (1991), evidence from Britain and America on MCTs serving a wide range of user groups during the 1970s and 1980s appears to be somewhat equivocal about their effectiveness (Kane, 1975; Brill, 1976; Payne, 1982; Westrin, 1986). On the one hand, studies supported claims that teams made more efficient use of resources by demonstrating improved collaboration between professionals, enhancement of specialist skills, more efficient use of unqualified staff, and the development of new specialist skills not tied to qualifications. The evidence suggested that service provision was made more effective by adopting an holistic approach to individualized work, systems-based solutions to individual problems, goal- rather than process-oriented methods, a more preventative approach through the early identification of problems, and more creative development of services. There were also conclusions that teams provided a satisfying environment in which to work: skills were used more appropriately, intellectual stimulation and exchange of ideas were more evident, and it was easier to create systems of mutual support and accountability. Underpinning all of these claims was the perhaps understated view that no single professional group had, or could be deemed to have, a monopoly of expertise in community-based work. MCTs were deemed to be great 'levellers' in this respect, signalling the end of medical/psychiatric dominance in community services for people with learning disabilities.

Countervailing evidence suggested that the above advantages may have been overstated and other difficulties under-reported (Briggs, 1980; Dingwall, 1980; Lonsdale, Webb and Briggs, 1980; Huxley, 1985). The bridging of professional and organizational boundaries is commonly reported as an obstacle to clear lines of accountability and control, with team members facing potentially conflicting loyalties to their organization and to the team. There are administrative and communication costs in running MCTs which may reduce time for direct work with service users. Time spent in meetings does not necessarily reduce client contact time, as there is evidence to suggest that it may be increased by improved communication (Huxley, 1985). However, meetings need to be productive. If service development forms part of the role of the team, this can remove team members from direct work. There is also some basis for the claim that MCTs can become inward-looking, preoccupied with team processes and develop a professional hegemony to the detriment of service users (Dingwall, 1980). In the view of one commentator, the powerful forces within teams can lead to insularity and even a sense of hostility to the outside world (Stevenson, 1980). Moreover, the overlapping or blurring of professional roles within teams can occur haphazardly rather than as a result of deliberate policy. MCTs would appear, at the very least, to require highly skilled management capable of sorting out complex professional and organizational problems.

One of the early messages to emerge from this pre-AWS experience was the idea that MCTs were, or could be, a highly convenient way of overcoming long-running difficulties of managing the interface between health and social services. However, this does not necessarily recognize that many of the underlying difficulties were less to do with organizational structures and bureaucratic mechanisms than the source and nature of the values, competencies and power bases of the different professional groups and agencies being asked to work together. This issue is re-visited in subsequent chapters. Restructuring by fiat is no more likely to resolve such difficulties at the level of front-line practice than is an exhortation for joint work between senior officers.

Although supportive of teamworking in general, Webb and Hobdell (1980) have suggested that it is often prescribed without any sense of what it is that teamwork is supposed to achieve. For example, they identify two dissimilar purposes of teamwork: to overcome the disadvantages of specialization by increasing coordination, and to exploit the advantages of a division of labour by facilitating specialization. However, questions about compatibility of purposes arise in a number of areas: whether teams are expected to resolve conflicting purposes internally; whether one purpose is to be emphasized to the relative exclusion of the other; and in what ways team functioning should be linked to local services and communities and to arrangements for local planning. Already, it is easy to see how the 'internal mechanics' of MCTs could become a preoccupation to the detriment of their ultimate function to meet people's needs and wants.

MCTs under the AWS

The AWS readily acknowledged the past inaccessibility and poor coordination of services for individuals and families. Conflicting help was occasionally given by different professionals in touch with the same family. Moreover, there was not always a sensitive approach to individual needs (Welsh Office, 1983). MCTs were seen as part of the solution to these difficulties, although recommendations were guarded by the recognition that 'it is not possible to identify a unique organisational solution to these problems' (Welsh Office, 1983, para. 6.4.4). Nevertheless, the AWS anticipated the advantages of people working together in teams, sharing an administrative base and secretarial support, and having a common method of organizing work. In this way, MCTs were seen not only as providing a single point of contact for people, but also as an organizational approach to serve the best interests of service users and families.

The functions of MCTs were spelt out within the AWS fairly prescriptively, and included: (1) provision of support and advice to parents of newly-diagnosed mentally handicapped children; (2) preparation and rolling forward of an individual plan for each person; (3) mobilization of community resources; (4) promotion of contacts between individuals, their families and local voluntary services in relation to the use of new services; (5) provision of regular practical advice and guidance to parents and care staff to help them to teach people skills and enable them to deal effectively with difficulties; (6) provision of practical help to individuals and families; (7) provision of advice and advocacy; (8) provision in the team office of a central point of contact and information; (9) transmission to employing authorities of information about deficiencies in local service provision; and (10) participation in the planning of local service developments (Welsh Office, 1983, para. 6.4.9).

In regard to the above, MCTs were expected to meet requirements for direct work (1, 5, 6), engage in individual planning (2), develop new resources and creative ways of using them (3, 4), provide a single point of contact for individuals (8), offer advocacy (7), and participate in local planning (9 and 10). In the face of the earlier reported challenges of multi-disciplinary teamwork, the AWS had extraordinarily high expectations for MCTs. In the absence of clear evidence about the viability of MCTs at this point in time, or the availability of a demonstration model, these specifications could be construed as a major gamble. On the other hand, the operational alternatives were neither obvious nor being articulated. As a result, there was a tendency for AWS expectations for teams to be read as a prescription. The best way for counties to secure funding for the professional infrastructure was to follow what the AWS proposed to the letter. Although one county fundamentally redrew its arrangements some years later, all Welsh counties started off by creating some form of MCT.

An all-Wales survey of MCTs in 1987 (McGrath, 1991) showed that only one of the 37 teams in existence at that time predated the AWS. Hence, the Welsh MCTs were very new and, in many respects, still heavily involved in 'learning by doing'. Staff development programmes tailored to the needs of MCT staff took time to take root (Ash and Woods, 1987; Brown, 1990). Between them, Welsh MCTs employed over 300 staff by 1987. Unlike the MCTs in England in 1981 which had been mostly health-based (Plank, 1982), Welsh teams were all located within social services departments. Their size, composition and responsibilities varied considerably. Teams in six counties had responsibility for all people with learning disabilities, whereas those in the remaining two served primarily or only adults. Children in these counties were the responsibility of social workers in area social services teams. (Subsequent to the survey one of these counties established MCTs for children paralleling those for adults.) Teams covered populations averaging from 52 000 in the most rural districts to 86 000 in more urban localities, except for one county with exceptionally large catchment populations averaging

181 000. The majority of teams were larger than their English counter-parts, which typically had three of four workers (Plank, 1982). Ten of the Welsh teams had less than six members, eighteen had six to eleven members and nine had twelve or more members. Four traits were held in common. Team members were described as having shared aims; there were distinctive roles for team members; there were mechanisms facili-tating joint work and all teams regarded themselves as teams. Neverthe-less, there proved to be a variety of teamworking models.

McGrath's (1991) survey characterized teams in terms of composition, leadership and community orientation. In terms of composition, there were 'basic' teams (14%) consisting of community nurses and social workers; 'professionally-oriented' teams (38%) which included members of other professional disciplines such as clinical psychologists, speech therapists, occupational therapists, physiotherapists or health visitors; 'service-oriented' teams (35%) with service organizers such as family aide or respite care coordinators complementing other core staff; and 'integrated' teams (14%) composed of nurses, social workers, other professionals and service organizers. Administrative staff were present in all but one team. Team composition gave a first indication of county prior-ities in the role and function of teams, though these changed over time, reflecting the adoption of successful arrangements elsewhere. For example, by 1991 all teams had progressed towards integrating social work, community nursing, the services of other therapists and family aide or respite care organizers. However, other innovations were not always adopted. The highly regarded welfare rights officers present in all MCTs in one county were not replicated elsewhere. Despite there being respon-sibility for children in six counties, in only three counties has there been any specific education liaison post linked to the MCT (two at team level and one at county level). Given the liaison difficulties with schools present in some areas, more formal liaison arrangements might have been more widely beneficial.

A variety of arrangements were noted regarding the leadership of teams. About a quarter (24%) were found to be leaderless with no-one in overall charge of team members, (subsequently all these teams moved to a model incorporating a team leader); all teams in one county (14%) had a coordinator responsible for all social services staff but with no control over health staff; 43% had team coordinators with day-to-day responsi-bility for all team members and managerial control of social services staff (fieldworkers and service organizers); and, finally, 19% had service coordi-nators whose managerial responsibilities for social services staff extended to day and/or residential staff.

A number of factors were implicated in shaping decisions about the composition and leadership of MCTs. First, there was still a lack of theoretical or empirical knowledge about the appropriate balance of professionals within teams. How the different professional groups perceived models of care, individual needs and professional priorities was largely to be determined. There were important political considerations about the matching of resources to achieve a reasonable balance of responsibilities between health and social services. Finally, some of the specialist staff required were simply not available. Speech therapy and physiotherapy posts in particular were often unfilled, reflecting national staff shortages in these disciplines.

The achievements of MCTs

Claims about the achievement of teams under the AWS to a large degree reflect the earlier literature and helped to confirm that they improved resource efficiency, fostered a more holistic, individual needs-led way of working, and provided a satisfying environment in which to work. These outcomes were far from universal, but they were more likely to be noted by team members when certain conditions prevailed (McGrath, 1991). Most in evidence was the unity of purpose created by a commitment to the principles of the AWS. Not only did this apply to MCTs but to other interest groups such as families and voluntary organizations, thereby helping to broaden collaboration. Agreement about the three core AWS principles enabled professional differences to be set aside or placed in their proper context. Moreover, such unity of purpose could be galvanized into a powerful force directed towards changing services to serve the interests of individuals in more appropriate ways. This process was further assisted when team members had been given access to joint training.

The use of a shared work base was of pivotal importance for it created a culture of cooperation and often made the difference between whether or not team members had regular opportunities to consult each other. Running in parallel with this was the value attached to having a shared database. Indeed, this was typically the product of occupying the same work base. Representing a commitment to the pooling of data from different sources about the needs and circumstances of individuals and their families, it provided an important source of information which could assist individual and local planning. The mechanism uniting data with action, however, was some form of individual planning or shared action planning, supported by designated key workers, for it was this that brought together interested parties as partners and set the context for working out realistic plans to meet the needs and preferences of individuals.

One of the contentious issues thrown up by the work of MCTs was that of role blurring. The values-led approach, reinforced by the growing adoption of normalization training, facilitated both professional alliances and co-working with the voluntary sector and community which had not been particularly widespread before (Grant and Jenkins, 1990). The crossing of professional boundaries was, perhaps, inevitable as workers strove to move away from off-the-peg responses to people's needs and towards more creative ways of working together. At worst, however, role blurring could be the result of one professional group undertaking the work of another for which it was not trained. This has remained the subject of dispute, exacerbated by a move by the health authorities from the early 1990s to restrict their staff to work related to 'health gains' only. The consequence of this shift, together with the introduction of care management, has narrowed the focus of health professionals and reduced role blurring.

Coordinating inter-professional work within teams was considerably easier than that involving collaboration with other professionals. Four groups of externally-based staff were important to the work of MCTs: generic social workers and social services staff in day centres and hostels; health professionals working with pre-school children; special school staff; and therapists. Overall, joint working with these groups was more likely where MCTs were able to offer professional skills, resources and support; where there was a commitment to collaboration; where a forum existed for interaction outside of specific case discussions; where formal links were deliberately created to stream-line communication, for example by designating one person as having a liaison role; and where there were clear parameters for collaborative action.

The indirect work of MCTs was much in evidence. This comprised activities like mobilizing community resources, facilitating voluntary sector initiatives, engaging in welfare rights work, and developing new services such as family respite and family aide services. Indirect work was commonly reported by team members to be among the most important achievements of teams. Progress on this front was more marked where there was an investment in designated service development workers.

Two structural factors were found to facilitate almost all of the reported achievements of MCTs. The first of these was the existence of clear, delegated financial and professional responsibilities. Lack of clarity in responsibilities simply led to confusion, duplication of effort or a rather loose laissez-faire system where team members worked in isolation from one another. Teams with access to contingency budgets for procuring or pump-priming creative new services or initiatives were at an advantage for they were better able to fine-tune services to the needs of individuals. However, this also placed a premium on the need for financial management and budgetary planning support, something which has been thrown into stark relief by the more finance-driven care-managed community care reforms. Secondly, MCTs with a team coordinator were more able to maintain a strategic steer of local developments and help to ensure that fieldwork, domiciliary, day and residential services were propelled by the same values and visions. This worked best where coordinators retained responsibility for all team members, irrespective of professional identity and employing agency, as well as other local learning disability services. In this situation, however, there were indications that the day-to-day management of MCT members required a separate team leader as the coordinator role was otherwise too broad for one person.

Briefly stated, these were the local structures and the outline processes established to provide a coordinated approach to the meeting of individual needs. The mechanism tying MCTs to their clientele, i.e. individual planning, needs some further explanation.

Individual planning

The vision of the AWS was of a service tailored to the individual needs and wishes of each person and family, facilitated by the interweaving of informal and voluntary organized support, but based on the full involvement of each person in the preparation, implementation and monitoring of their own care or support. The individual plan (IP) was put forward as the main foundation upon which these aims would be achieved. The original expectations were for 'all professionals concerned with the individual to meet at regular (six monthly) intervals, together with the client and family, to plan the short- and long-term aims for that person'; and further that 'plans must not at any stage be the product of professional assessment alone'. More recently, the Welsh Office has stated that 'everyone who wants one should have an individual plan co-ordinating care throughout their life and properly reflecting their needs and wishes' (Welsh Office, 1996).

These aspirations were embodied in the initial AWS county plans throughout Wales. Some core principles can be identified underlying the various individual planning systems that were developed – the involvement of the person with a learning disability and usually his or her carers; gaining an understanding of the service user's perceptions of their needs; systematic goal planning aiming at increased choice and independence of the service user; the production of an individual plan as an outcome of the IP meeting; and clearly specified responsibilities for implementing the goals set which could also involve the appointment of a named service provider to coordinate the plan's implementation (Brechin and Swain, 1986; Blunden, Evans and Humphreys, 1987; Jenkins et al., 1988). In Wales, the individual planning system developed in the NIMROD scheme (Blunden, 1980; Blunden, Evans and Humphreys, 1987) was very influential in how counties first approached the task of setting up IP systems. At the IP meeting, short- and long-term goals would be planned and those present would agree who was to undertake the various tasks necessary to achieve these goals. The NIMROD system stressed the preparation time necessary before an IP meeting in order to establish rapport with the service user, to understand his or her strengths and needs, and to help the service user communicate his or her aspirations. IPs were not only the main vehicle for individual planning; they were also envisaged as the primary source of data on service deficiencies which were to be fed back into the strategic planning system.

Experience of individual planning

With a vast backlog of work when first established, MCTs experienced early difficulties in progressing towards the idea of IPs for all. By 1987, 68% of teams had done either no IPs or had done them for less than 10% of users (McGrath, 1991). Only five of the thirty-seven MCTs claimed a 25% or greater coverage. Three years later a family survey found little advance with only 11% of carers identifying an IP meeting in the previous twelve months, though other forms of meeting were recorded, e.g. case review, service review, case conference (McGrath, Grant and Ramcharan, 1993). This figure, however, concealed considerable variation in the prevalence of IPs between counties (from 3% to 30%), reflecting both the priority accorded IPs by senior managers and the available staffing levels in MCTs. A four district survey by Evans et al. (1994), which included people living in different types of residence as well as the family home, reported higher coverage of IPs, but there had still only been a marginal increase in coverage from 29% to 33% over a period of four years.

There were many reasons for the slow progress in implementing IPs. In the main these were to do with either the lack of resources and under-developed infrastructures or with concerns about the IP model (McGrath, 1991). Apart from the time required for a full IP and the maintenance of regular reviews, team members did not want to raise service users' and carers' expectations in vain and they were often unwilling to set up IPs when they knew that resources, such as respite care or appropriate day services, were unavailable. Adherence to the original IP guidelines by team members made time-consuming and complex organizational demands of the system, and these were regarded as impractical and unnec-essary for all users. Users and carers were frequently described as daunted by the large and lengthy meetings which could too easily become profes-sionally dominated (Berry, 1986; Humphreys, 1986). Some team members have argued that the decisions to have an IP meeting and who attends it should be up to the service user rather than professionals. However, only a small proportion of service users are capable of advocating for themselves (see Chapter 5). With advocacy schemes being in short supply, it was therefore still easy for the system to ignore the service user's voice. For service users deemed to be appropriately supported, the need for IPs was less important. However, it still raises the question of how best to ensure that everyone's needs and circumstances can be appropriately reviewed.

An evaluative study of the NIMROD system (Humphreys *et al.*, 1985) led to revised guidelines (Blunden, Evans and Humphreys, 1987). First, a distinction was made between a direct service provider and a 'plan coordi-nator', noting that there are situations where it would be appropriate to separate the roles. Secondly, less emphasis was placed on the IP meeting provided that inter-professional or inter-agency issues were resolved outside this forum. Counties began to experiment with different IP models and simplified approaches where the nature of the IP meeting and process were determined more transparently by the views and perspectives of the service user. Efforts at total coverage were abandoned in favour of estab-lishing priority groups for IPs. These typically included school-leavers, those moving into more independent living situations or facing some other major life changes. In retrospect this perhaps provided an early signal about the kind of debates to emerge much later regarding requirements for eligibility criteria surrounding needs assessments following implemen-tation of the NHS and Community Care Act 1990, and about the opera-tional difficulties of feeding the results of IP processes into strategic planning (see Chapters 3 and 11).

In light of the above, key workers were often left to adopt a variety of approaches to planning at the individual case level, as one social worker explained:

With children I've got a couple of statutory child care cases which are dealt with differently. With other children that are not statutory child care cases I tend to just fit into the school reviews, but then I don't actually think much of those so that's done purely for my own benefit because I haven't got time to do individual plans for everybody. If I don't think that's working or there's a poor relationship between the school and the families, I have done an individual plan. Those that haven't got any of those things don't have any formal plans. I mean there is a lot of planning that goes on in the sense that I will go to a family and discuss a whole range of services, make a note of those, write them up in my file and go back and say 'I've been able to do. . .'. So informal planning takes place. With two other people I use a kind of old-fashioned case review meeting every year or whatever. About half a dozen have said they don't want planning anyway. But the others don't get it.

Regardless of what processes were followed, it was therefore still not inevitable that inter-agency coordination and a tailored response to individual need would be the end result, as the same social worker illustrated:

It's very difficult because a lot of the services we are identifying in the individual plan are provided by agencies that are not accountable to me or to the CMHT or even to social services, so I have no clout as a key worker. . . So I can do individual plans with people but the plans have no status in the sense that they're not a contract.

The warning shot being fired here is really about the central importance of authority and accountability in any set of arrangements. Planning processes of any type were likely to be ineffectual unless backed by a commitment to deliver what was promised within an agreed framework of accountability. In the worker's view these inter-agency arrangements were clearly not in place, leaving both herself and her clients disempowered.

Nevertheless, in relation to the reported benefits of IP systems, McGrath's (1991) MCT survey suggested endorsement of four prior claims: they were client-centred, with service users involved in their own life planning; they were goal-oriented, making progress easier to evaluate; they facilitated service coordination, although as we have seen they could not guarantee it; and they offered a planning base, reflecting the needs of individuals. On the other hand, active participation of service users within IPs was reportedly low (Humphreys and Blunden, 1987), though in some parts of the UK it would appear that service users and their families could sometimes find themselves excluded altogether (Laws, Bolt and Gibbs, 1988). Case studies of younger disabled people continued to illustrate the challenges of user involvement in needs assessment (Day, 1994), especially in relation to proven methods of interaction for people with speech difficulties or social impairment, inhibitions about needs assessment itself, lack of experience and low expectations of parental carers, and the perpetuation of a service-driven, 'forms-led' approach to assessment. Once again, the AWS was to provide a foretaste of difficulties which have continued to press upon the assessment experiences of care managers in the transition to the 'new' community care (Ellis, 1993).

Two other sets of issues impinged on the smooth working of IP systems. First, forms of independent advocacy, although promulgated in the AWS as an important priority for the voluntary sector, took several years to take root. There were difficulties associated with obtaining AWS funding for advocacy projects. There was a sense of ambivalence about whether it was appropriate for central government, as opposed to the independent sector, directly to fund this activity. Furthermore, the relationship between professional and independent advocacy had not been clearly specified in the original AWS document. Neither has it been clarified in any subsequent AWS documentation. As a consequence, fewer individuals have been helped or supported to speak for themselves, either as their own advocates or through partnership schemes or citizen advocacy, than might have been envisaged as necessary to facilitate the fuller participation of service users in individual planning. More is said about this in Chapter 5. Secondly, key workers often reported themselves as having insufficient authority to problem-solve or make arrangements across agency boundaries. In such circumstances, preferred plans for individuals either had to be jettisoned or individuals were left with less desirable options. This raises questions about the determination of service packages and how they were evaluated.

The packaging of services

One of the major paradigm shifts required by the AWS which directly implicated MCT members, service users and families was the move from a service- to a needs-led planning and intervention model. Through the IP process, it was anticipated that it would be possible to create or 'fine-tune' service packages that offered a closer 'fit' with people's individual needs and wants rather than to slot people into the available services. In this there were parallels with early experimentation with case management in the UK (Challis and Davies, 1986).

Two issues are addressed here: first, how did the newly established arrangements under the AWS shape who got what services, and secondly, what factors mediated people's judgements about the quality of services? Findings are based on a seven district survey, carried out during 1990/91, of all service users who were living at home with families (McGrath, Grant and Ramcharan, 1991; Grant, McGrath and Ramcharan, 1994). The survey was based on a mailing shot which had a 76% response rate with 752 family respondents and was designed to provide some initial indications about the relationship between service processes and outcomes. At this point, the findings are generalizable only to people living in the family home. More is said about the relationship between services and the quality of people's lives in Chapters 5–8.

An analysis of personal influences in service packaging suggested that services tended to be targeted at children, adults with low physical capacities and carers with high stress levels (McGrath, Ramcharan and Grant, 1993). These factors were major determinants of the scope of service packages. Persons with severe challenging behaviour seemed to be less prominent as a priority group in this regard. There was, however, a strong link between challenging behaviour and carer stress, suggesting that the latter may have been used as a proxy indicator of the former by practitioners. However, even in 1990/91 when the survey took place, challenging behaviour services were still under development in many localities, thus placing restrictions on the options available. Respite or family aide services were commonly accessed by families in these circumstances.

Relatively little informal help from outside the household was apparent. Paradoxically, this was even less evident where challenging behaviour had been reported, once again highlighting the vulnerability of this group of service users and families. The needs of this particular group had been identified as a priority for national action by the All Wales Advisory Panel (1991) in its *Challenges and Responses* report.

Having identified which groups of individuals were targeted for intervention in service packaging terms, we do not wish to suggest that this was the product of a deficit model in which the personal characteristics of individuals were the sole considerations. Nevertheless, the emphasis on an analysis of individual needs can lead in this direction. The danger, of course, is the possibility of neglecting social and ecological models which place a greater emphasis on environmental, cultural and political factors impinging on an individual's lifestyle.

The data also enabled the influence of the new planning arrangements on service delivery to be examined (McGrath, Ramcharan and Grant, 1993). Only 21% of respondents believed that there was an agreed plan worked out for themselves and their relative. However, 48% reported having been involved in some kind of meeting with professionals to discuss their relative in the last twelve months. Of these, about a quarter were said to be IPs, 42% were reviews divided roughly equally between school and day centres, 18% were case conferences and the remainder could not be categorized. Family carers had genuine difficulty separating the status of different meetings and this was not made any easier if little written information was forwarded to them about what had been agreed. Even so, only about 11% of the sample had something they recognized as an IP and just under 30% had a service review or case conference. Fewer than two-thirds (64%) of respondents believed that they had a key worker. In addition to the personnel characteristics raised above, the presence of a key worker and whether family members had attended planning meetings about their relative in the last year were dominant factors influencing the number of services received and professionals visiting. There was some support for the view that the predispositions of family members to formal services also influenced the range of services and professionals seen. A belief by families in self-reliance or a stated unwillingness on their part to look to professionals for help were both shown to be relevant here. Subsequent case studies illustrated just how difficult it could be for key workers to turn round the beliefs and value positions of some families when there had been problematic or rejecting experiences with services in the past.

Defining the personal or system factors that mediate who gets what services gives an indication of priority groups and filtering mechanisms. How services are appraised for their quality raises some other issues. A range of criteria were drawn up as the basis on which to form judgements about service quality. These fell into three groups: overall views about services in terms of perceived importance and satisfaction ratings; views about unmet needs expressed in terms of whether more was required to allow the family to lead a more normal life, to nurture the service user's independence, or to address identified service shortfalls; and finally a range of indicators about family stress including expressed feelings of

Table 4.1 Relationships between service process factors and criteria for appraising service packages

Service process factors	General appraisal		Service shortfall				Carer stress		
	Satisfaction with services	Importance of services	Sufficiency of professional help	More help to sustain 'normal' family life	More help to sustain user independence	Aggregate unmet service needs	Isolation	Health affected	Social restrictions
Extra contact required	***		***	***	***	***	***	***	
Proactive visiting preferred	***	***		***	*	***	***	***	*
Perceived empathy with carer	***	***	***	**	***	***	***	*	**
Perceived empathy with user	***	***	***	**	***	***		**	**
Reluctance to call professionals	***	***	***	**	***	***	***	*	**
Reported agreed service plan	***	***	***	*					
Recent involvement in care plan	***	***	**	**			*	**	
Presence of key worker	***	***	***						

Chi square *P* values ***<.001 ** .01 *<.05

Note: In summary, a number of service process factors were strongly associated with a range of positive service outcomes. Empathetic qualities perceived in workers, a preference for a proactive visiting pattern, the absence of reluctance about calling on professionals and no stated need for contact with professionals beyond that normally expected were all associated with positive service outcomes.

isolation, effects of caring on physical and emotional health, and experiences of social restriction in the lives of family carers (McGrath, Grant and Ramcharan, 1991).

Carers' positive appraisal of services and general satisfaction were related strongly to the total number of services received and to the organizational factors discussed above – the presence of a key worker, knowledge of a service plan and involvement in an individual planning meeting. A high correlation was found between the provision of advice and information and satisfaction ratings with services (McGrath, Grant and Ramcharan, 1991). However, evidence that all the ingredients of a service package were in place was far from synonymous with how the package itself was appraised (Table 4.1). What emerged with considerable force was the influence of carers' perceptions of professionals' ability to empathize with them and with service users, the importance of which cannot be overstated. Despite ring-fenced funding for new services, there were, and continue to be, significant resource shortfalls. The ability to explain why everything was not possible, while still working in partnership with individuals and families, turned often on the understanding and respect that had developed between the parties involved. The time over which the relationship between practitioner and both carers and user had developed was an important consideration in this context. Many carers, commenting warmly on a previous key worker, complained of the high turn-over of staff, pointing to the difficulty of building up a trusting relationship with a new worker who was perhaps only seen infrequently.

These findings suggest the importance of an understanding of service quality appraisal, i.e. of relationship factors rather than merely structural arrangements. However, the measures used here are best seen as intermediate outcomes – they are the product, directly or indirectly, of what services seek to do. They may, nevertheless, tell us little about what service users or carers want or value.

Before commenting further on this issue, two illustrations of relationships between key workers, service users and carers demonstrate the importance of understanding each person's history of contact with services.

Mr and Mrs Andrews had recently retired but were still supporting their daughter, Brenda (in her thirties), at home. Brenda was the youngest child (sic) in a large family. She attended a new, locally-based training unit on weekdays and was developing a close relationship with a family aide who took her out on a regular basis. Brenda's parents, however, had rather different views about the dynamics of their relationship with Fran, the key worker, as the following interview extract illustrates.

Interviewer: Would you say that you can express your views quite openly to Fran and feel that she will respond sensibly?

Mrs A: I get on alright with Fran because I moan to her every time she comes.

Mr A: I feel that perhaps she doesn't take to me too kindly because I tend to rock the system as well. She is part of the system so I think she tends not to look upon me too kindly sometimes in that respect. If the system is wrong I feel somebody must say so and the system must be put right.

Mrs A: She has been quite helpful the few times that she has been here, I must say that about her. She listened. I was grateful when I explained about Brenda and her epilepsy because it does worry me, but she was trying to say well perhaps everything will be alright, we will get things sorted out when I come back because of this group they now have for people with epilepsy.

Mr A: I see it a little differently. She is a trained nurse to start with isn't she? She sees epilepsy every day of her life in an institutional setting. It's not a great problem for her there and she tends to come to us with a sort of professional attitude you know, we will sort this out professionally. To a professional, where you have got all the facilities and everything in an institution, that is OK, you can cope. Here in the house very often you won't do. You feel absolutely useless in trying to help her.

Interviewer: On a different level, more on an emotional type feeling level between yourselves and the key worker, would you say that you could speak to her as you might a close friend, for example?

Mrs A: I could.

Mr A: You could. I don't know that I could really, to be honest with you.

Even from a short extract like this, taken from a much longer discussion with the family, it is possible to gain some idea of how a family's perception of the key worker's role can carry assumptions about the way that the key worker should act and perform. In the case of the Andrews family it is difficult to see how the key worker could begin to reconcile the differing positions taken up by Brenda's parents. For Mr Andrews, his rather dismissive attitude was linked to his perception of earlier failings connected to the individual plan:

Interviewer: It sounds as if it has been some time since there was something resembling an individual plan?

Mr A: It is two years. More than that maybe.

Mrs A: The key worker has been here about twelve months.

Mr A: We were invited to her last IP.

Interviewer: Right, so would you say that you now have an overall view of what the services are trying to achieve for Brenda?

Mr A: No, I haven't got a clue of what they are doing with her and this is what has always annoyed me. I don't know what they are doing, how they see her. It is at least a three way thing, the parents, the Unit, and there is a tutor as well, and we all see her in different ways and I think it is not one person's job. It is together that we must work to achieve a result. We went to this IP and we arrived in there and there is her tutor who must apologise for the absence of various others, unavoidably detained or whatever. Let's go home, let's be honest. What is the point if they can't take that bit of time. It is an appointment made and if they can't be there to meet that appointment... As far as we are concerned it is a very important occasion when we are making a plan, or we should be trying to make a plan together.

Taking another case, some further glimpses are possible into the need for flexibility about how individual planning was approached. Tony had been living in lodgings for six years after spending most of his life in a large hospital. Tony's landlord and landlady, Rob and Helen, treated Tony as very much part of the family and basically gave him the complete run of the house. Rob and Helen organized Tony's laundry and his finances and had helped him to take out a sensible insurance policy to protect his long-term savings. In her key worker role, Sue reckoned that she dealt with 'every aspect' of Tony's life, although much of this centred on his health because of the many problems Tony had in this respect. With the vagaries of Tony's health and his tendency to change his mind about plans, Sue had given up working to an IP system. Tony could be very stubborn and obsessional and his frequent changes of mind tended to undermine everyone else's best efforts to help him. Sue did not view this as failure however. The IP approach in this instance had proved to be too formal. Sue, therefore, found it more appropriate to visit and review at regular intervals. This more informal approach seemed to suit Tony who had a close relationship with Sue. Although Tony was very happy in his lodgings, he was without a job or any kind of structured day activity, having been 'expelled' from the local day centre because of his behaviour. Sue was still working on this problem but without much apparent success.

In this second case, continuity of relationships between the key worker and the service user was an important ingredient in the relationship of trust and understanding that had been built up. However, this was not always possible. Discontinuities in working relationships were a 'fact of life' though some, being seen as the product of poor service designs, ill thought-out organizational arrangements or a still inadequate resource base, by definition, were more avoidable than others. Insufficient author- ity to problem-solve, as in the first case, or the time and procedures required to access resources and funding, or poor management were given as reasons by MCT staff for dissatisfaction. These difficulties were seen as disempowering and some MCT staff gave notice that they were consider- ing a career move to distance themselves from the situation. Some others talked about the stress of working with 'difficult' individuals or families on their caseload who were overly demanding.

We therefore end this abbreviated account with a little more about the lives of Brenda and Tony in order to show where attempts at service packaging still fall short of helping people achieve more widespread community involvement.

In a number of respects Brenda's lifestyle is like that of many of her peers who are still living at home with parents. Aged 33, she attends a community-based day service which involves a mixture of educational, leisure and occupational activities. Although organized leisure and educa- tional activities take Brenda out into the community, this usually means in the company of a group from the training unit. She has quite an exten- sive friendship network consisting mostly of other colleagues from day services. Brenda has had a succession of boyfriends but no lasting or serious personal relationship has resulted to date. She enjoys a close relationship with her siblings, one of whom, a sister, has offered to look after her in the longer term. Brenda, however, can be quite single-minded, even stubborn, and has indicated that she would like to live in supported housing somewhere nearby so that she can have a more independent life. In consultation her key worker has offered her the opportunity to move into community housing but Brenda said that it was not quite what she was looking for. She has subsequently indicated that she would prefer her own flat. Her change of mind has been interpreted as a sign of ambivalence and uncertainty about a move so the key worker is continuing to review all the options. Brenda's key worker is proceeding at a pace that she feels Brenda and her parents can cope with in searching out and testing the alternatives. This is one reason why the pace of change in moving people into more appropriate housing can be so slow.

In the meantime Brenda is not unhappy living in the parental home. Her mother and father, both recently retired but involved in voluntary work, encourage her to do her own washing and ironing. They are committed to helping her to acquire domestic and everyday living skills and competencies, though they find themselves having to watch Brenda quite closely because of her epilepsy. This can be stressful for them, and they are very conscious of becoming over-protective as a result. Balancing the desire to help Brenda towards greater independence and autonomy against their own tendency to over-protectiveness represents a central struggle for Brenda's parents.

After living most of his life in hospital, Tony moved in as a lodger at Rob and Helen's home six years ago. He has the complete run of the house and is very happy with the lodging arrangement. Under no circumstances would he consider returning to live in the hospital. In this regard resettlement has been a great success. He gets much pleasure from the company he keeps at home and he feels part of the family.

Rob and Helen help to look after Tony's medicines. Because they do not charge Tony a great deal for his lodgings, they have been able to assist him to put some of his weekly income into a long-term savings account, giving him a degree of financial security in later life. It is not surprising that Tony feels very secure in his home environment. Despite his asthma and heart problems Tony gets out and about a lot. He has had a family aide worker for two years and enjoys his company but has not made more friends on their sorties into the community. He frequently uses the bus by himself to go into town to shop and visit favourite pubs. He meets many acquaintances on these excursions and enjoys stopping to talk, joke and pass the time of day. Time however is one of Tony's problems. He has lots of it which he has to structure for himself. Given his expulsion from a traditional day service, he is without daytime occupation. In his view he left because he was pestered too much by colleagues at the training centre: 'Some boys and girls get onto me sometimes... They call me all the time they do... I asked them what they want and they said they want money off me all the time'. Although he also admits that he was bored much of the time at the centre he has expressed interest in returning there. So far this has met with firm resistance from the day service concerned. Lack of paid work restricts his weekly income, which he resents.

Rob and Helen involve Tony in local church activities, help him to make decisions about what clothes to buy and even take him on holiday. Because of Tony's health problems, often related to his failure to use his inhaler, Rob and Helen have become used to dealing with emergencies and periodically have to pick him up from the local district general hospital following shopping trips. Rob and Helen can be seen as surrogate relatives, nursing attendants, financial advisors, holiday companions and gatekeepers for Tony to all sorts of services. In practice they have become Tony's benefactors. Without their support it is difficult to see how Tony could survive in the community.

These two brief case descriptions help to illustrate a number of developmental challenges for service packaging:

1   Despite the efforts put into consulting with service users and families about the design of support packages progress can be very slow or gradual because (a) some individuals can only proceed at a certain speed and they may need time to think about the possible impacts change would have on their lifestyles; (b) without warning they can have a change of mind about preferred options which necessitates more work from the key worker; (c) finding out what people want can be very time-consuming and far from straightforward.

2   There are structural and design deficiencies with services which limit the ability of key workers to deliver individualized, needs-led services. In some parts of the country there is still a heavy emphasis on segregated day services and even where alternative day services are available they are not always community integrated. Meanwhile, some individuals can still find themselves ejected from services for questionable reasons, leaving them with no replacement service at all.

3   Limited income due to a lack of paid work places financial restrictions on people's lives. This need not necessarily be so (Chapter 8).

4   Individuals can face great difficulty in forming close and enduring relationships with non-disabled persons and there is still a heavy reliance on relationships mediated by close family members or by services. Even with Tony who had the self-confidence and autonomy to move around the community, meeting many acquaintances, there was little sign of personal friends or close personal relationships. The key worker's reliance on a family aide worker as a befriender had only made limited inroads in this respect.

5   Families often make private plans about future care about which services can remain blissfully ignorant. IP or care management models need to be able to take account of the ties people have with others and to assess their meaningfulness and value to them.

6   Coping strategies of families need to be assessed for their effectiveness. What works needs to be reinforced. Sometimes family struggles, in the case of the Andrews family that of balancing enablement and control, are not worked upon by key workers even when recognized. They can too easily be seen as intractable.

Reflections on teamworking

The factors described in relation to MCTs which helped shape their achievements have a wider application to teamworking in different contexts and with different client groups. The factors – commitment to core values and principles, joint training, shared work base, shared data base, forms of individual or shared action planning, key worker systems, controlled role blurring, designated service development workers, clear, delegated financial and professional responsibilities, and a team coordinator – are not tied to any one type of team model. The prescriptions suggested by Ovretveit (1995) in his account of coordinated teamwork and care management emphasize many of the same points. Important though these are, it would be dangerous to pursue their application mechanistically. As Brown and Wistow (1990) have argued, '. . .the adoption of CMHTs as a unitary organisational "fix" for a diversity of, frequently ill-diagnosed, organisational requirements necessarily leads to less than optimal solutions in the field. In short, the design of CMHTs needs to follow a process of task analysis', (p. 120). A major advantage for the Welsh teams was that they were propelled by the principles of the AWS and by a reasonably clear set of objectives. Nevertheless, the precise roles of the teams were often ill-defined and the team staffing and management did not always match their responsibilities. In addition, the low level of individual planning undermined their link to local and county strategic planning.

Even with the agenda set by the AWS, team members constantly had to balance direct work with individuals against the possible longer-term gains of more strategic work. In this connection, there was frequently a tension being played out by MCT members between service development at the case level, driven by individual planning where it had been done, and service development at a service sector or locality level. The case level approach is perhaps the more 'pure' of the two since, in theory, it demands an individually customized response. Service sector or locality-based development work, often more efficient in use of staff time, sometimes reflected the known needs of a group of users. It could, however, result in schemes or projects into which people were slotted, thereby replicating rather more simplistic menu-driven approaches of the past. Schemes offered the prospect of providing for a wider range of choices for individuals and families where there was little or no choice before, and this was welcomed, but there remain some doubts as to whether such service choices are informed by models which are sufficiently sensitive to people's individual needs (Chapters 5–8).

The brief suggested by the AWS for MCTs was challenging in other ways. In retrospect, the function of services in relation to the community at large was undoubtedly not spelt out clearly enough. Hence, the operationalization of something as vague as 'mobilizing community resources', one of the identified core tasks for teams, had no ready template to guide what was to be accomplished. Human, capital, economic, emotional and intellectual factors are implicated in 'resources', but how they were to be secured, by whom, at what cost, and to what ends, remain questions exercising many people's minds. It is, therefore, difficult to form a complete judgement about what teams actually achieved in terms of mobilizing community resources except in the barest of material details. The 'new' tangible services developed were the clearest manifestation of this activity, though they were often the result of 'top-down' planning processes. Prospectively, more attention could be paid to the interweaving of services with the personal networks of individuals and the communities of interest to which they are tied (Barclay, 1984) to ensure that people are enabled to become a part of the community and contribute to it, instead of merely having a presence in it. The insights and lessons offered by forms of community social work (Darvill and Smale, 1990; Hadley and Leidy, 1996) should not be lost in this connection.

The findings raise questions about whether the right priority groups were being targeted for more intensive service packages. Given the apparent marginalization of people with challenging behaviours from those receiving more intensive services at the time of the survey the answer is almost certainly 'no'. Service arrangements have continued to evolve (Chapters 6–8). Now there are fewer people resident in hospital and many more living in ordinary housing in the community; there is a greater diversity of day services and there has been an exponential growth (from an admittedly low base) in the number of families receiving domiciliary and respite services. In addition to these important changes, the population with learning disability is 'greying' in many countries at a very rapid rate (Seltzer, Krauss and Janicki, 1994) which will create new demands on generic and specialist services for older people and on those families who continue to look after their relatives as adults. Hence the priorities now and even in the near future may look quite different. This places a premium on MCTs having the databases and the ties to higher management to help them form such judgements.

The workload demands upon MCT members were very considerable, less because of the sheer weight of client numbers and more because of the intensity, diversity and long-term nature of the work involved. Staff, therefore, developed informal eligibility criteria for groups needing IPs, presaging the care management arrangements which followed the NHS and Community Care Act 1990 (Social Services Inspectorate, 1991). Such a move is difficult to square with the Welsh Office (1996, p. 4) view that 'everyone who wants one should have an "individual plan". . .'. Whether or not the original eligibility criteria were based on individual need or service need, streamlining IPs further is probably not a sensible option as it risks simplifying them to a level that would be wasteful and ineffective for their intended purpose. In the present economic climate, additional staffing for MCTs seems unlikely. The implication would seem to be that some sort of enforced priority setting is unavoidable, even though it risks setting a tiered service. Stated more optimistically, it could be argued that the form, scope and content of individual planning should be entirely dependent upon individual circumstances.

The two case illustrations provide a reminder that people's lives are about more than just individual needs. In helping people to become community citizens, it is important to have an action plan for dealing with structural and environmental factors which are capable of producing disability (Oliver, 1996), otherwise solutions will rely unduly, as they have in the past, on approaches propelled by individual pathology.

In relation to understanding how people construe the determinants of service quality, we have to ask whether we fully understand people's evaluative frameworks and whether the way researchers or professionals look at and describe services is necessarily the same as those of service users and families. This has implications for the way service processes are identified and used in analytic terms. This is a continuing challenge given that service systems are under more or less constant change. The following chapters examine more closely issues about the relationship between services and people's everyday lives and work experiences.

References

All Wales Advisory Panel (1991). *Challenges and Responses: a Report on Services in Support of Adults with Mental Handicaps with Exceptionally Challenging Behaviours, Mental Illnesses or Who Offend.* Cardiff: Welsh Office.

Ash, A. and Woods, P. (1987). Courses for horses: foundation course for community mental handicap team members. In: *Community Mental Handicap Teams: Theory and Practice.* (G. Grant, S. Humphreys and M. McGrath, eds) pp. 119–130. Kidderminster: BIMH Publications.

Ayer, S. and Alaszewski, A. (1984). *Community Care and the Mentally Handicapped.* London: Croom Helm.

Barclay, P. (1984). *The Roles and Tasks of Social Workers.* London: Allen and Unwin.

Bayley, M. (1973). *Mental Handicap and Community Care.* London: Routledge and Kegan Paul.

Berry, I. (1986). Individual programme plans and the All-Wales Strategy: Some content and process issues. In: *Community Mental Handicap Teams: Theory and Practice.* (G. Grant, S. Humphreys and M. McGrath, eds) pp. 93–101. Kidderminster: BIMH Publications.

Blunden, R. (1980). *Individual Plans for Mentally Handicapped People: a Draft Procedural Guide.* Cardiff: Mental Handicap in Wales Applied Research Unit, University of Wales College of Medicine.

Blunden, R., Evans, G. and Humphreys, S. (1987). *Planning with Individuals: an Outline Guide.* Cardiff: Mental Handicap in Wales Applied Research Unit, University of Wales College of Medicine.

Brechin, A. and Swain, J. (1986). *Changing Relationships: Shared Action Planning with People with a Mental Handicap.* London: Harper and Row.

Briggs, T. L. (1980). Obstacles to implementing the team approach in social service agencies. In: *Teamwork in the Personal Social Services and Health Care.* (S. Lonsdale, A. Webb and T. L. Briggs, eds) pp. 75–89. London: Croom Helm.

Brill, N. I. (1976). *Teamwork: Working Together in the Human Services.* Philadelphia: Lippincott.

Brown, H. (1990). Training for community mental handicap teams. In: *The Roles and Tasks of Community Mental Handicap Teams.* (S. Brown and G. Wistow, eds) pp. 105–112. Aldershot: Avebury.

Brown, S. and Wistow, G. (1990). *The Roles and Tasks of Community Mental Handicap Teams.* Aldershot: Avebury.

Challis, D. and Davies, B. (1986). *Case Management in Community Care.* Aldershot: Gower.

Darvill, G. and Smale, G. (1990). *Partners in Empowerment: Networks of Innovation in Social Work.* London: National Institute of Social Work.

Day, P. R. (1994). Ambiguity and user involvement: issues arising in assessments of young people and their carers. *British Journal of Social Work,* **24**, 577–596.

Department of Health and Social Security (DHSS) (1976). *Report of the Committee on Child Health Services: Fit for the Future. Cmnd. 6684.* London: HMSO.

Department of Health and Social Security (DHSS) (1979). *Report of the Committee of Inquiry into Mental Handicap Nursing and Care, Vol. 1, Cmnd. 7468.* London: HMSO.

Dingwall, R. (1980). Problems of teamwork in primary care. In: *Teamwork in the Personal Social Services and Health Care.* (S. Lonsdale, A. Webb and T. L. Briggs, eds) pp. 111–137. London: Croom Helm.

Ellis, K. (1993). *Squaring the Circle: User and Carer Participation in Needs Assessment.* York: Joseph Rowntree Foundation.

Evans, G., Todd, S., Beyer, S. *et al.* (1994). Assessing the impact of the All Wales Mental Handicap Strategy: a survey of four districts. *Journal of Intellectual Disability Research*, **38**, 109–133.

Glendinning, C. (1983). *Unshared Care*. London: Routledge and Kegan Paul.

Grant, G. and Jenkins, S. (1990). CMHTs: involving voluntary organisations and the community. In: *The Roles and Tasks of Community Mental Handicap Teams*. (S. Brown and G. Wistow, eds) pp. 72–94. Aldershot: Avebury.

Grant, G., McGrath, M. and Ramcharan, P. (1994). How family and informal supporters appraise service quality. *International Journal of Disability, Development and Education*, **41**, 127–141.

Hadley, R. and Leidy, B. (1996). Community social work in a market environment: a British-American exchange of technologies and experience. *British Journal of Social Work*, **26**, 823–842.

Humphreys, S. (1986). Individual planning in NIMROD: results of an evaluation of the system four years on. In: *Community Mental Handicap Teams: Theory and Practice*. (G. Grant, S. Humphreys and M. McGrath, eds) pp. 78–92. Kidderminster: BIMH Publications.

Humphreys, S. and Blunden, R. (1987). A collaborative evaluation of an individual plan system. *British Journal of Mental Subnormality*, **33**, 19–30.

Humphreys, S., Blunden, R., Wilson, C. *et al.* (1985). *Planning for Progress: a Collaborative Evaluation of the Individual Planning System in NIMROD*. Cardiff: Mental Handicap in Wales Applied Research Unit, University of Wales College of Medicine.

Huxley, P. (1985). *Social Work Practice in Mental Health*. Aldershot: Gower.

Jenkins, J., Felce, D., Toogood, S. *et al.* (1988). *Individual Programme Planning*. Kidderminster: BIMH Publications.

Kane, R. A. (1975). *Inter-professional Teamwork. Social Work Manpower Monograph no. 8*. Syracuse, New York: Syracuse University School of Social Work.

Laws, M., Bolt, L. and Gibbs, V. (1988). Implementing change in a mental handicap hospital using an individual plan system. *Mental Handicap*, **16**, 74–76.

Lonsdale, S., Webb, A. and Briggs, T. L. (1980). *Teamwork in the Personal Social Services and Health Care*. London: Croom Helm.

McGrath, M. (1991). *Multi-disciplinary Teamwork: Community Mental Handicap Teams*. Aldershot: Avebury.

McGrath, M., Grant, G. and Ramcharan, P. (1991). *Service Packages: Factors Affecting Carers' Appraisals of Intermediate Outcomes*. Bangor: Centre for Social Policy Research and Development, University of Wales Bangor.

McGrath, M., Grant, G. and Ramcharan, P. (1993). *System Influences in Service Packaging for People with a Learning Disability and their Carers*. Bangor: Centre for Social Policy Research and Development, University of Wales Bangor.

McGrath, M., Ramcharan, P. and Grant, G. (1993). *Personal Influences in Service Packaging for People with Learning Disability and their Carers*. Bangor: Centre for Social Policy Research and Development, University of Wales Bangor.

Mansell, J. (1990). The natural history of the community mental handicap team. In: *The Roles and Tasks of Community Mental Handicap Teams*. (S. Brown and G. Wistow, eds) pp. 1–9. Aldershot: Avebury.

Oliver, M. (1996). *Understanding Disability: From Theory to Practice*. London: Macmillan.

Øvretveit, J. (1995). *Coordinating Community Care: Multidisciplinary Teams and Care Management*. Buckingham: Open University Press.

Payne, M. (1982). *Working in Teams*. London: Macmillan.

Plank, M. (1982). *Teams for Mentally Handicapped People*. London: Campaign for Mental Handicap.

Seltzer, M. M., Krauss, M. W. and Janicki, M. (1994). *Life Course Perspectives on Adulthood and Old Age*. Washington DC: American Association on Mental Retardation.

Simon, G. B. (1981) *Local Services for Mentally Handicapped People*. Kidderminster: BIMH Publications.

Social Services Inspectorate (1991). *Assessment and Care Management: Practitioners' Guide.* London: HMSO.

Stevenson, O. (1980). Social services teams in the United Kingdom. In: *Teamwork in the Personal Social Services and Health Care.* (S. Lonsdale, A. Webb and T. L. Briggs, eds) pp. 9–31. London: Croom Helm.

Webb, A. and Hobdell, M. (1980). Coordination and teamwork in the health and social services. In: *Teamwork in the Personal Social Services and Health Care.* (S. Lonsdale, A. Webb and T. L. Briggs, eds) pp. 97–110. London: Croom Helm.

Welsh Office (1983). *All Wales Strategy for the Development of Services for Mentally Handicapped People.* Cardiff: Welsh Office.

Welsh Office (1996). *The Welsh Mental Handicap Strategy: Guidance 1994.* Cardiff: Welsh Office.

Westrin, C-G. (1986). *Primary Health Care: Cooperation Between Health and Welfare Personnel.* Vienna: Centre for Social Welfare Training and Research.

Wilkin, D. (1979). *Caring for the Mentally Handicapped Child.* London: Croom Helm.

Chapter 5

Consumer involvement and advocacy

Consumer involvement and consultation were both introduced as tenets of the AWS. Attention to them as processes which fundamentally underpin service delivery has evolved in the subsequent twelve years. This chapter examines how they have been taken up and implemented. It is based on an analysis of research findings, policy documents, practice guidance and other commentaries.

It might be argued that planning, prioritization, management and review of services before the AWS was largely characterized by a 'received wisdom' model in which professionals held most of the decision-making power. Moving more towards consumer control, the 'consultation' model is one in which local authorities take consumer views into account when making decisions. Then there is true 'involvement', where consumers will not only be consulted but will be given a voice throughout the decision-making process. Nevertheless, decision-making essentially rests with the local authority. Further along the consumerist path lies the 'participation' model in which consumers have equal status as partners in decision-making. Their views are not only heard, but their opinions carry weight. Finally there is an 'ownership' model in which consumers exercise control over the services they want and dictate the ways in which they are delivered. Consumerism in each of the three periods of the AWS considered below is analysed against this continuum to establish the stage of development reached.

It is argued that, although there was a stimulus to develop beyond the initial AWS intention of consultation and involvement towards full participation, experience across Wales was variable. Consumerist ideals were accomplished at different levels in relation to the planning, management and review of services. Evidence suggests that limitations in the structures provided for participation under the AWS, as well as the motivation of the statutory sector, left users and carers with limited power or control over the services they received. Moreover, progress towards building a more general culture of participation in practice has been weakened by recent changes in community care legislation, local government reorganization and by dilution of central commitment to the AWS following its re-launch.

Involvement, consultation and the AWS

By the time of the AWS there was a recognition of '...compelling arguments for increased consumer participation if the goal is a more efficient and responsive service' (McGrath, 1989, p. 85). In an early review of the literature, Grant (1985) reported that, theoretically, participation led to a democratization of decision-making, was a means of developing a mutual understanding between key stakeholders in the service relationship, put a check on bureaucratic power, and promoted decisions which reflected consumer needs, wants and rights more closely. It was no less than a right of citizenship (Hadley and Hatch, 1981; Smith and Jones, 1981; Richardson, 1983). Through such strategies, it was shown that the difference between expressed consumer need and statutory agency response could be addressed (George and Wilding, 1976; Wilkin 1979; Pahl and Quine, 1984).

The AWS made a number of statements about the importance of consultation and involvement. These included the exhortation of social services to work closely with health, education and voluntary organizations as well as other relevant service providers and consumers. 'In particular, formal and informal arrangements must be made to involve the representatives of mentally handicapped people and their families in the planning and management of services' (Welsh Office, 1983, para. 6.3.4ii). The development of advocacy schemes arranged through voluntary organizations was also envisaged as providing an independent voice for people with learning disabilities. Moreover, the '...day-to-day monitoring of the quality and development of services will be the responsibility of individual service providers and consumers' (Welsh Office, 1983, para. 6.2.8). As such, the desire to involve as many people as possible in the process of 'fine-tuning' a strategy for Wales was regarded as an essential feature of the planning system outlined in the AWS.

The approach to user and carer participation in individual, local and county planning has already been described in Chapters 3 and 4. In summary, involvement of representatives of people with learning disabilities and their families in planning and management and in the monitoring and review of services was to be organized at local and county levels. The Welsh Office did not prescribe the relevant structures, arguing instead that they should 'build upon existing arrangements' within each county. Individual planning for all people with learning disabilities in Wales was seen as a vital means of providing the necessary information about the collective needs of all individuals upon which service priorities could be decided.

We now describe how these intentions were put into practice. As an heuristic device, three periods are identified which represent changes in emphasis in the implementation and the effects of consumer involvement and advocacy: Reaction 1983–1986, Rapprochement 1987–1991, and Retrenchment and Reorganization thereafter.

Reaction 1983–1986

As was explained in Chapter 3, the period allowed for completing initial AWS county plans was too short. This was partly because local authorities had little experience of consumer involvement, either of family and informal carers or the representatives of people with learning disabilities, and how to establish this in service planning and management. The importance of consumer consultation and involvement in planning was underlined by the Welsh Office rejection of many initial county plans on the grounds of insufficiently developed mechanisms for consultation. During the early stages there were a number of heated exchanges between counties and the Welsh Office about precisely what 'full and adequate' consultation meant (Grant, 1990).

Mechanisms for involvement and consultation at county and local level which emerged in the early years can be summarized thus (see Beyer *et al.*, 1986). Each county had a form of County Planning group. In two counties, these were subgroups of the Joint Care Planning Teams (JCPTs) and in six they were separately constituted. Each of these county planning groups reported to JCPTs which were themselves accountable to Joint Consultative Committees made up of health, education, social services and members of District or County Councils. The local planning mechanisms varied a great deal between counties, being formed on the basis of geographical areas coterminous with multidisciplinary community team catchments, age range of service users or policy or service dimensions, such as day care, education, community services and monitoring. All these local groups were envisaged as feeding into the county planning process.

Much of the evidence relating to the effect of representation in these planning tiers during this early period of the AWS comes from research undertaken in one county, Gwynedd. Clearly one needs to be cautious about overgeneralization, but a number of themes emerged which were reflected in other counties. The local planning groups in Gwynedd were initially organized with an open structure so that all carers from the area might attend and great efforts were made to prompt carers to become involved through advertising. At its height, 30–40% of carers reported attending at least one local planning group meeting (Humphreys, 1987). It is therefore necessary to bear in mind that there was a very considerable silent majority who were unable or unwilling to take their place as representatives in planning.

Only 25% of those who attended planning meetings felt positive about the experience and attendance levels subsequently declined. McGrath (1989) found that 63% of carers had little interest in contributing to wider planning. Reasons for the lack of interest included delays in producing plans, difficulties in progressing plans through numerous committees, difficulties in allowing adequate consultation within planning cycles and the financial year, lack of confidence, feelings that meetings were badly organized, repetitive and made little progress and a belief that their views as carers were being disregarded (McGrath, 1989).

Parents seeking immediate tangible benefits were soon disheartened by the slow progress as were those who tended to challenge the status quo and dealt with bureaucracies with impatience. Those most likely to remain involved were least likely to rock the boat and were tolerant or philosophical about a range of difficulties which undermined effective participation (Humphreys, 1987). Professionals in inter-agency planning meetings were less likely to argue points in front of parent representatives

(McGrath, 1988). So, although it was noted that such meetings had a different tone (Evans *et al.*, 1986), statutory sector representatives were more likely to meet and discuss issues outside of the meetings themselves. Moreover, when faced with issues which were said to have important ramifications for organizational, strategic and financial considerations, parents at county planning level were reported as seldom attempting to override or confront the judgement of executive officers. Grant (1985) likened such participants to 'junior partners', who are more easily accommodated within bureaucratic organizations because their mode of participation does not unduly disturb the status quo.

In the early years, the breadth of voluntary organizations was not well represented, with many Mencap representatives involved but few from other organizations. In Gwynedd, the voluntary sector representative was from a non-learning disability focused organization, though most of the other parent representatives were active in Mencap. Unless agencies retained a clear distinction about the constituencies that were being represented, it could become extremely confusing about whether parents were representing their own views, voluntary organization views or both. In addition, carers were often at a disadvantage in their lack of knowledge of statutory structures and procedures and some professionals saw their presence as tokenistic (McGrath and Grant, 1992). The AWS had specified the need to involve the representatives of people with learning disabilities, indicating that carers might legitimately represent the views of people with learning disabilities. This was unsatisfactory, especially since carers were found to be representing carer, particularly parental, interests rather than those of people with learning disability themselves (McGrath and Grant, 1992).

From these early experiences McGrath (1989) concluded that small informal local meetings were more likely to increase the level of consultation, involvement and/or participation. Attendance was facilitated by support with transport, evening meetings, home support for relatives with learning disabilities and appropriate training to maximize the effect of representatives' contributions. Such issues were, of course, relevant throughout the AWS period and addressed to varying extents by different counties.

The relationship between carer representatives at local and county planning levels posed problems for the AWS vision of cooperation between planning tiers. The evidence from Gwynedd indicated a number of difficulties with stormy relationships between parents and service representatives being reported and a parental view that service representatives at county level were remote or secretive and provided little feedback (McGrath, 1988). While parents on county planning groups were reported to have gained a closer understanding of the limitations placed upon statutory agencies, those at local planning level often saw parents at county level as having become part of the establishment and as having lost their independent voice. Carers remained fragmented and lacked cohesion during this period (Todd *et al.*, 1997).

A reorganization of planning took place in Gwynedd at the end of the Reaction phase to deal with some of these criticisms. Local planning groups were given a closed committee structure. Open meetings were held for carers twice a year only. A Mencap representative to the county planning group was elected in place of the non-learning disability voluntary organization representative. Detailed guidelines were published about the relationships between local and county planning groups. An Area Managers' Group, made up of different professionals, was put in place to advise the planning tiers in relation to service needs and priorities.

However, as reported in Chapter 4, the low level of individual plan (IP) implementation meant that most estimates of needs were crude guesses. Plans were the product of carers' and professionals' impressions of need or suggestions for alternative types of services. While this reflected the early development phase of MCTs, low IP implementation was an enduring factor. In addition, carer representatives were more likely to want to discuss immediate needs rather than service ideals and to call for the expansion or enhancement of traditional services rather than the development of radical alternatives (Beyer *et al.*, 1986; Todd *et al.*, 1997). Representation in planning, therefore, sometimes brought forward proposals which did not fit well with AWS principles (McGrath and Grant, 1992). Such a conservative stance went hand-in-hand with many carers' fears that their caring role would expand rather than contract under the AWS. Without trust that new services would be provided and that different services would deliver better outcomes, carers tended to want more of what they knew in order to alleviate what they saw as their burden of care. Such perceptions were strengthened by the fact that they often saw new ideas as too idealistic and divorced from reality. Thus, in Gwynedd for example, carers resisted professionals' views about the value of funding advocacy.

Unlike family carer representation, people with learning disabilities were, '. . .conspicuous by their absence' (SCOVO, 1986, p. 7) during the Reaction phase. As the Welsh Office reported, '. . .there has been little direct involvement in planning services by mentally handicapped people' (Welsh Office, 1987, p. 22), leading to the conclusion that the ideals of the AWS could not be achieved until people with learning disabilities were fully involved as partners. A major reason for this absence was that there were few groups which represented the views of people with learning disabilities when the AWS was launched. Indeed only four self-advocacy groups existed at the end of 1986 and not one citizen advocacy project had yet emerged. The Welsh Office Three Year Strategy Review neither mentioned citizen advocacy as a priority, nor discussed ways by which service users might develop independent support for the representation of their views and expectations.

However, the Welsh Office role was central in promoting consumer representation within local agencies and parental representation in line with the principles of the AWS. In fact, such representation is unlikely to have emerged without the AWS and Welsh Office leadership. The Welsh Office marked its commitment to consultation and involvement by its rejection of plans based on inadequate consultation and called for more representation of people with learning disabilities in planning in its review of progress after the first three years. This review also sought clarification of the basis of carer representation and better mechanisms for soliciting the views of 'constituency' members, that is, those on whose behalf representations were being made (Welsh Office, 1987, para. 27). It was further suggested that the Welsh Office itself would meet with Planning Teams once a year to '. . .enable parents, representatives of mentally handicapped people and voluntary organizations to make their views known directly to the Department. . . The expectation would be that mentally handicapped people themselves can make their views known at these meetings' (Welsh Office, 1987, para. 45).

The importance of the Reaction phase was, therefore, that it exposed inherent weaknesses in the received wisdom model of service design. The new county and local planning groups made possible not only joint planning among statutory and voluntary sector representatives, but also opportunities for the inclusion of both carers and people with learning disabilities. These opportunities were exploited only partially during the Reaction phase, but they set the occasion for a more thorough development of consumer involvement in the period which was to follow.

The issues of the representative basis and degree of influence exercised by carer representatives were brought to the fore during the Reaction phase. For example, the change in Gwynedd from the initial open consultation to a closed committee structure meant that fewer carers were involved in the decision-making process. This raised the question of how the active minority consulted 'constituency members' to ascertain the views of the majority.

Moreover, the presence of carers on local and county planning groups prompts the question of how much they contributed to the early decisions made. If one takes the premise that planning groups are jointly responsible for decision-making, it is possible to suggest that carers had established, at least, a degree of involvement at county level. However, if the premise is that group members are severally responsible for decision-making, it is by no means clear that carers carried the necessary authority or weight to push their decisions through in the face of statutory sector opposition. Indeed, it was observed that carers at county level did not often exert pressure or seek to influence decisions as a group. It has also been suggested that the motivation and values of statutory sector members differed between counties, and that they were not always geared towards supporting carers and users within the planning process (McGrath and Grant, 1992).

However, carers were at least involved in decision-making at local and county levels by the end of the Reaction phase, even if decision-making power continued to rest with service personnel. For people with learning disabilities, even minimal consultation was lacking. The original AWS call for 'representatives of people with a mental handicap' to be involved was severely criticized as it became apparent that carers who had taken on this representative role were at times working to a different agenda than people with learning disabilities might adopt. That few people with learning disabilities were in any way consulted or involved was a major failure of this period. Indeed they had not even established a presence on planning forums.

While the Reaction phase was geared to establishing representation in planning, other areas where the AWS saw the need for consultation and involvement, notably in monitoring and review of services, were not yet a focus of attention. There were some early indications of carer representation on service management structures and quality action groups. These were to develop further in subsequent years. By the end of the Reaction phase, local and county planning groups were sticking to their tasks and actively debating the nature of consultation, involvement and participation in the planning process so that, over time, attitudes changed and the ideal of consumer participation became much more taken for granted. Retrospectively, one education representative reflecting on county planning at this time said that 'the first phase was about putting people together, getting people to work for a common aim...I suppose it was about changing peoples' perspectives on the possible' (Todd *et al.*, 1997).

Rapprochement 1986–1991

The Reaction phase saw the development of relevant structures, a language of consultation and involvement and, later, a concern to address some of the difficulties experienced in making the culture of consumerism a reality. This culture was strengthened during the period of Rapprochement. Indeed, the issue of participation as defined in the second paragraph of this chapter, a concept not used in the original AWS document, began to take the place of the weaker notions of involvement and consultation. During this period, policies concerned with devolving decision-making to consumers were gaining favour more generally (Griffiths, 1988; Audit Commission, 1989). With a growing emphasis on user participation, as well as a fine-tuning of mechanisms already in place, the Rapprochement years could be viewed as the 'golden' period of participatory policy, practice and experience under the AWS.

Follow-up research in Gwynedd found that the focus of planning groups had shifted from planning to the implementation and review of new services (McGrath and Grant, 1992). Because of this, carers were now more involved than before in monitoring how local projects were developing. The greater accountability within the reorganized planning system was beginning to pay dividends, although the gap between local and county level action still needed to be bridged. Carers on local planning groups still perceived those on the county forum to be part of the establishment. In turn, carers at county level suggested that the plans put forward by those at local level lacked financial realism.

At the same time, research on a participation project running in another county reported that representatives from only 89 of the 280 families entitled to attend local planning meetings did so between 1986 and 1989 (Davies, 1990). While these levels were higher than found in Gwynedd earlier, the majority of carers were infrequent participants. Further, they were not necessarily representative of carers. 'Non-attenders seldom had access to a car. . .and were twice to three times as likely to be single carers than the rest. The typical representative is the parent of a handicapped person aged between 21 and 30. . .non-attenders were twice as likely to be parents of people over 30 and nearly three times as likely to be relatives of people over 40. . .a measure of cumulative hardship resulted in 77% of non-attenders scoring above average compared with 40% of others' (Davies, 1990, p. 17).

However, nationally it was generally felt that carers had had some impact upon the course of the AWS and that they represented a more powerful force than they had done before. One member of social services staff involved in planning reflected that . . . 'It's been good at county level because parents can actually, because of their numbers, outvote professionals if they wanted to. They certainly have had an input in planning, and their views are not the same as professionals' (Todd et al., 1997). Evidence from county annual reports indicates considerable, though widely dispersed, innovation and opportunism in seeking to involve parents in planning and consultation. For example, there were reports of surveys of parents' wishes, more localized community meetings, the establishment of project management groups, the appointment of participation officers, the emergence of local working groups for specific projects, the strengthening of voluntary sector forums and the development of quality action groups. Carers were further credited with the early and dramatic emergence of family support services, respite services and the growth of parent representative bodies.

In one area covering two districts in Gwynedd, voluntary organizations were responsible for managing one-third of new projects funded under the AWS and families could claim an active involvement in all of these, in roles other than that of service recipient (McGrath and Grant, 1992). Even discounting more varied relationships between service providers and families in the remaining two-thirds of projects, this represented an unprecedented increase from a base of almost zero before the AWS. Another promising indicator was that the services concerned covered a wide spectrum from the operation of special needs play-groups to short-term care projects, alternative day opportunities and citizen advocacy.

As McGrath (1989, p. 76) observed, 'Participation is more likely to be meaningful when it can be grounded in participants' experiences. For many carers, planning meetings became at times irrelevant, either focusing on abstract concepts or using language they did not fully understand'. Representation in local services, where decisions brought immediate and tangible changes in the structure and operation of a service, was, therefore, more likely to appear meaningful to those representatives who had become involved.

While carer representation had widened, there was growing questioning of the conflict of interest arising when carers were taken as representatives of people with learning disabilities. In 1989, there were still very few people with learning disabilities on planning forums, and none at all in four of the eight counties. Only 21 people with learning disabilities sat as members on the 39 local planning groups then in existence (Welsh Office, 1989).

Self-advocacy grew in the Rapprochement phase. From a base of only two groups in 1985, there were over 30 in operation by the end of 1991 and 58 by 1994. A review of 46 of these 58 groups (Ramcharan et al., 1996) indicated that the growth in the number of self-advocacy groups and their representation on local and county planning forums varied between counties (Figure 5.1). Involvement in county planning was not as

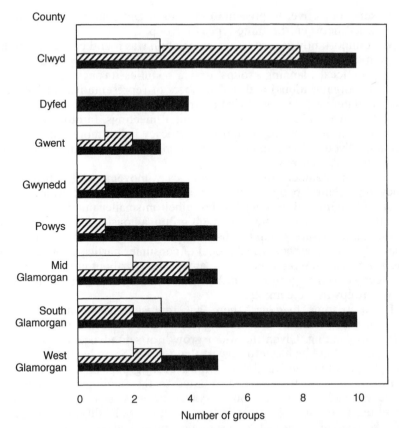

Figure 5.1 The number of self-advocacy groups in each county and the numbers of groups represented on local and county planning forums. ■ Number of self-advocacy groups in each county; ▨ number of groups with representation in local planning; □ number of groups with representation in county planning

widespread as at the local level with 34 groups (76%) having no representation.

Eleven groups (25%) termed themselves 'People First Groups', 16 (30%) 'Self-advocacy Groups' and 17 (39%) 'User Groups', the latter comprising various service user committees and in-hospital groups. All groups shared the idea that they spoke up for themselves. People First groups tended to be outward looking, claiming to represent people with learning disabilities on a number of forums. Self-advocacy groups had a stronger emphasis on learning about new advocacy skills and about their rights. User groups tended to be more inward-looking, seeking to change the services which their members received. People First groups had 28 representatives who participated in local planning, self-advocacy groups had 18 and user groups had nine. People First groups had 13 representatives who participated in county planning, self-advocacy groups had two and user groups five. Representation in local and county planning therefore varied between the three types of group.

Most importantly, a very strong association was found between whether a group was funded (usually through AWS monies disbursed through county or local planning groups, or via counties through specialist self-advocacy organizations) and the numbers of representatives at local and county planning levels. Participants from funded groups were also more likely to have paid supporters with them at meetings. In other words, the commitment of a county to fund self-advocacy led to more self-advocates being involved in local and county planning as well as better support for them to fulfil their roles.

Roles for members of the self-advocacy movement also broadened. They represented people with learning disabilities in the wider People First movement and in other forums, albeit in smaller numbers, as representatives on a supported employment group, a housing association group, a community leisure group for disabled people and a parents' forum. This goes beyond the service-based model of consumer participation set out by the AWS. The AWS did not make any proposals about cross-fertilization between consumer groups, nor about the need for representation in non-AWS groups in the community.

There is some evidence then that representatives within the self-advocacy movement were beginning to establish a presence, if not involvement, in planning. Given the wider growth of self-advocacy in Britain as a whole, it would be hasty to suggest that the AWS can be wholly credited with the growth in the number of self-advocacy groups in Wales. However, growth does seem to have been related to the funding which has been made available for such groups. Advocacy in Wales is likely to have benefited from the AWS both in terms of the availability of that funding and the general culture of representation promoted by the AWS.

As the Rapprochement period proceeded, the presence of people with learning disabilities in planning was beginning to be taken for granted and this, in itself, was seen as a successful AWS outcome. Few data exist to assess the extent to which contributions by representatives with learning disabilities in either local or county planning were meaningful or influential, and measuring this is notoriously difficult (Richardson, 1983). In one analysis of the meaningfulness of user representation conducted in a day service setting in Wales, Davies (1991) concluded that only 23% of users were capable of functioning reasonably in such a setting, that 31% might do so with sufficient training and another 20% with considerable training and support. A further indicator of the meaningfulness of participation levels obtained by reviewing minutes from planning meetings in one county found that, while consumers constituted 24% of those present, they made only 3% of contributions. In comparison, parents constituted 21% of those present and made 14% of contributions, voluntary sector representatives constituted 16% of those present and made 12% of contributions, while statutory agency representatives constituted 42% of those present and made 65% of contributions (Welsh Office, 1989). As the Welsh Office report commented, 'Consumer involvement takes the form of physical presence, but falls a long way short of participation' (Welsh Office, 1989, para. 26).

A genuine question remains concerning the extent to which people with learning disabilities actually influenced priorities for the provision of services. Interviews with people with learning disabilities point to views ranging from them being given an important say to their points of view being seldom taken into account (Todd *et al.*, 1997). The biggest contribution was possibly that meetings had become more sociable and less impersonal. It might be argued that having gained a presence in planning so late in the day, many of the key decisions on service priorities had already been taken.

A similar difficulty exists in gauging the meaningfulness of user participation in the management of services and its effectiveness in changing services in line with people's wants and needs. The publication *Still a Small Voice* (Welsh Office, 1989) which reported a survey of the extent of choice among 755 residents in 98 residential settings sheds some light on this. It showed 'in fairly stark terms how much more residents in domestic settings control their own lives. Houses and flats in which just one, two or three people live together reveal a massively higher degree of consumer involvement' (Welsh Office, 1989, para. 15). The authors concluded that 'by-and-large it is clear that settings opened since 1985 do provide for residents to be more fully involved in controlling their own lives than has ever been the case before' (Welsh Office, 1989, para. 17). Thus, services set up under AWS principles are likely to extend choice and improve a range of outcomes for their users. It might therefore be argued that the approach taken to the design and operation of services has an immediacy and relevance to the experience and choice of service users which are at least as important as that derived through formalized systems of consultation or participation.

Towards the end of the Rapprochement period the All Wales Advisory Panel (AWAP) Consumer Involvement Sub-Group argued that undue emphasis had been placed during the AWS period on consumer involvement in service planning as opposed to management, monitoring and review. The group also pointed to the continuing 'major imbalance in the extent to which parents ...(as opposed to) ...people with mental handicap are able to exercise influence on service planning and delivery' (AWAP, 1991, p. 12).

The AWAP report reiterated ideas, even at this late stage, about optimizing the participation of people with learning disabilities in planning, drawing on good practices across the counties. These involved: the need for preparation and support; preliminary work on the agenda; personal supports at meetings; co-holding of offices; providing transport and the flexible use of delegated budgets for these purposes; and, following the lead of some counties, the appointment of participation officers. In relation to parents, it was suggested that there should be more community-based meetings for families, consumer surveys, project management committees with parents represented, special officers for participation and involvement, local working groups to draw up project proposals, quality action groups, monitoring and evaluation groups at county level as well as a strengthening of the voluntary sector. It was suggested that parents should be valued and given practical support and assistance to participate in meetings as well as being treated as equal partners, a point taken up by Grant (1997). Jargon should be avoided, meetings should be less formal and organized around a stable group of contributors whose roles should be clearly stated.

Importantly, in thinking arguably not contained in the original AWS, the AWAP report also suggested that 'there is one further group of stakeholders . . . namely ordinary members of the community . . . As the Strategy becomes more fully implemented, people with mental handicap will start to move away from being "service users" or "consumers" and will simply become ordinary citizens' (AWAP, 1991, p. 6). Furthermore, the report concluded that 'some consumer involvement strategies have been harder to implement than others including the establishment of citizen advocacy projects to provide independent representation' (AWAP, 1991, p. 11).

Like self-advocacy, citizen advocacy initiatives were developed during the Rapprochement period and their growth continued subsequently. The first project providing citizen advocacy for people with learning disabilities in Wales was not functioning until 1988. Three more followed in 1989 with two further projects funded in 1993, the funding for one of these being withdrawn two years later. The projects were geographically scattered and covered only a small proportion of Wales. It has proved difficult to recruit advocates. In 1992, a particularly high point in terms of advocate numbers, the four longest established projects had a total of 50 advocates. Their total funding was £124 500, around £2500 per advocate per annum. Compared to the 8886 adults with learning disabilities over 16 years of age recorded on health and social services registers in Wales in 1992 (Welsh Office, 1993), this number is insignificant. Even within the catchment areas they served, the availability of advocates was low. For example, the project with the most citizen advocates (27) and the smallest catchment area of all projects in Wales served an area which had over 300 registered adults with a learning disability, together with a hospital population that was still over 100 (Ramcharan, 1995a).

While some citizen advocates have helped to secure further services for their partners and have been involved with their partners in individual planning, resettlement or case review meetings, none has supported any partners on local or county planning groups. Without exception, those partners able to express themselves have registered positive feelings towards their advocates. However, evidence indicates that no long-term friendships apart from those made with the citizen advocate have yet developed out of the partnerships (Ramcharan, 1995a). While presence in the community has therefore increased, there remains some way to go before an integrated community experience and support for partners is produced.

Although the AWS saw the need for the independent funding of advocacy, all but one scheme in Wales were initially funded by AWS monies directed through county planning groups. These arrangements have been a source of concern for the projects who wished to exert their independence, but have nevertheless been unable to attract funds from other sources. Counties have exercised influence through their funding. Examples include the withdrawal of funding because of disagreements about the extent to which their county's users had been provided with a service and because of inadequate recruitment of advocates; funding being directed through a resettlement grant with a related direction as to whom the project should prioritize; targets being set for advocate recruitment because of a lack of success after three years functioning and suspension of a project while a review was undertaken. Partnerships in the project which had recruited few advocates had moved towards a befriending relationship over time. Instrumental work by citizen advocates, that is, problem-solving, tended to be crisis oriented rather than proactive, with none of the advocates keeping track of individual planning meetings attended by their partners, nor in some cases the services their partners were receiving (Ramcharan, 1995b). While these experiences might lead the citizen advocacy movement to bemoan the fact that they were not independently funded, one can understand the worries implicit in county responses to the slow growth of advocate numbers. Moreover, one might question whether the lack of independence in their funding constituted their sole, or even most serious, limitation.

Among carer representatives, the evidence from the Rapprochement period highlighted a growing voice in prompting services such as family support, respite and alternative day opportunities. The focus at local and county planning group level had moved away from planning to implementation and review. Moreover, it was found that there was a flourishing involvement at service level as new services came on stream, in management, monitoring and quality assurance. With the expansion of carer representative bodies, more carers were involved at local level in these activities and it therefore became more likely that those at local and county planning levels were being better informed about how local services were functioning. Problems still remained with the links between carer representatives at local and county levels. Moreover, there is no evidence to point to any increase in their involvement in areas such as financial planning and decision-making, structuring planning systems or producing plans for service needs. In short, the configuration of carer representation had changed, marking a shift to involvement at local grass-roots and service provision level.

The longer established carer involvement began to be matched by the participation of people with learning disabilities, encouraged by the growth of the self-advocacy movement. Through their participation in such groups, people with learning disabilities generated their own agenda. Counties which had funded self-advocacy were more likely to have representatives on local and county planning groups. Issues about the extent to which people in self-advocacy groups, those likely to be most able to express their views, were able to represent the views of other people with learning disabilities were never addressed. Moreover, while local and county planning meetings were said to become more sociable and less impersonal as more people with learning disabilities entered representative roles, there are conflicting interpretations of whether their presence led to involvement, let alone participation on equal terms. The data taken from the minutes of such meetings would, if extrapolated, indicate a low level of involvement despite the growing numbers present, and certainly a lower level of involvement than carer representatives have. Moreover, data seemed to indicate that if choice were an arbiter of better outcomes, then particular services were likely to increase such choice independent of the existence of planning forums.

This may be just as well as representatives with learning disabilities were still falling far short of the ideal of full participation to which service personnel had 'hung their colours'. It also appeared easier to involve people and to engage their interest as partners in decision-making at the service level. Perhaps salutary is the fact that such local involvement came with the growth in carer groups and the self-advocacy movement. It might be argued that parents' forums and self-advocacy groups themselves emerged because of the opportunities for involvement that were on offer, as well as the culture of the AWS and its funding base.

In summary, a culture of pursuing the ideal of participation had emerged during the Rapprochement phase, moving intentions beyond the original aims of the AWS. However, participation in practice remained limited and the experience at local and county planning forums, while arguably reaching involvement for carers, had not developed much beyond consultation for people with learning disabilities. There were positive signs that user and carer involvement in management and review of services was increasing. Self-advocacy was also growing, though the carer voice in planning still predominated over that of users. A general dearth of IPs still existed and led to the maintenance of traditional decision-making. Citizen advocacy was almost non-existent. Despite the Rapprochement years of the AWS being those in which involvement, consultation and participation reached their height, community integration and full citizenship through participation were still far from being accomplished. Although the Welsh Office remained supportive of any movement towards consumer participation, their central concerns had, by the end of this phase, turned to pushing through more tangible service changes, particularly hospital resettlement and changes in day services. Their stance had returned to that typical of central British policy-making, exhortation without taking on the responsibility to effect change.

Retrenchment and reorganization

Between 1991 and the end of the first phase of the AWS in 1993, the arrangements for planning, management and review remained largely unchanged. Both self-advocacy and citizen advocacy continued to grow. However, broad-ranging policy changes after 1991 reinforced the changing Welsh Office role. First and foremost, the local authorities and Welsh Office were beginning to shift their attentions to the implementation of the NHS and Community Care Act (NHSCCA), especially the new needs assessment and purchaser and provider arrangements. Under the new legislation, the plans relating to learning disability services were to be forwarded for inclusion in the overall social care plan, once they had been decided through existing planning structures. The Guidance which followed the re-launched AWS in 1994 stated that 'the joint planning process. . .must remain a central feature of the AWS. Particular care must be taken to ensure that the views and wishes of the individuals and their carers are taken into account' (Welsh Office, 1996, para. 12.1). The idea of 'taking views into account' is a weak statement compared to the culture of participation that had begun to emerge. The Welsh Office was now actively supporting measures which were less individually oriented and participative than service personnel wanted to sustain at local level.

Moreover, the NHSCCA was not as systematic in its policy for participation as the original AWS. While the apparent focus was again related to total levels of identified need, the idea of universal IPs was replaced by a prioritization of services for those most in need (Secretaries of State, 1989, para. 1.10). Indeed it is unnecessary for local authorities to undertake an assessment unless a need has been demonstrated. Furthermore, the legislation failed to state the ways in which advocacy initiatives might be supported and used to maximize participation. The ideals of participation have been diluted under new community care arrangements and the AWS is now largely subordinate to community care policy.

The change in focus brought by the new community care legislation has more recently been exacerbated by Local Government Reorganization (LGR) in Wales which had its shadow year in 1994–5 and which took effect from April 1996. The eight counties became 22 new unitary authorities and old systems of county planning have had to be replaced. Smaller Social Services Departments have combined community care client groups at more senior planning and management levels. The consequences of these changes for participative planning cannot be underestimated. One carer viewed LGR, and the diminished responsibility of the Welsh Office as, de facto, the end of the AWS.

In the early stages of the Strategy, we thought at long last something positive was being done for people. We were promised this, that and the other. We were invited to attend planning meetings and things started to happen. We now feel very disappointed and thoroughly let down.

Self-advocacy groups had aligned themselves to old county boundaries and needed to subdivide if they were to align themselves to the new unitary structures. There were fears that this would weaken current arrangements and make groups more vulnerable, although there were hopes that the movement had built sufficient cross-county and national alliances to facilitate mutual support as users regrouped. In this new climate, members of advocacy organizations aligned to the old counties have usually had to negotiate with several new unitary authorities to secure ongoing funding and there are grave concerns presently being expressed among these groups about their future. The changes in legislation have also prompted some projects originally geared to citizen advocacy to change their focus in order to sell their services within the new 'mixed economy of welfare', for example by taking on representation for users in complaints procedures.

In summary, as the AWS neared the end of its first ten years, a number of externally imposed changes in legislation and policy made the tenuously established mechanisms of involvement, consultation and participation vulnerable to reverse. In such a scenario the positive changes of the first ten years are likely to be undermined. The culture and structure of participation developed under the AWS up to 1991 may not be sustained.

Judging the overall effect of these changes to consultation, involvement and participation must await further research.

The AWS as a consumer-oriented policy

Progress towards consultation, involvement and participation has varied across counties in Wales. Despite this, it is true that a substantial movement away from the 'received wisdom' character of pre-AWS services has been widely achieved, although experience suggests that there has been an imbalance in the influence exercised by families as opposed to service users. While one focus of review comes from determining the extent to which the AWS succeeded in its own terms, another is to gauge the strengths and limitations of the AWS as a consumerist policy. Fundamental to any such review is the very nature and purpose of consumerist strategies. First, there is a question about the nature and success of the means through which consultation, involvement and participation are achieved. Secondly, there is a question about the aims and objectives of consumerist policies and whether they are primarily a vehicle for overcoming the organizational excesses of bureaucracy or directed towards the empowerment of service users.

Writers applying consumer principles to public services have drawn attention to essential dimensions of such a policy including access, choice, information, redress and representation (Potter, 1988). The paucity of individual plans implemented during the AWS years meant that the necessary information upon which informed decision-making was to be achieved was not available. This made ad hoc choices about service priorities possible which, without Welsh Office intervention, may have led to the expansion of existing services rather than to their replacement by new ones. That the necessary information about the needs of all those to be served was not available also heightened the importance of carer and user representatives consulting those they represented.

The evidence has shown that few families have an appetite for public meetings or for participation in planning meetings outside the ambit of IPs. Indications are that those who take up representative roles tend to be more articulate, middle class and to be carers of younger adults and they cannot, therefore, be relied upon to give expression to the full range of latent needs, interests and expectations in the community. By virtue of membership of county planning bodies, parents have been obliged to enter a negotiating and consultative role, for it is almost a contradiction in terms to adopt a pressure group stance from within. This seems to accord with the literature on voluntary organization involvement with local authorities which has indicated that groups having a close association with councils tended not to indulge in traditional lobbying. For those parents straddling the middle ground between the service world and the wider carer constituency, it was all too easy for them to feel isolated. They could not be expected to mirror all parental interests from their constituent areas, not only because some of these interests were incompatible, but because many needs and interests were unknown, as consultative structures were not in place.

Similar problems arise in the user constituency given that the self-advocacy movement is likely to provide representatives from among the most able. Logistical help, training and needs for support and the ambience of meetings were being worked upon in order to facilitate the contributions of representatives in local and county planning forums. In tackling these issues, the possibilities of maximizing access and choice within the planning system were at the very least being addressed, though to varying degrees between counties. Moreover, there was growing evidence towards the end of the Rapprochement years that the growth of grass-roots carer and user movements were beginning to widen consultation, involvement and participation, particularly in the management, monitoring and review of local services. In one county, a third of new services had service users and family members involved in their management committees, boards of directors, advisory or review groups.

Despite these positive signs the success of the AWS in its consumerist aims needs to be measured against the meaningfulness of user and carer representation and the extent to which consultation, involvement and participation were achieved. In this light McGrath (1988) noted that there was a tendency for parent members to defer to professional or administrative authority. As discussion moved from considerations of the structures for planning, systems of accountability and financial planning to issues relating more to individual projects or project proposals, parental contributions were seen to increase. For people with learning disabilities who achieved a presence on local and county planning later in the day, questions about the meaningfulness of their presence persist. On the basis of the review of minutes of planning meetings reported earlier the likelihood is that they were even less involved than family carers.

Overall, the evidence seems to point to a gradation in the success of consumerism under the AWS. As new services came on line, family carers and users were more willing to become involved in the management and review of these services. Participation in terms of decision-making as equal partners was most likely to occur at this level. At local and county planning level, commitment was less forthcoming. Within such groups, as discussions moved from talk about the quality of services and prioritizing services towards issues of strategic planning and financial control and accountability, contributions from family carers reduced. It would, therefore, seem less apt to describe the experience of carers in such groups as full participation. A significant degree of control over services, particularly regarding strategic management, financial issues and accountability remained in the hands of the statutory sector and the Welsh Office and was not susceptible to influence by carers and users.

If the outcome of the consumerist ideal in the AWS was geared towards overcoming some of the organizational excesses of bureaucracy, it managed this only partially for carers and very little for people with learning disabilities. It is hard to judge whether, if given more time to develop, the balance of power would have shifted from officers to these groups. It is easier to be more optimistic about the growing involvement at service level of both carers and users whose immediate stake in the services prompted higher levels of involvement and commitment to effecting change.

The findings show that people are more likely to seek involvement and participation when the stake they have is greater, and where the topics of discussion have an immediacy to their lives. In line with recent theoretical literature this seems to indicate the need to address a further level of consumerism beyond participation to one of 'ownership' in which control over services is exercised by service recipients and their advocates. The AWS did not set out to achieve or test this possibility. Rather, in its own terms, it did succeed in moving away from the 'received wisdom' model, even if the resultant consultation, involvement and participation were patchy across Wales and among different stakeholders and, even though the hierarchy of authority from professionals, to carers, to people with learning disabilities persisted.

References

All Wales Advisory Panel (AWAP) (1991). *Consumer Involvement and the All Wales Strategy: Report to the All Wales Advisory Panel from the Consumer Involvement Sub-group.* Cardiff: Welsh Office.

Audit Commission (1989). *Developing Community Care for Adults with a Mental Handicap, Occasional Papers No. 9.* London: HMSO.

Beyer, S., Evans, G., Todd, S. and Blunden, R. (1986). *Planning for the All Wales Strategy: A Review of Issues Arising in Welsh Counties.* Cardiff: Mental Handicap in Wales Applied Research Unit, University of Wales College of Medicine.

Davies, K. (1990). Some issues around consumer participation in service planning and management. In: *Individual Planning and the All Wales Strategy in the Light of the Community Care White Paper.* (P. Ramcharan, M. McGrath and G. Grant, eds) pp. 9–24. Bangor: Centre for Social Policy Research and Development, University of Wales Bangor.

Davies, K. (1991). *An Evaluation of the Rhondda Vanguard Participation Project.* Unpublished report available from The Mid Glamorgan Participation Project, 120A Aberrhondda Road, Porth, Rhondda.

Evans, G., Beyer, S., Todd, S. and Blunden, R. (1986). Planning for the All Wales Strategy. *Mental Handicap*, **14**, 108–110.

George, V. and Wilding, P. (1976). *Ideology and Social Welfare.* London: Routledge and Kegan Paul.

Grant, G. (1985). Towards participation in the All Wales Strategy: issues and processes. *Mental Handicap*, **13**, 51–54.

Grant, G. (1990). *Consumer Involvement and the All Wales Strategy: a Research Note for the All Wales Advisory Panel Sub-group on Consumer Involvement.* Bangor: Centre for Social Policy Research and Development, University of Wales Bangor.

Grant, G. (1997). Consulting to involve or consulting to empower? In: *Empowerment in Everyday Life: Learning Disability.* (P. Ramcharan, G. Roberts, G. Grant, and J. Borland, eds) pp. 121–143. London: Jessica Kingsley.

Griffiths, R. (1988). *Community Care: Agenda for Action.* London: HMSO.

Hadley, R. and Hatch, S. (1981). *Social Welfare and the Failure of the State: Centralised Social Services and Participatory Alternatives.* London: Allen and Unwin.

Humphreys, S. (1987). Participation in practice. *Social Policy and Administration*, **21**, 28–39.

McGrath, M. (1988). Inter-agency collaboration in the All Wales Strategy: initial comments on a Vanguard Area. *Social Policy and Administration*, **22**, 53–67.

McGrath, M. (1989). Consumer participation in service planning: the AWS experience. *Social Policy and Administration*, **23**, 67–89.

McGrath, M. and Grant, G. (1992). Supporting 'needs-led' services: implications for planning and management systems. *Journal of Social Policy*, **21**, 71–97.

Pahl, J. and Quine, L. (1984). *Families and Mentally Handicapped Children: a Study of Stress and of Service Response*. Canterbury: Health Services Research Unit, University of Kent at Canterbury.

Potter, J. (1988). Consumerism and the public sector: how well does the coat fit? *Public Administration*, **66**, 149–164.

Ramcharan, P. (1995a). Citizen advocacy and people with learning disabilities in Wales. In: *Empowerment in Community Care*. (R. Jack, ed.) pp. 222–241. London: Chapman and Hall.

Ramcharan, P. (1995b). *An Evaluation of Colwyn Citizen Advocacy Project*. Bangor: Centre for Social Policy Research and Development, University of Wales Bangor.

Ramcharan, P., Whittell, B., White, J. and Thomas, B. (1996). *The Growing Voice in Wales: People with a Learning Difficulty and Self-advocacy in Wales*. Bangor: People First Wales in association with Centre for Social Policy Research and Development, University of Wales Bangor.

Richardson, A. (1983). *Participation*. London: Routledge and Kegan Paul.

Secretaries of State for Health, Social Security, Wales and Scotland (1989). *Caring for People: Community Care in the Next Decade and Beyond*. London: HMSO.

Standing Conference of Voluntary Organisations for People with a Mental Handicap in Wales (SCOVO) (1986). *Evidence from Welsh Voluntary Organisations for the Welsh Office AWS Three Year Review*. Cardiff: SCOVO.

Smith, L. and Jones, D. (1981). *Deprivation, Participation and Community Action*. London: Routledge and Kegan Paul.

Todd, S., Felce, D., Beyer, S. *et al.* (1997). *Stakeholder Perspectives on the Course of the All Wales Strategy*. Cardiff: Welsh Centre for Learning Disabilities Applied Research Unit, University of Wales College of Medicine.

Welsh Office (1983). *All Wales Strategy for the Development of Services for Mentally Handicapped People*. Cardiff: Welsh Office.

Welsh Office (1987). *The All Wales Strategy for the Development of Services for Mentally Handicapped People: Review of Progress since March 1993*. Cardiff: Welsh Office.

Welsh Office (1989). *Still a Small Voice: Consumer Involvement in the All Wales Strategy*. Cardiff: Welsh Office.

Welsh Office (1993). *Activities of Social Services Departments: Year ended 31/3/92*. Cardiff: Welsh Office.

Welsh Office (1996). *The Welsh Mental Handicap Strategy: Guidance 1994*. Cardiff: Welsh Office.

Wilkin, D. (1979). *Caring for the Mentally Handicapped Child*. London: Croom Helm.

Chapter 6

Developing community residential services

The AWS endorsed the right of Welsh citizens to community residence irrespective of the nature or degree of their disabilities. About two-thirds of the 3100 people with learning disabilities living in residential services in Wales in 1983 lived in hospital. Few among the remainder lived in the small scale community accommodation envisaged by the AWS, virtually the only examples being the housing developments provided within the NIMROD service. The AWS signalled a wholesale change in the pattern of services. Ordinary housing stock was to provide the context for all residential services, with variation in staff support creating a spectrum of provision to suit individual need and ability. Other forms of residential service such as hostels, hospitals or special units were not consistent with AWS principles and would not attract development funding.

We referred to the potential twin aims of the AWS in this area in Chapters 2 and 3 as to serve people in need in the community and to reprovide for people in inappropriately large and outmoded settings, implying resettlement both from the hospitals and traditional hostels. However, these aims were separated and accorded different priorities in planning. Resettlement from hospital was left to one side initially. Hospital populations had been declining in England and Wales in any case. The rate of decline accelerated in England from about 1984 onwards but not in Wales (Ericsson and Mansell, 1996). The AWS had little effect on the speed of hospital reform throughout the 1980s. Priorities lay elsewhere, for example in establishing social services led joint planning, the provision of multidisciplinary community teams and the development of family support.

The assumption that there was a focus on responding to the previously unmet needs of people living with their families in the community is questionable. If there had been significant development, one would have expected to see a shift in where people lived, with fewer living in family households and more in service supported settings. This would have resulted in an overall increase in the level of provision. There is no evidence to support the idea that these changes occurred. The hospital census (DHSS, 1972) showed that there were 104 hospital residents per 100 000 total population in Wales in 1970. Our most recent stocktake of national provision showed that hospital, local authority, private and voluntary sector residential services, combined, provided 98 places per 100 000 total population in 1995. This reinforces the impression gained in our earlier survey of the impact of the AWS in four districts between 1986 and 1990. While there had been changes in the nature of provision, the scale of provision and the balance in where people lived between private households and service settings remained the same.

What, in fact, appears to have been the early priority was resettlement from social services hostels. Between 1983 and 1988, local authorities and private and voluntary bodies opened 101 new settings, increasing the number of residential services other than the hospitals from 80 to 181 (Beyer, Todd and Felce, 1991). Developments were mainly small, consistent with AWS guidance, although new private provision still tended towards larger size. The emphasis on hostel resettlement was reflected in the fact that the number of people accommodated by local authorities did not increase dramatically between 1983 and 1987, rising from 676 to 736, despite the sector opening the largest number of new homes (45). Hostel sizes reduced as groups moved out. The median size of staffed local authority accommodation fell from 20 in 1983 to six by 1988.

Set against the ambition summarized in the first paragraph and the funding advantages of the AWS, the impression that progress has been below expectation created pressures to speed reform. As we discussed in Chapter 3, the resource investment provided by the AWS afforded the opportunity to develop community services for all people in need. Comprehensive community-oriented plans could have fuelled a 'community-pull' transition from hospital and hostel care as well as meeting local need. However, county planning was not sufficiently strategic nor linked to hospital resettlement. Comprehensive plans were not formulated and the lead agencies showed a reluctance to assume true leadership. In the end, and perhaps by default, 'hospital-push' resettlement was reactively developed as the continued institutional presence threatened to tarnish the AWS's reputation. Even now, twelve years after the launch of the AWS, a quarter of the people living in residential services live in hospital. No large hospital in Wales has closed at the time of writing and there is doubt as to whether complete institutional closure will be achieved. In the words of one person already resettled:

I wouldn't want to go back. Since I have moved out I've got my own space. They should hurry up and get all people left in hospitals into houses. Why have they allowed some people to move out and not others?

We will return to the interplay between the expansion of community services and the reduction of those which predated the AWS in the next section. We now direct our attention to the issue of service quality. The quality of the new community services is, arguably, as important as their availability. The expectation of improved opportunity and support in decent housing in the community leading to a much more typical and rewarding quality of life has underpinned the reform movement. These expectations were confirmed from research which began to be reported during the first years of the AWS (e.g. see references in Felce, 1989 and Lowe and de Paiva, 1991). In a Welsh context, the NIMROD evaluation had special significance. People living in its community housing services, most resettled from hospital, made significantly better progress in skills than did two comparison groups remaining in hospital. Family and friendship contact increased for those resettled and they made significantly more use of community amenities than did hospital residents. However, revenue costs were higher (Davies *et al.*, 1991) consistent with research which has found a general tendency for the costs of small housing services to be greater than hospital costs (Wright and Haycox, 1985; Knapp *et al.*, 1992; Felce, 1994; Raynes *et al.*, 1994).

The reprovision which has occurred under the AWS has almost uniformly followed the small community housing model. In this respect, the AWS upheld a strong policy line. The true impact of the AWS might, therefore, be found in the quality of the new services rather than in their extensiveness or rate of development. However, that change over time brings progress should not be assumed. The detailed grain of the quality of what is being achieved can often get lost when change on a broad front is undertaken. Small size and a combination of an ordinary house, in an ordinary street, with ordinary people for support backed by high resource input became, in planning and policy terms, proxies for quality. Improved quality of outcome was an independently stated goal of the AWS but, notwithstanding the ideological and practical training on offer, it has been more a hoped-for by-product of the restructuring of services than a focus of strategic planning and management. It is right, therefore, that the quality of life of people receiving residential support should be the subject of evaluation. We devote the second half of this chapter to our research in this area and highlight an agenda for the continuing improvement of the quality of what is achieved.

Community housing developments and hospital reform

As we have argued in Chapter 3, the seeds of later difficulties lay in the failure to manage the interplay between social services and health in the early years of the AWS and to establish a comprehensive total population and total expenditure planning framework. While an initial focus on building up community provision may have been merited, such an orientation would not have been incompatible with resettling people from outmoded facilities, as earlier developments such as NIMROD had shown. In stark contrast to the NIMROD development, where services had been closely related to specific areas and the comprehensive needs of the total population encompassed, detailed demographic planning of the eventual pattern of services did not underpin the AWS.

Two factors seem relevant to explaining the early course of the AWS. A rhetorical emphasis on developing community services before pursuing hospital resettlement was strengthened by the decision to give social services departments lead-agency responsibility and by the immediate history of failure to gain health authority support for a policy which logically implied hospital closure. Ever since the shock of the Ely Hospital scandal, there had been a search for service development proposals which were sufficiently radical and forward looking to be credible. However, those put forward by the then health authorities retained too great an attachment to institutional models and organization. Choice of lead agency and the community development thrust of the AWS represented a means to move forward. Yet, putting the future of the large hospitals on hold burdened the AWS with an unresolved issue close to its core.

Social services did not have a track record of serving people with learning disabilities well, certainly not those with more severe disabilities. Undertaking comprehensive social care responsibilities represented a major challenge to officers and councillors alike. There is no evidence that the principle of comprehensiveness was clearly established. The AWS was a central initiative in response to a professional lobby for reform. It had weak political roots locally. Hesitancy was compounded by inevitable suspicions about hospital closure and Thatcherite cost-cutting in Labour dominated Wales, suspicions which have persisted to the present day. Local authorities were, therefore, slow in generating the total view which the AWS implied, and responded piecemeal with their own concerns foremost. It is perhaps no great surprise that early action involved reform of their own directly-managed hostel provision.

Lessening dependence on institutional services was a stated aim of the AWS. Resettlement from hostels contributed to meeting this aim but, by the same token, and in a numerically more significant way, so would hospital resettlement. The AWS could only develop a partial view without health service commitment to institutional closure and a mechanism for bringing the inherent resources together with those invested in social care. Although the Welsh Office made a sustained effort to establish joint health and social service action, policy issues were not properly resolved either centrally or, in many counties in Wales, locally until late in the day. As we described earlier, the Welsh Office misdirected their first call for plans on the future of the hospitals solely to the health authorities. The attempt to correct this about the time of the mid-term review of the AWS by asking for hospital redevelopment plans to be annexed to joint county plans did not change the impression that hospital resettlement was distinct, an impression reinforced by the decision to back hospital resettlement by ear-marked funding.

Responsibilities for leading hospital resettlement remained unclear. The local authorities were lead agents with respect to the AWS. Health services were sitting tenants on the existing expenditure and the management and operation of the existing services. No arrangements were made for the transfer of financial or managerial control. Two counties with well-developed joint agency planning managed the closure of small hospitals within their own boundaries, but similar effective relationships were not in place to manage cross-border resettlement from the larger hospitals. The conditions for the production of fully integrated plans were not realized and the piecemeal planning of the first years continued. Even when, late in the life of the AWS, the prospect of the hospitals surviving the AWS created an imperative to act, plans which integrated hospital provision with meeting needs in the community were still not produced. Rather, hospital resettlement became an increasingly dominant focus of the AWS from the early 1990s onwards. The main expression of policy after 1993 has been the provision of funding to stimulate the reinvestment of hospital resources in the community, echoing the English Care in the Community demonstration projects of the second half of the 1980s (Knapp *et al.*, 1992).

The impact of the AWS up to the end of the 1980s

By 1988, some 614 places had been provided in ordinary housing, an increase of 580 from the base of 34 which existed in 1983. The number of people accommodated in the independent sector more than doubled. The provision of voluntary homes accelerated between 1987 and 1988 (20 new settings opened) as emerging partnerships flourished between voluntary bodies and housing associations working in tandem with the statutory sector. Some of these developments were for people moving out of hospital and represented direct arrangements between independent bodies and the health service. Others involved partnership between local authorities and voluntary bodies. By 1990, housing provision had increased to 986 places, a rate of development of 186 places per year over the previous two years compared to 116 per year between 1983 and 1988. Much of this increased activity was already in the system, although some could be attributed to the impact of the mid-term review. A number of voluntary agencies had come into being by this time to operate supported housing services in collaboration with housing associations. One such, Cartrefi Cymru, was explicitly formed to operate in any of the eight counties which wanted to use it. Its creation was stimulated by the Welsh Office out of concern for an inadequate variety of provider arrangements in all counties.

How changes in service delivery patterns up to 1990 affected service users and their families was gauged by a longitudinal study of people from four districts in four Welsh counties (Evans *et al.*, 1994). The districts themselves were not randomly drawn but were selected to represent important diversity found in Wales: rural and urban populations, depressed economy and relative affluence, stronger Welsh-speaking culture and greater Anglicization. Four hundred and four people were surveyed in 1986 and again in 1990. Overall, 165 people in 1986 (41%) and 168 in 1990 (42%) lived in some form of service setting, illustrating relative stability in the extent of provision and the balance between private household and service residence. Proportions of the sample in residential care across districts varied from 24% to 56%, a range which is great enough to suggest that local provision was still uneven and that where a person lived continued to determine their service options.

Figure 6.1 shows the balance of private housing and service residential provision in both years and the numbers of people changing where they lived in the intervening time. There was a growth in the provision of ordinary housing from six to 32 available places. The districts slightly under-represented the extent of development in Wales as a whole: a fifth of residential provision was in ordinary housing within the four districts compared to an estimated quarter generally at that time. Two districts had only a tenth of their total residential provision in the form of ordinary housing, while the other two had achieved about a quarter and a third respectively.

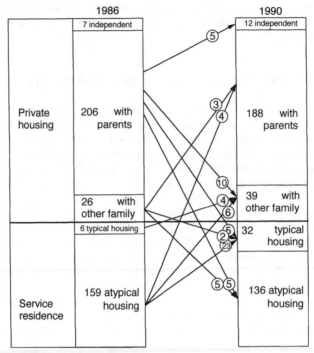

Figure 6.1 Change in residence of the sample during the middle four years of the All Wales Strategy, 1986–90

The expansion of ordinary housing met a diversity of need. Seven people moved from parental homes or the homes of other family members, while 23 moved from more traditional residential services: four from local authority hostels, eight from hospitals, four from private or voluntary sector settings with six or more places, and seven from other types of placement such as lodgings. The number of people living in hostels decreased from 23 to 12, those not going to ordinary housing moving mainly to private households to live with families. Hospital occupancy decreased from 65 to 44. Those leaving hospital but not going to ordinary housing moved mainly to large private or voluntary settings.

However, the development of ordinary housing was not being achieved quickly enough. At a rate of development similar to that achieved in the four years studied, it would take a further 21 years for the remaining 136 places in atypical housing to be replaced. More people (10) moved from private family households into atypical accommodation than into staffed housing (seven); an indicator of the ongoing tension as to whether new services were to result in reform of outmoded services or meet the needs of people previously unserved in the community. Fourteen people moved from service residences to family homes. Although these may have been moves of choice, such adults could still not be said to have homes of their own in the community and access to normal patterns of living in line with the principles of the AWS. However, principles are a weak device when faced with the long-standing rationing of services[1].

Into the 1990s and a growing emphasis on hospital resettlement

The pace of change accelerated at the end of the 1980s. The development of ordinary housing between 1988 and 1995 was at about twice the rate of the previous five years, increasing the number of places available from 614 to 1824. In total, Wales now had 633 housing services split between voluntary, private and local authority providers in approximately 2:2:1 ratio. The average size of residence was three, and this was similar across all provision sectors. Development in these latter years was dominated by the independent sector; local authorities operated more settings in 1995 than in 1988, but accommodated fewer people, 690 compared to about 740, some of whom still lived in the few remaining traditional hostels.

Expansion of ordinary housing provision by about 1200 places was associated with a 1000 drop in the hospital population (from just over 1700 in 1987 to about 700 in 1995). All of the original large hospitals remained, accommodating between about 80 and 200 residents each. The one hospital which had achieved rather more rapid reduction than the others had brought about the change in an unexpected way, given the emphasis of the AWS. The health authority had delegated control over commissioning to the provider trust which operated the hospital. Relationships with the social services department had all but broken down. Independent sector provision routes were deemed too slow and expensive. Hospital managers fostered development through the private sector. Many of the new arrangements involved ex-hospital staff becoming established as private proprietors. Ultimately, aspects of the payments being made were ruled *ultra vires*, but the fact that this process was sanctioned by the Welsh Office, albeit tacitly, illustrated the strength of the imperative to bring about institutional reform.

Meanwhile, the review of the first ten years of the AWS initiated a much tighter resource framework. Gone was the broad vision of comprehensive services, except in principle. In its place was a central funding strategy to achieve hospital resettlement within existing resources. The Welsh Office had become alarmed by the escalating costs of housing proposals. In the absence of a strategic plan setting out the eventual scale and pattern of services at a target total cost, the review of project proposals in the previous decade had not been subject to the financial discipline of a budget ceiling. Indeed, as there had been a failure to spend AWS allocations in the early years, the overall financial climate was not restrictive. The costs per place in submitted proposals tended to rise year by year and together with increasing costs for associated day service provision and the assumption that the majority of people to be resettled with higher support needs were yet to come, the financial projections calculated for completing hospital closure caused concern, particularly as they came at a time of restricted public expenditure.

Circular 30/94 (Welsh Office, 1994) asked authorities to draw up plans for alternative services for those in hospital within a cost framework set by existing expenditure. They were to identify deficiencies in this planned support and to estimate the additional cost of correcting them. Although all authorities indicated that acceptable reprovision required resources additional to those already within the institutions, costs per place were considerably reduced compared to those in recent submissions. After further consideration, an additional £5m was made available centrally to support the resettlement programme and authorities were again asked to draw up plans based on the resources available (Welsh Office, 1995). One county with a number of small hospitals within its boundaries submitted a plan which met the financial guideline. In total, the recurrent revenue required to implement the plans submitted exceeded that available by nearly £5m, an overshoot of about 16%.

At the time of writing, resettlement plans have been agreed which could potentially create alternative provision for over 500 of the 700 individuals still living in hospital. Resettlement from the three small hospitals in one county (about 85 people) should be completed by the end of 1997 and from two of the three large hospitals in South Wales (about 80 and 180 people respectively) by the end of 1997 and 1998. Some resettlement is to continue from the third large hospital in South Wales, but the main programme (about 200 people) will only start in 1998/9 as resources allow. The situation in relation to the one large hospital in North Wales (about 150 people) will be reviewed in three years time; resettlement will begin only as and when resources become available.

The quality of ordinary housing provision

Reprovision in Wales has been marked by more uniform adoption of the small house model than elsewhere in Britain. Whereas, mean setting sizes in the local authority and voluntary sectors in Wales were about four and three, the comparable figures in England were 13 and six (Department of Health, 1996). This suggests a greater commitment to ordinary housing and smallness of scale (four places or fewer) under the AWS compared to the more pragmatic deinstitutionalization policy pursued in England. The more resource rich investment climate has also resulted in more plentiful staffing. However, any claim to better quality of outcome is made without reference to evidence. Although service inputs may be indicative of outcome, research has shown that single service attributes such as small size or high staffing do not guarantee high quality (e.g. Landesman-Dwyer, Sackett and Kleinman, 1980; Landesman-Dwyer, 1981). They may not even be the most critical determinants of outcome (e.g. Hatton *et al.*, 1995). So, what evidence is there that the small staffed community house model has delivered the quality of life gains promised? There is now renewed resource-driven interest in the question. Commitment to the ordinary housing model has wavered as the resource framework has tightened, associated, as it is, with higher costs in the minds of commissioners.

From their review of the British deinstitutionalization research literature, Emerson and Hatton (1994) concluded that services based on
community housing were on the whole better than traditional hospitals.
Indicators compared related to the quality of the living environment,
community integration, constructive occupation, development and family
involvement. But comparison to the poorly resourced, often remote and
inappropriately designed institutions of the past is not a severe challenge.
Even then, some of the new services evaluated have not been found to be
significantly better on some indicators of development and activity than
those they replaced. Quality of outcome varies between small community
housing and so do revenue costs (see Knapp et al., 1992; Felce, 1994;
Raynes et al., 1994 for further discussion). A precise resource
input–quality output equation cannot be sustained. Management attention, therefore, to value for money remains an important consideration
not only from the perspective of husbanding resources but also out of a
concern for quality.

Our research on the quality of supported housing in Wales involved
measuring various dimensions of quality in 15 services between 1990 and
1992 (Perry and Felce, 1994; Felce and Perry, 1995). The houses were
drawn from four counties in South Wales and collectively served 57 adults.
They ranged in size from one to seven places. The houses were selected
to represent the spectrum of support needs[2]. Houses are numbered in
ascending order of the ability of the resident group in the figures and text
which follow.

Housing quality

Perhaps not surprisingly, newly provided ordinary housing services have
brought people reasonably decent material standards. The majority of
houses in our sample were homelike and well furnished. They scored
means of 62% and 64% of the totals possible on two scales which jointly
reflect the attractiveness of the settings, the standard, variety and perso-
nalization of their furnishings and decor, and their homeliness – the Physical Quality Scale (Conroy and Bradley, 1985) and the Characteristics of
the Physical Environment Scale (Rotegard, Hill and Bruininks, 1983).
These findings are consistent with a larger survey undertaken in England
(Raynes et al., 1994) and with the general conclusion from Emerson's and
Hatton's (1994) review. However, it is important to note that variation in
our study (ranges, 49–72% and 28–88% respectively) was related to the
abilities of the people served. Less able residents tended to live in less
homelike settings.

Staffing input and staff:resident contact

Service planners or commissioners have generally been willing to allocate
higher staffing levels in new community developments than were found
in the existing institutions (see Knapp et al., 1992), a trend which built
on increasing staff:resident ratios in the hospitals throughout the 1970s
and early 1980s (Office of Health Economics, 1986). Daytime staff hours
per week per resident varied in the researched settings from six to 157

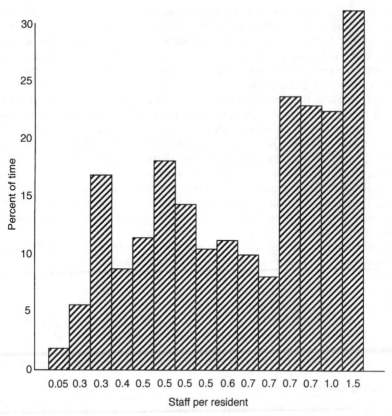

Figure 6.2 Total staff contact per resident in relation to numbers of staff per resident

(mean, 63), with a significant inverse relationship being found with resident abilities. Staffing in Houses 1–6, which served residents with the greater impairments, were more than double those in the remainder (an average of 93 hours per week per resident compared to 42). The pattern was not perfect though, reflecting the impact of other factors such as very small size and variation across different commissioning or provider agencies.

Differences in staffing level were carried through into differences in the extent of staff contact residents received only at the extremes. No significant relationship exists if the data for the houses with the highest and lowest staffing levels are excluded (Figure 6.2). Staff contact received by residents varied greatly among houses with similar staff:resident ratios and similar levels of staff contact were also found between houses with markedly different staff:resident ratios (Figure 6.3). A decreasing return from the addition of staff was apparent. In common with much other research, staff in houses for more able people interacted more with residents than those in houses for less able people, despite the presumed need of the latter for greater support.

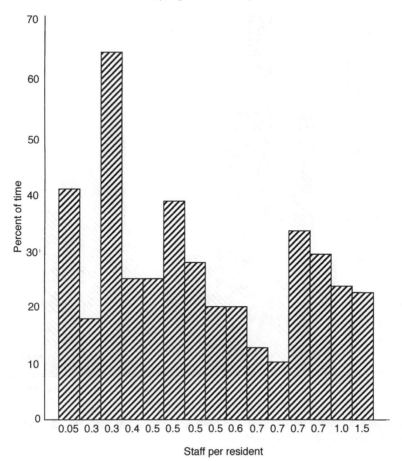

Figure 6.3 Per cent of time contacting residents per staff in relation to numbers of staff per resident

The quality of staff support

High staffing levels testify to the importance attached to what staff do in working with residents. We assessed the quality of staff support by measuring not only the amount of contact residents received but also the level of assistance they were given to conduct activities (Figure 6.4). On average, each resident received contact from staff for 15% of the time (range, 2–31%) – about 9 minutes in every hour – typically in the form of conversation. They received assistance for less than two minutes in every hour (15% of staff contact). The degree of reliance on spoken language and the low level of practical help is of course particularly disadvantageous for people with more severe and pervasive disabilities. Most people in Houses 1–6 lacked well-developed language, had social impairments and were not proficient in basic self-help skills.

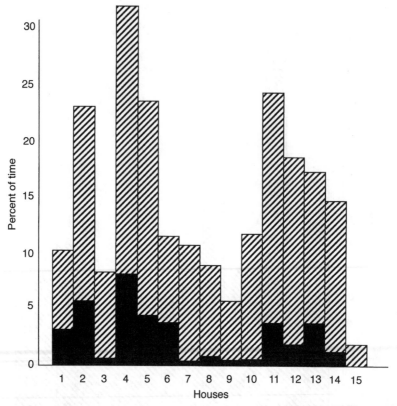

Figure 6.4 Total staff contact and staff assistance per resident. ■ Staff assistance; ▨ other staff contact

Although residents in Houses 1–6 received more staff contact (mean: 18% vs 12%) and more assistance (mean: 4% vs 1.5%) than their counterparts in Houses 7–15, there was not a significant correlation between staff activity and resident disability. Assistance at a level of a few minutes per hour is clearly insufficient as will be shown next.

Resident activity

Residents spent more time interacting with staff than with each other. Social interaction between residents in Houses 1–6 was not observed to any appreciable extent, but it was low among even some of the more able residents, such as those in Houses 14 and 15.

The overall activity levels of residents (combining social engagement with participation in personal (self-care), leisure and household (domestic) activities) varied between five- and six-fold across the houses (Figure 6.5). At the upper end, residents enjoyed the high levels of occupation which characterize most people's lives. At the other, the level of involvement in activity found (less than 10 minutes per hour)

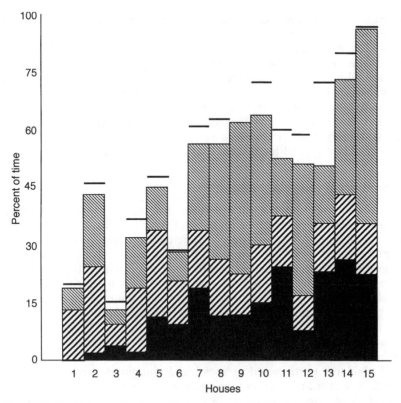

Figure 6.5 Resident engagement in activity. ▨ Leisure activity; ▱ personal activity; ■ domestic activity

gives cause for serious concern. As would be expected, engagement in self-care activity was relatively constant across houses. Engagement in other forms of activity (leisure and household) was highly related to resident ability. Indeed, as would be expected from the low levels of assistance being given to residents, variation in the overall level of participation in activity was effectively determined by differences in what residents could do for themselves. Despite the assumed environmental advantages of ordinary housing, resident participation in running their own households (engagement in domestic activity) was virtually non-existent in Houses 1–4 and low in many others. Leisure was the largest component of activity for more able residents, much of it watching television.

Development, autonomy and choice

There was little evidence of formal methods being adopted to assess or promote individual development in the housing services. Change over time measured by repeating the Adaptive Behavior Scale (Nihira *et al.*, 1974) was on average positive but considerable variability made interpretation difficult. The findings suggest that developmental growth is by no means certain, even in community services (Felce and Perry, 1996).

The extent of autonomy and choice residents enjoyed is difficult to assess when residents lack the language to give their own views, as was the case with most of the people researched. Staff were interviewed using a number of simple scales and their responses indicated high levels of autonomy and choice over basic concerns of day-to-day living. However, external assessment during the course of a PASS evaluation[3] suggested that autonomy and choice were still severely constrained compared to what would be typical for ordinary citizens living at home.

Community and social integration

The isolation of many institutions from any sizeable community and the distance imposed between residents and their families and friends have been highlighted for many years as barriers to community inclusion and maintenance of social relationships. Promotion of community and social integration has been a central rationale of the move to the community. We explored these aspects of the residents' lives by asking staff to fill in diaries of community excursions and social contacts over the course of a month. In addition, staff were interviewed about resident integration using the Index of Community Integration (ICI), a scale which Raynes *et al.* (1994) had used in their survey of residential provision in England[4].

All residents participated in social and community activities to some extent. However, integration was variable. The results on the ICI ranged from 20% of possible score to 73% with a mean of 55%. On average, therefore, residents experienced about half of the community or social opportunities included within the scope of the scale. Residents in two houses (1 and 3) engaged in a particularly restricted range of activities. The average frequency of community activities recorded in the diaries varied from 10 to 45 per person per month (mean 18). On the whole, settings with less able residents had lower frequencies than those with more able residents. Social activities which involved going out or staying with friends or family or entertaining them at home were less frequent than community activities (i.e. the use of community amenities) for residents in all houses bar House 15. They ranged from an average of 3 to 20 per person per month with a mean of 8. Some residents had very restricted social lives. As we comment in other chapters, most people with learning disabilities have gained a greater community presence but their social participation remains limited.

Compared to the ICI mean of 44% found in the Raynes *et al.* survey in England, integration in community services in Wales was marginally better. Community use was slightly less than had been reported in the Andover and NIMROD research (de Kock *et al.*, 1988; Lowe and de Paiva, 1991) but the frequency of social events was slightly greater than in the former and than was reported for the Care in the Community demonstration projects (Knapp *et al.*, 1992). Notwithstanding this, increasing the social inclusion of people with severe learning disabilities is one of the more difficult outcomes to achieve.

Normalization

As normalization has provided one of the rationales for service redevelopment (see Chapter 2), it is appropriate to evaluate the resulting provision in such terms. Wolfensberger and Glenn (1975) devised the evaluation tool, PASS, to assess the extent of conformity of a service to the normalization principle. It comprises 50 rating scales concerned with physical and social integration, age- and culture-appropriateness, developmental growth, quality of setting, the foundation of service design, management and administration. It has been a controversial measure as scores are combined using weights solely of the authors' choosing to represent the importance of the issues. Importance is related to normalization for 34 of the ratings and to desirable management and administration practices for 16 of the ratings. It is difficult to validate the assumptions made as the scale is defined on a concept which is not operationalized in measurable terms in any other way. However, the picture obtained across the 14 houses which we were able to evaluate (one withdrew from further participation in the study) is consistent with the interpretation of the other indicators so far presented.

PASS ratings are arranged in clusters and a summary of the findings across all of the houses for these clusters is shown in Figure 6.6 (see also Felce and Perry, 1997). Ratings concerned with the physical context of the services vis à vis community resources and populations were reasonably high as were those concerned with environmental quality. The 50% mark represents minimally acceptable standards according to the scale's authors, given the way that we have recast the PASS scoring system. The locations of 12 of the 14 houses scored were assessed at or above this level, as were the building characteristics of 10 and the quality of setting of seven.

In contrast, the clarity and intensity of organization to do with meeting resident needs was assessed as poor, in many cases decidedly so. Only four

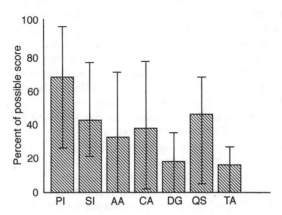

Figure 6.6 Scores on PASS 3 for 14 houses. PI, physical intergration; SI, social integration; AA, age-appropriate interpretations and structures; CA, culture-appropriate interpretations and structures; DG, developmental growth; QS, quality of setting; TA, total administration; I, range of scores

houses scored 50% or above on the age-appropriate interpretations and structures rating cluster and seven scored below 25%. No service scored 50% or above on their approach to developmental growth, and 12 scored below 25%. In particular, every service received the lowest level assessment on the rating, *intensity of relevant programming*, which addresses how well services identify and respond to specific developmental and other needs of their users. This finding is consistent with the lack of a systematic approach to resident development discussed earlier. It also mirrors the finding that the extent of resident participation in activity depended mainly on their own abilities.

In addition, the majority of administrative issues received very low scores, an unanticipated finding which may reflect the stage of service development reached at the time of evaluation. All of the houses studied were recent developments, operating in a far from comprehensive pattern of services and without a well coordinated pattern of local support. Use of generic resources and consumer and public participation in the operation and management of the services were, at best, embryonic. Issues such as education of the public and manpower development had not been defined as part of the individual service's relationship with wider society. Moreover, a lack of innovation, an absence of academic links or research activity, ad hoc staff development and poor self-evaluation and renewal mechanisms were consistent with a low emphasis on working methods and core competencies. In addition, the managerial base of services was under review with the introduction of the purchaser/provider split and the encouragement of a mixed economy of services.

Implications for improving quality

This research and the more general review of Emerson and Hatton (1994) have demonstrated that improved resident experience or development have not always accompanied the creation of the more preferable environmental and resource context of typical ordinary housing services. Bratt and Johnston (1988) have referred to the kind of services provided by routine service operation as part of widespread reform as 'second generation' projects, contrasting them to the earlier round of specially developed 'model' services backed by research. They suggested that the quality of what was provided could be adversely affected by the sheer scale and rapidity of later change in what has been an exodus of about 29 250 people from hospital in England and Wales between 1980 and 1992 (Emerson and Hatton, 1994). Specifically in their own study, they referred to an absence of any defined approach to developmental or other outcomes for residents, as if the changed environment itself was believed to be a sufficient condition for other outcomes to follow.

We now know that this is not the case, at least not to the extent which is consistent with the high principles and aspirations of the AWS and the general rhetoric which has surrounded the move to the community. The simple 'ordinary house, ordinary street, ordinary staff' model, the change from a medical to social care model and the ideological or values-based training which followed the dissemination of normalization have not proved sufficient to deliver typical lifestyles, especially where people with more severe disabilities are concerned. Many of the quality of life indicators studied in our research were related to the ability of residents. These included the homeliness of the environment, frequency of social contacts and community integration, extent of constructive occupation, and most PASS scores other than those related to the physical characteristics and location of the houses and administrative concerns. Providing a high quality of life to people with the most substantial disabilities remains a challenge to be tackled.

Our sample of Welsh houses does in fact seem to have achieved a higher degree of individually-oriented care, given residents greater choice over matters of day-to-day concern and provided a better platform for community activity than the community facilities in England surveyed by Raynes *et al.* (1994). This survey included residential options of a larger size than those we studied and the differences in results will be viewed by many as consistent with the expectation that more individually responsive and integrative services do result from smaller scale. Community and social integration were not, however, much improved over levels reported for the earlier model projects despite a progressive move to smaller scale and higher staffing. Better ways of embedding support services in the social worlds of our communities need to be found.

Quality with respect to supporting age-appropriate activity and development was particularly vulnerable in services for people with the greatest disabilities. Such people also had the most limited social lives. The nature of staff support of residents and the extent of resident engagement in activity, compared across people of equivalent ability, was clearly different in the houses studied here than in some of the early demonstration projects, despite their size, environmental and resource advantages (see discussion in Felce and Perry, 1995). The extent of assistance given to people by staff is probably the key determinant of participation in activity other than the abilities of the people themselves (Felce, 1996). So, while much credit should be given to planners and providers for making sure that supported housing services are of high quality and well resourced, more needs to be done to structure the delivery of support to take advantage of their inherent opportunities. In view of this, Felce (1991), Mansell and Beasley (1993), McGill and Toogood (1994) and Emerson and Hatton (1994) have argued that the implementation of an 'active support' model through clearly defined structures for planning staff and resident activity and for the delivery of practical help to residents to meet the behavioural demands of commonplace situations is an essential component of high quality provision, at least for those with more substantial disabilities. Our recent research to test 'active support' in practice has found that it leads to significant increases in the assistance residents receive which in turn leads to significant increases in their constructive occupation (Jones *et al.*, 1997).

Further, even though groupings are now on a much more human scale, this does not mean that there are not still concerns about the process by which people come to live together, their status and their rights within their accommodation, their degree of control over their lifestyle and how their needed support is arranged. Recent perspectives, exemplified by the 'supported living' paradigm (Kinsella, 1993), have continued to push forward the extent to which people with disabilities are extended choices and circumstances which other people in our society take for granted. People are much more likely to be tenants in their accommodation now than at the beginning of the 1980s, but the legal protection of tenancy should be extended to all. More effort has been given to determining groupings in other than an arbitrary way in recent years than before and this has been coupled with a greater flexibility in resourcing. However, particularly when services come under pressure, as they have in the final stages of planning resettlement under the AWS, they can too easily adopt formulaic, standard approaches, accepting a predetermined size, constraining groupings to fit the chosen number and allocating a fixed quota of staff.

Supported living emphasizes the primacy of planning for and with individuals and the importance of deciding groupings and service size to suit their needs and wishes. It also emphasizes the logic of determining support in relation to individual need and promotes the role of services not only as a direct provider of resources, structures and processes, but also as a catalyst to enhance the benefit derived from the individual's network of natural support and the resources of the community. Promotion of typical choices and the exercise of individual control are paramount. In this context, separating the provision of housing from the provision of support is an important safeguard to personal determination. It should be possible for people to review and change their support arrangements without having to move and vice versa. The nature of residential services will, therefore, undoubtedly undergo further revision in seeking to help people with learning disabilities attain fulfilling and satisfying lives. However, this does not mean that one should look at past reform with too critical an eye. Understanding about how to act in the best interests of people with learning disabilities has grown as a result of what has been done and will surely continue to do so.

We leave the last word to people who live fairly independently in the community. They talk about having a home, having control and making choices, and about living with others and the need for companionship.

I like living here. It is near the shops and I go out more ... I like living here because it is my own home and I have more choice of what I do.

Sometimes I feel I can't cope and it's a bit much for me. Sometimes I think I can't say these things to other people about why I don't like it because they'll take the house back. I've got friends who I talk to about it. I'd like to be on my own but I'm happy with Jane.

I didn't really choose to come and live here ... I chose all the stuff (furnishings, decor etc.).

(Do you like living here?) I don't know ... I wish I could leave the bungalow ... I'd like to go to (town where lived before) with (sister) and (her daughter) ... I miss them.

(My flat is) fully private. I only get a visit from my landlord for the rent, that's all ... (social services staff) come in to see me, how I am ... I'm actually autistic see.

I was told this about three years ago ... I looked it up in the dictionary and it meant that I am in my own world ... I think that's why ... I wanted to be myself all the time.

I like the company. I like the area ... I was born (in the area) and my father was a policeman years ago. My mum used to live (here) ... this is my home town.

I like living at home now and helping to do the dinner and the tea.

(Do you like living here?) Sometimes ... sometimes very lonely ... go home, put the radio on. Yes, my mother died, see.

You've got to think about the future ... I wouldn't like a place on my own. I would like to share with somebody. I like company. My sister's different from me. She likes to be on her own ... (but) ... I'd like somebody coming in to see us.

I'd like to talk to someone in the evenings. Nobody ever visits.

I'd like to see more people drop in. I speak to the bird sometimes. Other people think I'm talking to myself but I'm speaking my problems to the bird.

Notes

1. Certainly, no government in Britain has yet faced the implications for the national exchequer of the considerable expansion of provision which would be required if adults with learning disabilities were to be supported to live independently of their families from an age when it is more usual to leave the parental home.
2. Few residents in three houses (Houses 1–3) were continent or possessed the abilities to feed, dress, wash or speak in sentences; they had Adaptive Behavior Scale scores (Nihira et al., 1974) typical of the lowest quartile of the range. Residents in a further three houses (Houses 4–6) had greater self-help skills but they too had little spoken language. Most of the people in the sample with challenging or stereotypic behaviours or the triad of social impairments (Wing and Gould, 1978) also lived in these six houses. Residents in the other houses were more able; they generally had good self-help skills and could speak in sentences. Residents living in Houses 13–15 had Adaptive Behavior Scale scores typical of the highest quartile of the range.
3. Program Analysis of Service Systems (Wolfensberger and Glenn, 1975).
4. The ICI establishes whether or not a resident has participated in 14 listed activities in the course of the previous four weeks (three concerned with social activities – having someone for a meal, guests to stay or going for an overnight stay; and 11 with community use – going shopping, using a bus and going to a hairdresser, cinema, cafe, pub, church, sports event, social club, concert or play, or bank). A fifteenth item is concerned with whether or not the person has been on holiday in the last year. The percentage of items scored as occurring for each resident in each house was averaged to give an overall percentage.

References

Beyer, S., Todd, S. and Felce, D. (1991). The implementation of the All-Wales Mental Handicap Strategy, 1983–1988. *Mental Handicap Research*, **4**, 115–140.

Bratt, A. and Johnston, R. (1988). Changes in lifestyle for young adults with profound handicaps following discharge from hospital care into a 'second generation' housing project. *Mental Handicap Research*, **1**, 49–74.

Conroy, J. W. and Bradley, V. J. (1985). *The Pennhurst Longitudinal Study: a Report of Five Years Research and Analysis*. Philadelphia: Temple University Developmental Disabilities Center.

Davies, L., Felce, D., Lowe, K. and de Paiva, S. (1991). The evaluation of NIMROD, a community based services for people with a mental handicap: revenue costs. *Health Services Management Research*, **4**, 170–180.

de Kock, U., Saxby, H., Thomas, M. and Felce, D. (1988). Community and family contact: an evaluation of small community homes for severely and profoundly mentally handicapped adults. *Mental Handicap Research*, **1**, 127–140.

Department of Health (1996). *Residential Accommodation. Detailed Statistics on Residential Care Homes and Local Authority Supported Residents. England 1995*. London: HMSO.

Department of Health and Social Security (DHSS) (1972). *Census of Mentally Handicapped Patients in Hospital in England and Wales at the End of 1970*. London: HMSO.

Emerson, E. and Hatton, C. (1994). *Moving Out: Relocation from Hospital to Community*. London: HMSO.

Ericsson, K. and Mansell, J. (1996) Towards deinstitutionalization. In: *Deinstitutionalization and Community Living. Intellectual Disability Services in Britain, Scandinavia and the USA*, (J. Mansell and K. Ericsson, eds) pp. 1–16. London: Chapman and Hall.

Evans, G., Todd, S., Beyer, S. *et al.* (1994). Assessing the impact of the All-Wales Strategy. *Journal of Intellectual Disability Research*, **38**, 109–33.

Felce, D. (1989). *Staffed Housing for Adults with Severe and Profound Mental Handicaps: the Andover Project*. Kidderminster: BIMH Publications.

Felce, D. (1991). Using behavioural principles in the development of effective housing services for adults with severe or profound mental handicaps. In: *The Challenge of Severe Mental Handicap: a Behaviour Analytic Perspective*, (R. Remington, ed.) pp. 285–316. Chichester: John Wiley and Sons.

Felce, D. (1994). Costs, quality and staffing in services for people with severe learning disabilities. *Journal of Mental Health*, **3**, 495–506.

Felce, D. (1996). The quality of support for ordinary living: staff:resident interactions and resident activity. In: *Deinstitutionalization and Community Living: Intellectual Disability Services in Britain, Scandinavia and the USA*, (J. Mansell and K. Ericcson, eds) pp. 117–133. London: Chapman and Hall.

Felce, D. and Perry, J. (1995). The extent of support for ordinary living provided in staffed housing: the relationship between staffing levels, resident dependency, staff:resident interactions and resident activity patterns. *Social Science and Medicine*, **40**, 799–810.

Felce, D. and Perry, J. (1996). Adaptive behaviour gains in ordinary housing for people with learning disabilities. *Journal of Applied Research in Intellectual Disabilities*, **9**, 101–114.

Felce, D. and Perry, J. (1997). A PASS 3 evaluation of community residences in Wales. *Mental Retardation*, **35**, 170–176.

Hatton, C., Emerson, E., Robertson, J. *et al.* (1995). *An Evaluation of the Quality and Costs of Services for Adults with Severe Learning Disabilities and Sensory Impairments*. Manchester: Hester Adrian Research Centre, University of Manchester.

Jones, E., Perry, J., Lowe, K. *et al.* (1997). *Opportunity and the Promotion of Activity among Adults with Severe Learning Disabilities Living in Community Housing: the Impact of Training Staff in Active Support*. Cardiff: Welsh Centre for Learning Disabilities Applied Research Unit, University of Wales College of Medicine.

Kinsella, P. (1993). *Supported Living: a New Paradigm*. Manchester: National Development Team.

Knapp, M., Cambridge, P., Thomason, C. *et al.* (1992). *Care in the Community: Challenge and Demonstration*. Aldershot: Ashgate.

Landesman-Dwyer, S. (1981). Living in the community. *American Journal of Mental Deficiency*, **86**, 223–234.

Landesman-Dwyer, S., Sackett, G. P. and Kleinman, J. S. (1980). Relationship of size to resident and staff behavior in small community home residences. *American Journal of Mental Deficiency*, **85**, 6–17.

Lowe, K. and de Paiva, S. (1991). *NIMROD: an Overview*. London: HMSO.

McGill, P. and Toogood, A. (1994). Organising community placements. In: *Severe Learning Disabilities and Challenging Behaviours: Designing High Quality Services*, (E. Emerson, P. McGill and J. Mansell, eds) pp. 232–259. London: Chapman and Hall.

Mansell, J. and Beasley, F. (1993). Small staffed houses for people with a severe learning disability and challenging behaviour. *British Journal of Social Work*, **23**, 329–344.

Nihira, K., Foster, R., Shellhaas, M. and Leland, H. (1974). *AAMD Adaptive Behaviour Scale*. Washington DC: American Association on Mental Deficiency.

Office of Health Economics (1986). *Mental Handicap: Partnership in the Community?* London: Office of Health Economics/Mencap.

Perry, J. and Felce, D. (1994). Outcomes of ordinary housing services in Wales: objective indicators. *Mental Handicap Research*, **7**, 286–311.

Raynes, N., Wright, K., Shiell, A. and Pettipher, C. (1994). *The Cost and Quality of Community Residential Care*. London: David Fulton Publishers.

Rotegard, L. L., Hill, B. K. and Bruininks, R. H. (1983). Environmental characteristics of residential facilities for mentally retarded persons in the United States. *American Journal of Mental Deficiency*, **88**, 49–56.

Welsh Office (1994). *Welsh Office Circular 30/94*. Cardiff: Welsh Office.

Welsh Office (1995). *Welsh Office Circular 7/95*. Cardiff: Welsh Office.

Wing, L. and Gould, J. (1978). Systematic recording of behaviors and skills of retarded and psychotic children. *Journal of Autism and Childhood Schizophrenia*, **8**, 79–97.

Wolfensberger, W. and Glenn, L. (1975). *Programme Analysis of Service Systems: Handbook and Manual (3rd edn)*. Toronto: National Institute on Mental Retardation.

Wright, K. and Haycox, A. (1985). *Costs of Alternative Forms of NHS Care for Mentally Handicapped Persons*. York: Centre for Health Economics, University of York.

Chapter 7

The development and impact of family support on carers and people with learning disabilities

One of the central objectives of the AWS was to develop a range of support for people with learning disabilities and their families. Previous research had shown that parents of people with learning disabilities had minimal access to services (Bayley, 1973) and that available support was often inadequate (Oswin, 1984). The AWS sought to rectify these problems through two different means: the increased availability of practical support services (for example domiciliary support and short-term care) and the development of networks of informal support within the community. The AWS, and previously the Jay Report (DHSS, 1979), emphasized that relief from some of the day-to-day pressures of caregiving would strengthen family capacities to care.

Although support services became integral components in idealized accounts of comprehensive community-based service (see IDC, 1982), it was assumed that increasing levels of support would lead to improved outcomes for caregivers in overcoming some of the stresses associated with caregiving. In this respect, the AWS did not outline the nature of the difficulties families faced or how such difficulties were to be resolved beyond that of recognizing that families faced 'hardships' (Welsh Office, 1983, p. 2) and that 'short-term relief' (Welsh Office, 1983, p. 5) and 'a range of domiciliary support' (Welsh Office, 1983, p. 7) could provide 'breaks which would not otherwise be possible' (Welsh Office, 1983, p. 5). As it was claimed later, much of the literature on support services, of which the AWS was an example, lacked reference to any developed outcomes or quality measures which could be meaningfully connected to what services were seeking to achieve (Grant, McGrath and Ramcharan, 1994). Moreover, a detailed understanding of carers' experience upon which formulations of support might be developed was absent.

Since the launch of the AWS, many of the assumptions underlying support have been increasingly questioned. There has been an emerging recognition that not all social support, formal or informal, is beneficial (e.g. Ganster and Victor, 1988; Thoits, 1992; Ell, 1996). There is a growing understanding that intervention programmes must consider how events and circumstances within and outside of the family unit are related, and how they influence child, parent and family functioning (Dunst and Trivette, 1988). This has led to a call for an informed assessment of the dimensions, forms and types of support that influence child, parent and family functioning. Dunst and Trivette (1988) set out several critical parameters for research. These include the need to disaggregate the dimensions of support, the need to question whether all support is necessarily construed as supportive and an acknowledgement of the relevance of transactional perspectives to an understanding of impacts (see for example, Lazarus and Folkman, 1984).

Questions concerning the processes and aims of support services have led to a redefinition of research objectives. It is no longer sufficient to employ level of provision as a proxy for quality. Grant (1993) has argued that there is a need to move away from research which merely maps the size and density of support networks and to look more closely at several other dimensions: the nature of support offered, the social norms governing their functioning and their contextual and dynamic properties. Todd and Shearn (1996a) have argued much the same in relation to formal support. Robinson (1994) has also argued that research needs to examine the extent to which support has positive impacts upon the lifestyles of people with learning disabilities as well as their carers. Research on the NIMROD service demonstrated that support could enhance the lifestyles of people with learning disabilities through the provision of teaching opportunities and a wider range of day-to-day experiences of community life (Lowe and de Paiva, 1991). Support services have the potential to be an important mechanism to enhance community integration and quality of life of the individual.

This chapter seeks to describe the growth of support services and to examine some aspects of their effectiveness through data obtained from various research studies. It is recognized that the issues outlined above were not considered in the original AWS document. They do, however, seem worthy of clarification given that a defining feature of the AWS was its intention to offer not so much a blueprint for service reform but a 'touchstone for future developments in services' (Welsh Office, 1983, p. 1). The chapter also focuses on the changing experiences of family carers over their lifespan and that of their relative.

The growth and patterns of support services in Wales

The establishment of the NIMROD service in Cardiff provided a practical demonstration of the utility of a domiciliary support service to families (Humphreys, Lowe and de Paiva, 1986; Lowe, de Paiva and Humphreys, 1987; de Paiva and Lowe, 1988). This service was welcomed by families since it provided an important means of enabling parents and people with learning disabilities to spend more time apart and for each to engage in independent activities (Lowe, de Paiva and Humphreys, 1987). It offered a multifaceted input involving both respite for parents and the provision of an enhanced presence within their local communities for people with learning disabilities.

The NIMROD domiciliary support service was novel within Britain at the launch of the AWS, but was replicated throughout Wales over its course (Evans, 1990). Providing support to families through the development of domiciliary support was an area of significant service expansion under the AWS (Beyer, Todd and Felce, 1991; Perry *et al.*, 1998). In 1983, there were 41 families in Wales who received domiciliary support. By 1988, it was estimated that there were 1840 families receiving such support, and in 1995, 1914 families. Data from a longitudinal study of service use in four social service districts between 1986 and 1990 revealed that there was an expansion of availability of domiciliary support from 23% to 32% of families (Todd *et al.*, 1993a).

The growth of domiciliary support was an early and palpable example of service reform espoused by the AWS. This expansion of support was reflected also in major changes in the provision of short-term care. Between 1986 and 1990, there had been an increase, from 16% to 35%, in the proportion of families who had used short-term care in the four districts studied (Todd *et al.*, 1993a). By 1995, 2278 families in Wales used short-term care, almost twice as many families as in 1988 (Perry *et al.*, 1998). The development of short-term care in Wales was notable also for a radical change in the way this service was provided. Prior to, and also in the early years of the AWS, the bulk of short-term care was provided in hospital or hostel settings. In 1988, over 50% of short-term care still took place in such settings. By 1995, this had dropped to 18%. By then, short-term care was more likely to be provided in ordinary staffed housing or was family-based, 51% and 31% respectively. The development of short-term care in ordinary housing represented a significant move towards more typical settings with a hope that some of the ill-considered and damaging depersonalization and experiences noted by Oswin (1984) would be avoided. The development of family-based respite care was an even more positive departure from such problems (see Swift, Grant and McGrath, 1991).

The AWS can therefore be seen as making a positive response to the existing inadequacy of both the quantity and quality of short-term care (Bayley, 1973; Oswin, 1984; Hubert, 1991) and achieving a notable level of change in the direction set out in the AWS document. The development of short-term care and domiciliary support services between 1986 and 1990 led to a situation where there was a reduction in the proportion of families who had no access or made no use of one or other of these services, from 68% to 45% (Todd *et al.*, 1993a). Carers tended to take support services as the most easily identified success of the AWS (Todd *et al.*, 1993b). Such comments are supported by other studies which suggest that the development of support services are popular ones (Lowe and de Paiva, 1991; Swift, Grant and McGrath, 1991; Lowe, 1992). The nature of their impact upon families is considered later in this chapter.

However, there were some areas of concern which detracted from the gains provided by practical support services. Swift, Grant and McGrath (1991) reported that carers of people with challenging behaviour may be less well served by family-based respite than other children. Service provision for this group may be inadequate (McGrath and Grant, 1993), a worrying feature given that the presence of challenging behaviour has been shown to be associated with greater levels of carer stress (Quine and Pahl, 1985; Grant and McGrath, 1990) and with making many routine aspects of caregiving problematic for carers (Shearn and Todd, 1997a). Gains were further offset because day provision for adults which provides substantial, frequent and regular respite had altered. The level of full-time day occupation for adults fell from 78% to 68% between 1986 and 1990 (Evans *et al.*, 1994).

As noted above, the involvement of the local community in the lives of carers and people with learning disabilities was a central concern of the AWS. However, precise mechanisms for achieving this were not outlined in the AWS document. Evidence suggests that there was a decrease, from 51% to 42%, in the proportion of families who received support from informal sources between 1986 and 1990 (Todd *et al.*, 1993a). Informal support, as defined in this study, implied some form of practical support from kin not living in the family home or from neighbours or friends. Two factors were implicated here; the lessening availability of kinship support as families age and the lessening reliance on informal support as formal support becomes available. The decrease in informal support was moderated by the rate of development of formal support. Overall, there was a reduction, from 35% to 26%, in the proportion of families who reported not receiving support from either informal or formal sources (Todd *et al.*, 1993a). However, the extent of local community involvement in informal support was minimal as most informal support was provided by kin (Grant, 1993). Consistent with the above, Grant (1993) also found such support may contract over time. One third of families experienced considerable shrinkage in the numbers of kin providing support over a two-year period.

The reduction in levels of support over time is attributable to a number of life-course processes and the social norms governing family and social relationships (Grant, 1993). Todd and Shearn (1996a) reported that parents experience a change in the level of support that they can expect from other family members as they age. As their informal support networks diminish so parents may find that their caregiving responsibilities become greater. They may need to support other members of their family, including ageing relatives or grandchildren. The loss of significant supporters has a considerable impact upon family care-giving situations as outlined below. In the early years, parents received considerable help from their own parents with caregiving activities. However, this support diminished as their own parents died or became incapable of providing support:

When my mum died two years ago that was a really bad time for me. My husband had just lost his parents a few years before that. I used to ring my mum up two or three times a week. We were really close and I don't think I've ever gotten used to her being gone. She was really great with Karen, she'd look after her any time we asked her to. No fuss! Every so often when we get an invite to go out I think 'If only mum was here!' But she's not.

As well as possibly having to come to terms with the loss of parental support or even to the need to care for their own parents, many parents come to expect less of their non-disabled offspring in terms of practical support. Loss of support from one generation of the family is not necessarily replaced by other generations. Grant (1993) and Todd and Shearn (1996a) found that there were important rules governing the use of support from members of their personal networks and that caregivers adopted a normative framework to guide their help-seeking behaviours from family and friends. This was found to have three consequences. Older parents now offered their non-disabled children support rather than receiving it from them. Parents were keen to fulfil their normative responsibilities as grandparents and offer their offspring support in the same way that their own parents had done for them. Thus many parents were child-minding so as to allow their offspring or their spouses to seek and maintain employment. In addition, parents felt that they had given disproportionate attention to their child with learning disabilities when their non-disabled offspring were younger. They now felt that they wanted to make up for this and accordingly placed few demands upon them. They were also reluctant to ask for help from neighbours and friends. They felt that others might be able to cope with looking after a child but not with looking after an adult. Importantly, carers also felt a growing lack of opportunity to reciprocate child care arrangements with friends as they once had been able to do:

Our friends have brought their own kids up now and are finding their freedom. Their kids have flown the nest and they're off doing their own thing. The last thing they want is someone like us coming along and restricting their movements.

The types of support offered informally within families or as part of reciprocal relationships with the wider community may not be easily replaced by formal support services or through the fostering of new informal relationships which have not arisen naturally. Swift, Grant and McGrath (1991) observe that stimulating the potential of the community to provide support takes considerable time and effort. However, as we describe below, what is required is that support can be flexible and negotiable. At present these two characteristics are typically absent from formal support services. It is an open question whether it will prove easier to establish genuinely flexible and responsive formal support services or new types of informal support which have these characteristics. In either case, fresh effort needs to be devoted to reconceptualizing support and developing it in practice.

The caregiving career

In this section, we consider how the development of family support services has affected the lives of carers. Todd *et al.* (1993a) noted that 65% of a random sample of 404 people with learning disabilities lived in the parental home. Of this group, 27% were aged 30 or older and 15% of parents were aged 65 or older. Direct involvement in the parental role can, therefore, last several decades. There is a temporal dimension to caregiving, the significance of which is only beginning to be realized by researchers (Grant, 1986; Seltzer, Krauss and Heller, 1991; Taraborrelli, 1994; Nolan, Grant and Keady, 1996a; Todd and Shearn, 1996b).

Caregiving can be seen as a form of career which individuals not only enter and leave, but which involves many intermediate stages. The meaning and implications of caring are not fixed and new situations are encountered as people move through the life course from which new needs and wants emerge, and for which new coping strategies are required. In this respect, becoming a parent of a person with learning disabilities is much like any other career in that it involves entry to a social role, the path and parameters of which are not instantly known. Rather, as the years unfold and new experiences are encountered, carers re-evaluate their lives and revise decisions concerning how they manage their caregiving involvement. The concern with time and biography has also been raised in connection with people with chronic health conditions and impairments (Corbin and Strauss, 1988) and is relevant also for any analysis of carers' experiences (Todd and Shearn, 1996b).

A perspective which emphasizes personal careers and biographies also promotes the need to look at inter-relationships between different career lines (Spence and Lonner, 1978). Caregiving must be seen in a broader context of 'biographical work' (Bury, 1982; Charmaz, 1983, 1987; Corbin and Strauss, 1988). Much of the caregiving literature has tended to focus exclusively on the nature of the caregiving role and its constituent tasks in isolation from peoples' other roles or interests. Involvement in caregiving has, then, to be set alongside other involvements, for example, homemaking, marital, work and social roles. This was partially recognized in the AWS in that it sought through support to provide breaks from their parental roles which would not otherwise be possible.

Identification of learning disability and early counselling

Entrance to the caregiving career typically begins with disclosure of information to parents that their son or daughter has, or is expected to have, a learning disability (Booth, 1978). This is an area in which one might have expected to see some change given that one aim of the AWS was to promote a positive definition of learning disability. Furthermore, it is an area which has typically been badly handled in the past (Bicknell, 1988). None of the commissioned research we describe in this book deals directly with the important issue of disclosure of learning disability to parents and subsequent counselling. That said, a working party was established by the Standing Conference of Voluntary Organizations (SCOVO) during the period of the AWS to review disclosure and early counselling practices throughout Wales and to make recommendations for training and practice. The report (SCOVO, 1989) was based on the analysis of the views and experiences of parents, parent groups, voluntary organizations and front-line professionals.

The counselling needs of parents experiencing the use of ultrascan equipment in the detection of fetal problems or of those proceeding with terminations are not widely known but there appears to be a lack of procedural guidance for professionals in these situations. The report also showed that the majority of parents wish or prefer: (1) to be told together and as soon as possible, in a private place without interruptions, without an audience of staff; (2) to be told honestly and directly, but by someone who conveys warmth and understanding; (3) to have a period of privacy with each other after the initial disclosure interview; (4) to have an opportunity for follow-up interviews to ask further questions and receive information and advice; and (5) to have time and space to themselves to consider feelings about themselves and their child. Families providing evidence for the review reported that these principles were infrequently followed and a number were still upset years after the event by the manner in which disclosure had been managed. At this stage of their careers, carers are very much novices in their roles and lacking information about what is before them (see, for example, Taraborrelli, 1994).

Parents also indicated a desire for help that was competency enhancing, that is directed at helping them to exploit their own skills and resourcefulness in supporting their child, much in the way that Dunst, Trivette and Deal (1994) describe. Many talked of the particular value of self-help groups where they could exchange experiences with parents who had been 'down that road before'. Through joining such groups they were able to extend their social networks, deal directly with the sense of isolation or rejection that could overtake them and, in encountering parents in similar or worse situations than themselves, put their needs into perspective. As Nolan, Grant and Keady (1996b) have described, the opportunity to reframe one's understanding of problems and develop a sense of meaning from caring are qualities which enable people to cope better. Although the different professional groups submitting evidence for the review all affirmed the value of an interdisciplinary team approach, there was concern at the lack of qualifying and in-service post qualifying training for staff. Perhaps most disconcertingly of all, professional bodies were unable to demonstrate that they had given early counselling any priority within their policies or validated professional qualifying training programmes.

The issue of disclosure of learning disability is also relevant to another set of actors, namely people with learning disabilities. This issue has received less attention than the ways in which parents are informed about their offspring's impairment. The questions of how people with learning disabilities themselves 'discover' or are given information about their disability were posed in two separate studies; a study of life in a special school (Todd, 1995), a setting supposedly central in introducing people to what is typically viewed as a stigmatized identity (Shearer, 1981); and also a study of relationships between parents and their co-resident adult offspring with learning disabilities (Todd and Shearn, 1997), relationships which are central to the ways disabled people come to understand the moral and social implications which their impairments have for others (Schneider and Conrad, 1980; Scambler and Hopkins, 1986).

The data from these studies suggested that staff and parents were reluctant to deal directly with transmitting information concerning the meaning and implications of learning disability. A 'closed awareness context' (Glaser and Strauss, 1964) was found to exist in relationships between people with learning disabilities and their parents and staff. That is, parents and staff avoided telling people that they had a learning disability. They reported that they had chosen to conceal such information to protect people from what was thought would be emotionally damaging information. 'Learning disability' was perceived to be such a toxic identity that it would have a devastating impact upon individuals. Parents could recall the moment when such news had been delivered to them and did not wish their offspring to undergo such experiences themselves. Learning disability was also seen as a disqualifying identity: the many ordinary expectations which people with learning disability held for their own lives would be fragmented by disclosure. As one parent commented:

She doesn't know and thank God for that! It's a blessing as far as she's concerned. ... I'm grateful that she doesn't know! It makes life much easier for her. If Kathleen knew .... But she's happy. I don't think she'd be happy if she knew. Some of them [people with learning disabilities] do and that must be awful. She talks about getting married and having a job. I'm glad she doesn't know that she won't ever get married. ... She doesn't have to know that her life will not be like her brothers and sisters. Why should I depress her?

Parents felt that they lacked the expertise to deal effectively with the sensitivities of disclosure, while staff in the studied special school felt that disclosure was a parental responsibility. As a consequence, the information needs of people with learning disabilities have been overlooked. It was clear that learning disability was interpreted by parents and staff in the two studies as a powerfully stigmatizing identity that could not be revealed to individuals themselves. Paradoxically, by avoiding this issue the stigma of learning disability is defended rather than challenged. Many people with learning disabilities may be prevented from taking political action through individual planning meetings or advocacy groups of the type described in Chapters 4 and 5 since vital information is withheld from them. Such findings also indicate that the AWS did not necessarily lead to a shared and more positive definition of 'learning disability', a key component of its philosophy and objectives.

Rewarding and meaningful: a challenge to typical assumptions concerning caregiving

The AWS was based on a belief, typical of the period, that caregiving involved considerable hardships and strains for carers. There was a prevalent assumption that caregiving is generally a stressful and negative experience, and that this results from the nature of the tasks involved in caregiving. Voysey (1975), for example, refers to the 'constant burden', a view shared by many other authors. Caregiving, therefore, has been informed by an understanding of stress as the abiding and colonizing dimension of caregiving (Grant et al., 1998). There is little recognition in academic or professional discourse that the caregiving experience could be satisfying for many carers (Nolan, Grant and Keady, 1996b). From this perspective the primary role of support can be taken to be stress reduction typically through offering an interruption to or respite from a noxious situation. The alternative model does not deny the real pressures and demands of caregiving, but admits that they can be accompanied by many rewards and the fact that carers derive positive meanings from caring. However, and in line with prevailing assumptions, support services have not developed from such an understanding and there are few studies which have sought to identify the balance of stresses and rewards.

Grant *et al.* (1998) found that there were three overlapping dimensions of reward for carers. There was a range of satisfactions which derived from the nature of the interpersonal dynamic between carer and care-recipients, the intrapersonal orientation of the carer and the ways carers evaluated their efforts and the role caregiving played in their lives. The act of giving was a basic but major source of reward for carers. It was important that carers felt their relative was happy and derived pleasure from life. The perception that their relative was acquiring skills and independence was another factor leading to rewards for carers, as was the fact that the dignity of the relative was being maintained through their work. However, certain service routines around which caregivers were expected to conform could set out demands which implied that caregivers could not devote as much time as they wanted to the personal development of their relative (Shearn and Todd, 1997a). For example, the arrival of a school or day centre bus early in the morning left carers feeling they were rushing through activities. Given these externally imposed time constraints, it was often easier and quicker for caregivers to do tasks for their relative. Consequently, carers felt uncomfortable in not living up to their self-set development roles.

Some of the satisfactions carers derived were based upon views that their relative was seen as a valued individual rather than a problem. However, the values of professionals and those of carers may not be consistent, and often carers felt that professional frames of reference predominated. As there can be a palpable division between the aims and values of carers and those of services, support services may not be unreservedly welcomed. Service agencies and carers may not share a common approach to the individual with learning disability so that any collaborative approach to care is inhibited by conflicting views. As one carer noted:

I don't want them to see the handicap first. I want them to look at her and think, 'Gosh, she's lovely, she's happy, let's try, let's face the challenge, let's be more positive'. Don't just write her off because they might need to pick her up and put her on the toilet so many times a day or somebody might have to give up ten minutes to feed her during the lunchtime. I don't want that. I want her to be wanted wherever it is she goes, otherwise I don't want to know.

There was much scope for satisfying relationships to extend beyond the caregiving dyad to include other family members, friends and service personnel. These relationships offer carers the opportunity for their labours to be evaluated in a positive light. Such recognition can signify that carers have acquired considerable competence in dealing with challenging situations, although often they may feel that their knowledge is not always acknowledged by services (Nolan, Grant and Keady, 1996a). Shearn and Todd (1996) argue that services sometimes expect acquiescence to a set of professionally imposed standards which are not held by community members, thereby making carers' relationships with the community problematic. In resisting these standards, carers felt they ran the risk of being seen as over-protective and, by implication, responsible for thwarting the personal development of their relative.

Some of the difficulties carers experience in using support services (outlined below) are associated with a sense that their expertise is not recognized. Quite simply, carers are not treated as competent providers and planners of care despite their many years of involvement and coping in their role (Nolan, Grant and Keady, 1996a). The range of tasks which constitute caregiving are extensive and involve physical, emotional, social and public management, tasks which are underpinned by a detailed knowledge of their relative's needs, interests and aspirations (Shearn and Todd, 1997a). Carers' own knowledge may have been acquired without much professional advice as noted earlier, so that they have considerable pride in their craft, a pride which may make them less willing to adopt professional approaches which differ from their own (Nolan, Grant and Keady, 1996a). Service approaches which emphasize supplementing rather than replacing carers' expertise with professional bodies of knowledge are more likely to lead to effective and creative partnerships.

The level of their involvement in their caring roles left many carers feeling that caregiving provided a positive and meaningful purpose to their lives. Seen in this context, it is possible that any support has the potential to frustrate as well as enhance these rewards. As the research literature on caring increasingly emphasizes, subjective appraisals of caring and its objective characteristics are the medium through which stress and burden are felt (Lazarus and Folkman, 1984; Nolan, Grant and Keady, 1996a). This view is consistent with a transactional model of stress and highlights the importance of listening to and acting upon parental accounts of their situations and their needs and wants. Support which seeks to complement the goals carers set are more likely to have a positive impact.

Importantly, there needs to be some understanding of the aspirations of caregivers if services are to succeed in reinforcing what carers find rewarding. Empathy, therefore, is essential, as is the time and care required to build services around family needs. Emerging from the research with considerable force is the fact that carers' perceptions about the quality of services are directly linked to the extent to which they feel service professionals empathize with their situation and that of their relative. The importance of this attribute cannot be over-stated, since support services are often allocated on a pre-determined basis rather than being based upon a rounded view of the individual and family.

The arguments presented above call for more flexible, empathetic and family-controlled support such as those found to operate in family-based respite schemes (Stalker, 1990; NCH, 1991; Swift, Grant and McGrath, 1991). These developed in all parts of Wales during the AWS. Here the role of the service is to act as broker between family and host families (Swift, Grant and McGrath, 1991). That is, the role for services is to act as a mediator between families and natural or informal supporters. This may be time-consuming work but, in most cases, it pays long-term dividends in that it leads to a high level of satisfaction and contentment about the standard of care provided by host families. Despite the feelings of guilt at the 'relinquishing' of responsibilities that often accompanies initial use of respite, many families commented that the expert and protracted brokerage work of service workers had enabled them to feel that the key decisions were controlled by them. A number of families commented that the care was as good as they themselves provided. Additionally, many talked about the trust they had in the host family and in feelings of security they had knowing their child was in safe hands. Importantly, many attributed improvements in their child's demeanour and behaviour to their experiences of spending time with host families. Carers felt that they exercised choice in the selection of families and could, therefore, feel satisfied that selected families held common values and approaches to their relative.

Overcoming isolation

With the passage of time, carers will acquire some understanding of the implications of being a carer of a person with learning disabilities and its implications for their own lives. Being informed that a child has a disability is very likely to be experienced as a form of 'biographical disruption' (Bury, 1982) in that many taken for granted assumptions about one's life are called into question. Yet, for the most part, parents continue to seek to have their claims to the rights and obligations of typical parenthood legitimized by others (Voysey, 1975). As their children age, however, such struggles seem to become intensified (Todd and Shearn, 1996b) and call for a reappraisal of the direction their lives are taking. This section of the chapter examines the extent to which support services enable carers to reconcile different aspirations, in particular their involvement in caring and in other roles. While emphasis has been given to caring and its attendant stresses, there has been a tendency to overlook the fact that caregivers want more from their lives than being carers. For many carers, perhaps, the source of stress and tension in their lives lies not within the caregiving relationship itself but in the diminished extent to which they can develop networks and careers outside of being a carer.

Many carers do not express a need for support because of the physical tasks of caregiving. Rather, they value support more for the opportunities it might provide for overcoming the isolation or social restrictions of their situation, that is, as a bridge between the family home and the wider world. Todd and Shearn (1996a) described how some carers can become embroiled in situations where virtually all their activities had to be conducted in the company of their relative with learning disabilities. One mother felt that managing routine day-to-day tasks was an accomplishment of some note given her situation:

It just seems that we're spending too much time together and it's getting claustrophobic. It's like having a redundant or retired husband under your feet all day. ... You love them but you end up screaming for space. Seven days a week he's in the house. I used to be able to do things before, like meet a friend for coffee in town or do some shopping. Now Martin has to come everywhere with me, even to the hairdressers. But the top and bottom of it is, there's no space. I really feel that it's getting me down.

In such a situation, and as noted in the AWS, the introduction of domiciliary and respite services can be seen as making a positive contribution to carers' lives through providing breaks. Since many carers had endured periods when they had received little formal support and were aware of families who still had to endure such situations, the popularity of support services has tended to be high. Respite may be valued in this context simply for the fact that it provides 'time-out' from caring. However, this represents a passive view of respite in as much as it overlooks the constructive use to which liberated time is put. In this regard there appear to be two important domains; opportunities for work and socializing. However, before these domains can be accessed other tasks or responsibilities often have to be accomplished including: looking after other children, supporting kin who live outside of the carers' home, and seeing to their own personal needs and aspirations. For many, stress stems from the difficulties they experience in juggling a range of roles, responsibilities and aspirations, and the 'articulation work' (Strauss *et al.*, 1985) involved; that is, how caregivers are forced to juggle the different demands they encounter and the aspirations they hold (Shearn and Todd, 1997a). Here we find that carers' own allocation of time and energies can easily be subsumed by demands of care-work and of being a homemaker. Typically support makes these two domains of activity easier to integrate but it often has limited impact upon extending the opportunities carers have for wider social involvement. The data below suggest that support does little to subvert typically gendered caregiving responsibilities whereby any expression of self-interest is subordinated to social obligations. As Laws (1979, p. 129) argues: 'It is understood that when a woman undertakes the responsibility of parenthood, she subordinates her own needs, desires or priorities to the welfare of the child'.

Managing multiple careers

Employment

The ideology and practice of informal care rests upon and reinforces a sexual division of labour which leaves women largely responsible for the day-to-day work of keeping families going (Finch and Groves, 1983; Graham, 1984; Ungerson, 1987). Although the role of men as carers has tended to be overlooked (Arber and Gilbert, 1989), the majority of carers are women. The needs of mothers in particular were not highlighted in the AWS since the gendered nature of caregiving situations was not taken as problematic. Such a stance led to the employment situation of many mothers of people with learning disabilities being overlooked. The nature of the stereotyped roles of wife and mother lends support to a view that these roles should be women's primary orientations and the source of their fulfilment. Other roles, that is public roles such as employment, should be accepted by women themselves as secondary concerns (Delamont, 1980; Traustadottir, 1988). This ideology has been challenged over the past two decades so that there are changing patterns of women's participation in the world of paid work. Many women expect work or a paid career to figure in their lives; and employment is seen as a salient expression of their self-identities (Martin and Roberts, 1984). Increasingly, many mothers combine family and domestic work with paid employment, and the return to full-time work becomes more likely as their children age (Kiernan and Wicks, 1990).

However, this trend has not been replicated for mothers of children with learning disabilities. Their level of employment is significantly lower than for mothers in general (Breslau, Salvever and Staruch, 1982; Cooke, 1982; Glendinning, 1983). In a current study (Shearn and Todd, 1997b), we have found that few mothers are able to combine the roles of parent and employee, and if they can it is typically in part-time employment. Despite the increase in the provision of support services, only 31% of 72 mothers of children with learning disabilities surveyed in one county worked in any form of employment, and less than a fifth of these mothers (that is 6% of the sample) were in full-time employment. This compares to an employment rate of 67% for all mothers of similarly aged children in the county, two-fifths of whom work full-time. Many of the non-working mothers of the young children in the study (67%) reported that they wanted to work. Social policy concerning carers has tended to be framed in isolation from employment policy so that there is little realization of the importance of work to carers (Glendinning, 1983; Parker, 1990). Policy also fails to address the fact that their employment prospects remain limited even as their offspring age.

Many of the mothers regarded the possibility of working as unrealistic. They felt a strong social pressure that combining employment with motherhood would be placing their own needs before those of their children. Mothers sensed that the standard of ideal motherhood was more strictly applied to them than to mothers of non-disabled children.

All mothers are sometimes made to feel guilty if they go out. But if you're the mother of a handicapped child, they think you should be at home. They really think that you should be there with them *all* the time.

Mothers felt that their children's care needs meant that members of their informal networks were unable or unwilling to provide sufficient support to release them for work. They also faced a lack of affordable or appropriate day care and after-school care for their children. While some were able to work part-time, the extensiveness of school holidays created an insurmountable difficulty for mothers contemplating returning to or starting work. Support services such as domiciliary and respite care were not designed to overcome these difficulties. Potential employers might expect them to take more time off than their colleagues and mothers, therefore, considered themselves to be unattractive employees:

If I had a job, I'd have to be prepared to leave at the drop of a telephone call, and I'd have to be back at 3.30. How many people want to employ someone like me? It doesn't make me very desirable does it?

A small number of mothers in the study were managing full-time work and finding it extremely taxing. They felt they were seen as putting their family before their work commitments and were thus seen as 'poor employees'. With little formal or informal support at their disposal, they felt unable to derive benefit from work or caregiving and were failing to be successful in either domain. Combining caregiving and employment often leads to job termination and diminished self-worth (Phillips, 1995).

As one potential route by which to be seen not just as a carer but as a productive person in their own right, the absence of employment in carers' lives can lead to isolation, boredom, worthlessness, frustration and personal insecurity (Rothwell, 1980; Callender, 1992).

Realization that work is not a possible option strengthens over time. Initial discovery of some of the limitations occurs in the early years of parenthood. However, mothers do not give up employment aspirations. Their offsprings' adolescence often ushers in a need to revise their future plans and face the long-term implications of having a child with learning disabilities (Todd and Shearn, 1996b). Carers foresee a diminishing availability of informal support. They anticipate that adult day-care services are not likely to be as reliable as schooling, expectations which have been reinforced by the increasing sessional nature of such services. As a result, they come to give up any ambition of a working career and accept that their employment situation will perpetually mirror that of mothers of very young children.

Socializing

Employment offers one expression of individual identity. A broad range of informal social roles provides another (MacRae, 1990). Parents of adolescents and young adults with learning disabilities report that their lives are restricted in this area too. They found it difficult to do typical social activities, such as going to the cinema or theatre, or going for a meal or to a pub, either with each other or with friends. Time management was a persistent pressure (Todd and Shearn, 1996b) and often so difficult that it constituted a form of 'time panic' (Lyman and Scott, 1970):

My life revolves around the clock, on a time limit. It's not so bad, but sometimes you feel your life is spent in a cocoon of a couple of hours at a time. Life just seems governed by the clock. When I'm out I'm always wondering how much time I've got left.

Even with available day and domiciliary services, parents found it 'difficult to fit everything in' and divide their time appropriately between parenting, domestic and self-directed activities. They constructed timetables to get what needed to be accomplished done. Seldom did the time made available through day and domiciliary support meet their needs. They felt the need to be 'in the right place at the right time' or suffer moral censure about their commitment to caregiving. Thus parents tended to cut other activities short to avoid being late to resume responsibility for their offspring:

The earliest I could get anywhere would be about 10.30. And then I'd have to leave by 2.30 to make sure I'm home in time. I could leave a little bit later, but you have to bear in mind something might happen to the bus and Tom might get home before me.

Service support was generally ill-designed to resolve these problems and give parents access to the more normal social lives which they desired. Domiciliary support was typically provided on an inflexible schedule for fairly restricted periods with little negotiation with parents about its amount or timing. The time offered did not necessarily match the rhythm of community life so that parents were still effectively cut off from their peers. Moreover, arrangements were more set than those which could sometimes be established through informal social networks. It was not clear that having a really good time with one's friends was a legitimate reason for extending the period of support beyond that which was arranged. For all of these reasons, parents' opportunities to socialize were severely constrained compared to their peers:

We get two hours a week between 7.00 and 9.00 pm. Where can we go at that time of night? Anyway two hours is neither here nor there. Most of the time I'll sit in front of the TV. I need three, maybe four, hours. As it is, I have half an hour to get somewhere and half an hour to get back. That leaves me with one hour. If it's a birthday or our anniversary, we wait for Louise to go then rush out. But we can't relax because we're thinking we have to get back.

We manage to get out with our friends once every three weeks or so. We can be out there having a great laugh, maybe having a meal, and then someone will say, 'Let's go on somewhere else!' My hubby and I just look at each other and sigh, 'Sorry, but we've got to get back'.

Their situation in practice was reinforced by how others had come to see them, not as spouses, workers or friends but as predominantly carers. They were expected to conform to the standards for committed carers, being 'ever-accessible' and 'ever-available' (Zerubavel, 1981). Technology facilitated such a commitment and provided a symbolic reminder of the centrality of their caregiving roles. Many parents carried bleepers or car-phones with them to be contactable at all times:

I can say I shut myself off to a certain extent, but ... you're always waiting for the phone to ring. ... We've got a bleeper in case anything goes wrong when we're out. It makes you feel a bit safer. Just like being a doctor-on-call I suppose. ... When the phone goes, the first thing that you think of is: 'Please God, don't let it be the centre!'

In summary, available support seems to allow carers to see to basic domestic, home-making duties but not to promote wider involvement outside of the home. This ability to 'catch-up' was valued by carers who were all too aware of what life had been like without such support. However, support services were unable to satisfy the aspirations of carers who attached importance to wider social involvement. That is not to say that carers did not derive satisfaction from their caregiving role but that this sole function in life was insufficient. The gap between carer aspirations and the reality of their lives seems to be an important determinant of carer malaise. Support services need to be further refined if they are to reduce that gap. As it stands, carers cope with the ongoing tension of frustrated aspirations by ultimately surrendering them, an adjustment which adds to the felt costs of caregiving:

We used to feel cheated that our lives weren't going to turn out like our friends. But I think we accept it more now. I think we decided years ago that all we expect is for Sue to be happy. It's all we strive for. It's best to stay off the subject of other people. We've been down that road before. You don't have to keep banging yourself with a hammer to realize it hurts.

Older family carers

The life course of a carer for a person with learning disability as understood from our research is a long-term involvement which undergoes several transformations. For many, it is one which extends into their late years. However, there has been little indication that older people and their family carers have been identified as a priority group for services. Demographic and social changes provide some good reasons for being concerned about the capacity of families to continue supporting older people with learning disabilities. These include: (1) increasing life expectancy which is likely to prolong family caregiving even further and to implicate siblings during middle age to a greater extent than at present; (2) the changing ratio of older to younger families which will create the need to alter the balance of services and probably lead to an increase in service costs; and (3) a reduction of the proportion of caregivers to recipients. In addition, changes in the structure of the family and rates of divorce will have impacts which are less easy to assess at this time (Seltzer, Krauss and Heller, 1991). The importance of these trends was not anticipated by the AWS and issues about older people with learning disabilities and their families do not appear to have been addressed by subsequent policy. Generally, there is no clear vision of what a service system for older families should look like and what the balance between generic and specialist services should be. Yet, while many older carers have specific needs in later life, it should be recognized that some of the difficulties they encounter, especially social isolation, may be avoided if support were to be provided more effectively at an earlier stage.

There is some justification for claiming that older family carers and ipso facto those they support at home have been badly neglected by policy. Many are isolated socially and others have allowed themselves to become cut off from services so that they are ill-informed about potential options for continuing care (Grant, McGrath and Ramcharan, 1995). Ruth (53 years old), for example, was supported at home by her sister, Shirley, a professional working woman. Their relationship involved give and take on both sides. According to Shirley, the rewards and gratifications of looking after her sister had become more evident over the years. They had common friends with whom they shared leisure interests, something helped by their age-relatedness as siblings. Shirley, nevertheless, made some telling observations about how their social relations in the neighbourhood were being affected by residential instability and changes in personal mobility, meaning that they perceived a growing sense of isolation as their local community changed around them.

Studies show that there is a high dependency on maternal support and that, for people who remain co-resident with families, maternal support features more prominently as people age (Grant, 1986, 1993). Chapter 6 described how resettlement overtook meeting the needs of people living with families as the focus for the development of residential services in Wales. As residential provision did not become more available, there was as much emphasis on family carers continuing to look after their adult offspring as there ever had been. The everyday support needs of these carers may not have been fully recognized in AWS related service developments. Parents of older people with learning disabilities use fewer formal services. Parents of adults with learning disabilities aged 30 years or older had the lowest use of day services, domiciliary support and short-term care in the sample survey we conducted in four local government districts (Todd *et al.*, 1993a). Support networks change over the life cycle, for example through death, divorce, ill health and movement of family members. Such changes appear to diminish support in later life. Carers may come to depend on keeping their adult disabled relatives at home as they adjust to such changes (Grant, 1993; Todd and Shearn, 1996b). In other words, families may mature into a state of inter-dependence between carers and care-recipients. Carers feel that both their psychological survival and that of their relative are linked with their continuation in the role.

The growing investment they make in their caregiving roles may explain why older parents seem to report greater well-being than many younger carers or even older carers who come to this role later in their lives (Seltzer and Krauss, 1989). Their situation is compounded by their own anticipations of a life without this involvement. McLaughlin and Ritchie (1994) describe a similar phenomenon in a study of the lives of carers of elderly people. They found that the transition from carer to former carer was difficult if carers had been unable to maintain other social roles. Some parents are provided a glimpse of such a life when they use short-term care. For them, time away from their offspring does bring some reward and a replenishing of their energies. Importantly, however, they can experience a sense of waiting during such breaks for their son or daughter to return home:

If Nicky lived somewhere else I'd be devastated. I've had a week's holiday without him. The daytime wasn't too bad. I can say to myself 'Oh I've got two hours, maybe even four'. Then I can come home when I feel like it, have a shower, make some supper and go to bed. All without having to change bums. But I was lost in the night. It made me wonder what life would be like without him. It would be so completely different. I'd miss him so much and I'd have to make an effort to make new friends for myself. I'd just be lost.

In summary, becoming a carer should be seen as a long-term process. Its involvement is both enduring and changing in response to a wide variety of factors. While there has been an increase in the availability of support which goes some way to meeting concerns about the lack of support for carers (Twigg and Atkin, 1994), the support that is available may not be viewed as effective. Available support may not be sensitive to the difficulties many carers experience. It may also potentially undermine the rewards carers extract from their roles. There is a need therefore to recognize that any intervention needs to be planned, empathetic, comple-mentary to carers' own work and efforts and provide legitimacy to carers' wants for wider and meaningful social involvement. As Ellis (1993) has commented, this will require a fundamental re-appraisal of current profes-sional practices and approaches towards the family. The 1995 Carers (Recognition and Services) Act provides such an opportunity particularly if a broad understanding of carer needs can be brought to bear rather than one which is overly tied to the stress of caring.

Bridging the gap between people with learning disabilities and the community

Domiciliary services have incorporated a broad range of objectives for carers, including respite and practical support in the home. They have also inherited components of home teaching by a focus on skill acquisition. In addition, they have been promoted as a device for overcoming the routine exclusion from the everyday routines of their communities which is a fundamental difficulty in the lives of people with learning disabilities (Edgerton, 1967; Cheseldine and Jeffrey, 1981; McConkey, Walsh and Mulcahy, 1982; Todd, Evans and Beyer, 1990; Grant, McGrath and Ramcharan, 1995). In this section, we examine the effect that the development of domiciliary services has had upon the social lives of people with learning disabilities.

Studies have typically shown that there is a low level of contact between people with learning disabilities and non-disabled others, a feature which highlights discrimination and is found by people with learning disabilities to be unsatisfactory (Lowe, de Paiva and Humphreys, 1987). There is also evidence suggesting that many people become more isolated over time from the communities in which they live (Grant, 1993). For example, only a minority appear to have friends who are independent of their mothers' social networks or services. The social lives of people with learning disabilities are frequently constrained to and by members of their support networks (Grant, McGrath and Ramcharan, 1995). For Doris (74 years of age), life at home was subject to her older sister's house rules which included barred access, until quite recently, to anyone from social services. It took a crisis to sister Mary's health – a fall and consequent dizzy spells – to cause a reappraisal of this position. Nevertheless, Doris was still expected to be compliant to her sister's wishes and had no recognizable social network of her own. As caregivers age, they may feel less enthusiastic about providing their relative with social opportunities outside of the home (Shearn and Todd, 1997a).

The AWS made altering the nature of the social lives of people with learning disabilities a central concern. It sought to provide people with opportunities to 'become respected members of their communities' (Welsh Office, 1983, p. 2) and to enable 'people to blend with confidence into their communities' (Welsh Office, 1983, p. 6). Support services were seen as a mechanism for achieving such ends by broadening the leisure and social activities of people with learning disabilities outside the home. But what evidence is there that domiciliary support services have enabled people with learning disabilities to participate in a greater range of social activities and, as a consequence, to shift the composition of their social networks to include a greater representation of non-disabled people? The range of activities undertaken in typical community settings (community presence) and the nature of peoples' social networks (community participation) offer two related but independent indices of the extent of integration (Emerson and Petty, 1987), an over-riding aspiration of the AWS.

Data derived from an observational study of domiciliary support suggested that this service has had only partial success in overcoming some of these difficulties (Evans *et al.*, 1992). An important function of support worker activity involved establishing and maintaining their client's presence in the wider community. However, their success in achieving more than this basic goal was limited. Many sessions were based upon a simple conception to enhance the community integration such that being 'out in the community' was expressed as the central objective:

Sophie stated that one of her main aims with Mark was to 'get him out'. She felt he spent too much time indoors playing with toys. Their session involved a car journey into the town centre. They bought about half a dozen items. They then bought some chips and went to a park. Sophie pushed Mark on the swings for about 10–15 minutes, then returned to the car. Sophie described the main aim of the session as allowing the public to see people with learning disabilities so as to overcome any fears they may have of them.

A support worker could act as 'escort', 'activity manager' or 'co-participant' depending upon the extent to which their clients were sufficiently engaged in the prevailing activity. All support workers acted as 'escorts' to and from activities but few sessions involved support workers in this role alone. As their clients mainly did not maintain their own activities independently, support workers also operated at the two other levels. As an 'activity manager', they initially arranged an activity for their clients to do and periodically intervened to maintain it:

A group of three support workers were engaged in conversation with each other and stood around the counter of the cafe in a Youth Club. Their clients were playing pool, the game having been set-up by one of the support workers. From time to time, one of the support workers would tell their clients how to play the game. When the game of pool was finished, one support worker suggested that they get the dart-board out. The three support workers and their clients played darts together.

Although keen to be largely observers, support workers became co-participants when their clients would otherwise have nothing to do or when there was no other person available to take on the role. In some cases, being a 'co-participant' was inevitable, for example when going to a pub or going to town as the individual's sole companion:

We drive out to a pub by a river. In the pub we sit in a corner. It is reasonably crowded for a Friday evening. The conversation is largely one way, with Sophie asking Lucy about what she has been doing in the day centre; her family; her eyesight and her health. During the evening, Lucy talks to no-one else except Sophie and myself.

While support services may have made some in-roads in terms of improving the community presence of people with learning disabilities, arguably the more important measure of community participation or social affiliation has changed little. Although many of the activities undertaken were seen as a means of overcoming social impoverishment, there was little evidence that the activities undertaken led to more substantive ties with other people. Indeed, there was minimal contact with non-disabled people in the sessions we observed. Some places were chosen because they were known to be quiet, for example, a Youth club on an evening when there were likely to be few other people there. Others, such as pubs, shops or cafes, possessed the anonymity of open public access, but encouraged an inward-looking relationship between support worker and client. Interactions with other people were functional, transient and superficial.

That social participation is not easily achieved is consistent with research which has reported that many people with learning disabilities have few or no friends despite increased use of a wide range of community resources (e.g. Evans *et al.*, 1994; Grant, McGrath and Ramcharan, 1995). For the most part, family members, staff and other people with learning disabilities constitute people's support networks (Todd, Evans and Beyer, 1990). Grant, McGrath and Ramcharan (1995) argue that, although being ostensibly free to participate in community life, people's participation is largely regulated by service professionals or families, who control with whom they interact, and the manner and frequency of interaction. Quite often this type of control minimizes meaningful social contact and reflects an interpretation of learning disabilities by carers and staff as troublesome (Todd, 1995; Todd and Shearn, 1997). Todd (1995) described an outreach programme for young adults about to leave a special school with a dual educational purpose: to educate the community about people with learning disabilities and to allow people with learning disabilities to become familiar with the community. Staff, however, felt that the routines of community life were threatened by the presence of people with learning disabilities. They also felt that the community was potentially hostile towards their clients. Staff therefore interpreted their work as minimizing threats for both groups and this led them to confine their work to safe social spaces. This space was a kind of 'tourist bubble' where few interactions occurred. Staff operated as 'tour guides', allowing people with learning disabilities and others to be present in the same place but prevented association. As in the case of individuals out with their support workers, people with and without disabilities were not present for the same reasons or out to gain the same ends.

People with learning disabilities are not excluded people, denied access to the everyday places of the community. However, they are not fully included either. They are in a liminal stage (van Gennep, 1960; Murphy *et al.*, 1988), sharing physical space but lacking social associations. This situation prompts a greater need to think creatively about how relationships built upon authentic mutual interest can be achieved if people with learning disabilities are not to remain as onlookers or as 'perpetual tourists'. One shift may be towards services adopting an instrumental role in selecting and assisting non-disabled partners, who are real members of a community of interest such as a youth club or activity group, to support the involvement of people with disabilities. Such people may provide a better gateway to genuine participation for the person with disability than a member of staff acting as a guide or surrogate member of the community with only 'observer status'. The growth of family-based respite services illustrates how services can perform this connecting role (Beckford and Robinson, 1993) to good effect (Swift, Grant and McGrath, 1991; Flynn *et al.*, 1995).

The achievements of the AWS and looking to the future

Providing support to families was a key objective of the AWS and much has been done toward this end. Although there are some important gaps, for example, in the way disclosure to parents and people with learning disabilities themselves is handled, there have been important developments concerning the ways in which parents have been given support. There has been a dramatic growth in domiciliary and short-term care services, services designed to enhance the quality of life of carers and people with learning disabilities. Their development was a consequence of their prioritization in the early years of the AWS. For many carers, this diminished the experience of claustrophobic caregiving and eased some of the difficulties they encountered in managing time. However, important questions remain concerning the extent to which carers, as well as people with learning disabilities, are able to increase their social participation as a consequence of receiving support as currently conceived. Given the substantial growth of such services, there is now a need to re-examine their design and working so that intended social outcomes can be realized. Any such development must be based upon a more complete understanding of caregiving, and one reflecting its longitudinal nature, its rewards for carers and its association with other actual or potential aspects of carers' lives.

Our findings suggest that there are some important social domains from which carers feel excluded and it is this exclusion which contributes significantly to their distress. Support services seem not to be sensitive to such concerns. Carers felt that they often accessed community facilities at inappropriate times, making it difficult for them to spend time with friends. People with learning disabilities were also assisted to be present within community settings, but being out and about in the community in itself did not necessarily enhance their community participation. The needs of parents parallel the important quality of life concerns of people with learning disabilities which have driven policy development: employment, community participation and personal development. A more sophisticated policy on family support is required, one which establishes such quality of life concerns as legitimate and worthy of their share of social care resources.

Lessons learned in Wales indicate that the notion of 'support as respite' is as misleading and damaging for parents as it has been considered to be for people with learning disabilities (Robinson, 1994). The issue of maternal employment was raised in this chapter as a graphic illustration of the limitations carers experience despite changes in the level of support service provision. This example highlights some of the weaknesses in the way such services are perceived and how policies can be formulated in isolation from each other. There is a clear need to integrate employment policies with social policies concerning family care (Laczko and Noden, 1993). Consideration of measures which might make it easier for women to manage dual careers is noticeably absent from the policy agenda. It is, perhaps, noteworthy that while the AWS raised the issue of promoting equal employment opportunities for people with learning disabilities, the employment situation of parents, and of mothers in particular, was not discussed.

In conclusion, the AWS has been a catalyst in boosting the level of resources directed towards the goal of providing support. Progress can be seen as a first phase of development, from which much has been learned about the nature of effective support. It needs to be identity-affirming (Todd and Shearn, 1996b) and facilitative (Nolan, Grant and Keady, 1996a). Facilitative care implies that arrangements are worked out through an even relationship between carers and service providers. This requires some understanding of carers' aspirations and of the importance they attach to the various aspects of their lives. This is no different to the general rule that service provision should meet individual need. However, its importance is underscored by the fact that support services can have negative effects if their delivery threatens carers' self-esteem and personal satisfaction. It is possible for support to be identity-threatening (Todd and Shearn, 1996a) and obstructive (Nolan, Grant and Keady, 1996a). Service interventions within the family must show a measure of empathy for the rewards and dilemmas of caregiving and confer a measure of legitimacy upon carers' efforts and aspirations. Further research on the means of achieving such responsive services is required.

References

Arber, S. and Gilbert, G. N. (1989). Men: the forgotten carers. *Sociology*, **23**, 111–118.

Bayley, M. (1973). *Mental Handicap and Community Care*. London: Routledge and Kegan Paul.

Beckford, V. and Robinson, C. (1993). *Consolidation or Change? A Second Survey of Family Based Respite Care Services in the United Kingdom*. Bristol: Norah Fry Research Centre, University of Bristol.

Beyer. S., Todd, S. and Felce, D. (1991). The implementation of the All-Wales Mental Handicap Strategy. *Mental Handicap Research*, **4**, 115–140.

Bicknell, J. (1988). The psychopathology of handicap. In: *Living with Mental Handicap: Transitions in the Lives of People with Mental Handicaps*, (G. Horobin and D. May, eds) pp. 22–37. London: Jessica Kingsley.

Booth, T. (1978). From normal baby to handicapped child. *Sociology*, **12**, 203–221.

Breslau, N., Salvever, D. and Staruch, K. S. (1982). Women's labor force activity and responsibilities for disabled dependants: a study of families with disabled children. *Journal of Health and Social Behavior*, **23**, 169–183.

Bury, M. (1982). Chronic illness as biographical disruption. *Sociology of Health and Illness*, **4**, 167–182.

Callender, C. (1992). Redundancy, unemployment and poverty. In: *Women and Poverty in Britain in the 1990s*, (C. Glendinning and J. Millar, eds.) pp. 137–158. Hemel Hempstead, Herts: Harvester Wheatsheaf.

Charmaz, K. (1983). Loss of self: a fundamental form of suffering of the chronically ill. *Sociology of Health and Illness*, **5**, 168–195.

Charmaz, K. (1987). Struggling for a self: identity levels of the chronically ill. *Research in the Sociology of Health Care*, **6**, 283–321.

Cheseldine, S. E. and Jeffrey, D. M. (1981). Mentally handicapped adolescents: their use of leisure. *Journal of Mental Deficiency Research*, **25**, 49–59.

Cooke, K. (1982). *1970 Birth Cohort: Ten Year Follow-up Study. (Working Paper DHSS No. 108)*. York: Social Policy Research Unit, University of York.

Corbin, J. and Strauss, A. (1988). *Unending Work and Care*. San Francisco: Jossey-Bass.

Delamont, S. (1980). *The Sociology of Women*. London: George Allen and Unwin.

de Paiva, S. and Lowe, K. (1988). *Community Care Workers: an Examination of the Changes in Clients' Skills and Use of Facilities*. Cardiff: Mental Handicap in Wales Applied Research Unit, University of Wales College of Medicine.

Department of Health and Social Security (DHSS) (1979). *Report of the Committee of Inquiry into Mental Handicap Nursing and Care*. London: HMSO.

Dunst, C. and Trivette, C. M. (1988). Toward experimental evaluation of the family, infant and preschool program. In: *Evaluating Family Programs*, (H. B. Weiss and F. H. Jacobs, eds) pp. 315–346. New York: Aldine de Gruyter.

Dunst, C. J., Trivette, C. M. and Deal, A. G. (1994). *Supporting and Strengthening Families: Volume 1 Methods, Strategies and Practices*. Cambridge MA: Brookline Books.

Edgerton, R. B. (1967). *The Cloak of Competence: Stigma in the Lives of the Mentally Retarded*. Berkeley: University of California Press.

Ell, K. (1996). Social networks, social support and coping with serious illness: the family connection. *Social Science and Medicine*, **42**, 173–183.

Ellis, K. (1993). *Squaring the Circle: User and Carer Participation in Needs Assessment*. York: Joseph Rowntree Foundation.

Emerson, E. B. and Petty, G. M. H. (1987). Enhancing the social relevance of evaluation practice. *Disability, Handicap and Society*, **2**, 151–162.

Evans, G. (1990). *Providing Support to Individuals at Home and their Locality*. Cardiff: Mental Handicap in Wales Applied Research Unit, University of Wales College of Medicine.

Evans, G., Felce, D., de Paiva, S. and Todd, S. (1992). Observing the delivery of a domiciliary support service. *Disability, Handicap and Society*, **7**, 19–34.

Evans, G., Todd, S., Beyer, S. *et al*. (1994). Assessing the impact of the All-Wales Strategy. *Journal of Intellectual Disability Research*, **38**, 109–133.

Finch, J. and Groves, D. (1983). *A Labour of Love: Women, Work and Caring*. London: Routledge and Kegan Paul.

Flynn, M., Cotterill, L., Hayes, L. and Sloper, T. (1995). *Respite Services for Adult Citizens with Learning Disabilities*. Manchester: National Development Team.

Ganster, D. C. and Victor, B. (1988). The impact of social support on mental and physical health. *British Journal of Medical Psychology*, **61**, 17–36.

Glaser, B. and Strauss, A. (1964). Awareness contexts and social interaction. *American Sociological Review*, **29**, 669–679.

Glendinning, C. (1983). *Unshared Care: Parents and their Disabled Children*. London: Routledge and Kegan Paul.

Graham, H. (1984). *Women, Health and the Family*. London: Harvester.

Grant, G. (1986). Older carers, inter-dependence and care of mentally handicapped adults. *Ageing and Society*, **6**, 333–351.

Grant, G. (1993). Support networks and transitions over two years among adults with a mental handicap. *Mental Handicap Research*, **6**, 36–55.

Grant, G. and McGrath, M. (1990). Need for respite-care services for caregivers of persons with mental retardation. *American Journal on Mental Retardation*, **94**, 638–648.

Grant, G., McGrath, M. and Ramcharan, P. (1994). How family and informal supporters appraise service quality. *International Journal of Disability, Development and Education*, **41**, 127–141.

Grant, G., McGrath, M. and Ramcharan, P. (1995). Community inclusion of older people with learning disabilities. *Care in Place*, **2**, 29–44.

Grant, G., Ramcharan, P. and McGrath, M. *et al*. (1998). Rewards and gratifications among family caregivers: towards a refined model of caring and coping. *Journal of Intellectual Disability Research*, **42**, 58–71.

Hubert, J. (1991). *Home-bound: Crisis in the Care of Young People with Severe Learning Difficulties*. London: King's Fund Centre.

Humphreys, S., Lowe, K. and de Paiva, S. (1986). *Community Care Workers: a Description of the Community Care Worker*. Cardiff: Mental Handicap in Wales Applied Research Unit, University of Wales College of Medicine.

Independent Development Council for People with Mental Handicap (IDC) (1982). *Elements of a Comprehensive Service for People with a Mental Handicap*. London: King's Fund Centre.

Kiernan, K. and Wicks, M. (1990). *Family Change and Future*. York: Joseph Rowntree Foundation.

Laczko, F. and Noden, S. (1993). Combining paid work with eldercare: the implications for social policy. *Health and Social Care in the Community*, **1**, 81–89.

Laws, J. L. (1979). *The Second X: Sex Role and Social Role*. New York: Norton.

Lazarus, R. S. and Folkman, S. (1984). *Stress, Appraisal and Coping*. New York: Springer.

Lowe, K. (1992). Community-based services: what consumers think. *British Journal of Mental Subnormality*, **38**, 6–14.

Lowe, K. and de Paiva, S. (1991). *NIMROD: an Overview*. London: HMSO.

Lowe, K., de Paiva, S. and Humphreys, S. (1987). *Community Care Workers: Key Issues in Providing a Domiciliary Support Service*. Cardiff: Mental Handicap in Wales Applied Research Unit, University of Wales College of Medicine.

Lyman, S. and Scott, M. (1970). *A Sociology of the Absurd*. Pacific Palisades: Goodyear.

McConkey, R., Walsh, P. and Mulcahy, M. (1982). Mentally handicapped adults living in the community: a survey conducted in and around the city of Dublin. *Mental Handicap*, **11**, 57–59.

McGrath, M. and Grant, G. (1993). The life-cycle and support networks of families with a mentally handicapped member. *Disability, Handicap and Society*, **8**, 25–41.

McLaughlin, E. and Ritchie, J. (1994). Legacies of caring: the experiences and circumstances of ex-carers. *Health and Social Care in the Community*, **2**, 241–253.

MacRae, H. (1990). Older women and identity maintenance in later life. *Canadian Journal on Aging*, **9**, 248–267.

Martin, J. and Roberts, C. (1984). *Women and Employment: a Lifetime Perspective*. London: HMSO.

Murphy, R. F., Scher, J., Murphy, Y. and Mack, R. (1988). Physical disability and social limitability: a study in the rituals of adversity. *Social Science and Medicine*, **26**, 235–242.

National Children's Home (NCH) (1991). *Sharing the Caring: Respite Care for Children and Families*. London: NCH.

Nolan, M., Grant, G. and Keady, J. (1996a). *Understanding Family Care: a Multidimensional Model of Caring and Coping*. Buckingham: Open University Press.

Nolan, M., Grant, G. and Keady, J. (1996b). The Carers' Act: realising the potential. *British Journal of Community Health Nursing*, **1**, 317–321.

Oswin, M. (1984). *They Keep Going Away*. London: King's Fund Publishing Office.

Parker, G. (1990). *With Due Care and Attention: a Review of the Literature on Informal Care*. London: Family Policy Studies Centre.

Perry, J., Felce, D., Beyer, S. and Todd, S. (1998). Strategic service change: development of core services in Wales, 1983–1995. *Journal of Applied Research in Intellectual Disability*, **11**, 15–33.

Phillips, J. (1995). *Working Carers*. Aldershot: Avebury.

Quine, L. and Pahl, J. (1985). Examining the causes of stress in families with mentally handicapped children. *British Journal of Social Work*, **15**, 501–517.

Robinson, C. (1994). Making the break from respite care. *British Journal of Learning Disabilities*, **22**, 42–45.

Rothwell, S. (1980). United Kingdom. In: *Women Returning to Work*, (A. M. Yohalem, ed.) pp. 160–216. London: Frances Pinter Ltd.

Scambler, G. and Hopkins, A. (1986). Being epileptic: coming to terms with stigma. *Sociology of Health and Illness*, **8**, 26–43.

Schneider, J. and Conrad, P. (1980). In the closet with illness: epilepsy, stigma potential and information control. *Social Problems*, **28**, 32–44.

Seltzer, M. M. and Krauss, M. W. (1989). Aging parents with mentally retarded children: family risk factors and sources of support, *American Journal of Mental Retardation*, **94**, 303–312.

Seltzer, M. M., Krauss, M. W. and Heller, T. (1991). Family caregiving over the life course. In: *Ageing and Developmental Disabilities: Challenges for the 1990s*, (M. P. Janicki and

M. M. Seltzer, eds) pp. 3–24. Washington DC: American Association on Mental Retardation.

Shearer, A. (1981). *Disability: Whose Handicap?* Oxford: Basil Blackwell.

Shearn, J. and Todd, S. (1996). Identities at risk: the relationships parents and their coresident adult offspring with learning disabilities have with each other and their social worlds. *European Journal on Mental Disability*, **3**, 47–60.

Shearn, J. and Todd, S. (1997a). Parental work: an account of the day to day activities of parents of adults with learning disabilities. *Journal of Intellectual Disability Research*, **41**, 285–301.

Shearn, J. and Todd, S. (1997b). Mothers want work and support too. *Llais*, **44**, 3–6.

Spence, D. L. and Lonner, T. D. (1978). Career set: a resource through transitions and crises. *International Journal of Aging and Human Development*, **9**, 51–65.

Stalker, K. (1990). *Share the Care: an Evaluation of a Family-based Respite Care Service*. London: Jessica Kingsley.

Standing Council of Voluntary Organizations for People with a Mental Handicap in Wales (SCOVO) (1989). *Parents Deserve Better: a Review Report on Early Counselling in Wales*. Cardiff: SCOVO.

Strauss, A., Fagerhaugh, S., Suczek, B. and Weiner, C. (1985). *The Social Organisation of Medical Work*. Chicago: University of Chicago Press.

Swift, P., Grant, G. and McGrath, M. (1991). *Home to Home: a Review of Family-based Respite Care in Dyfed*. Bangor: Centre for Social Policy Research and Development, University of Wales Bangor.

Taraborrelli, P. (1994). Innocents, converts and old hands: the experiences of Alzheimer's disease caregivers. In: *Qualitative Studies in Health and Medicine*, (M. Bloor and P. Taraborrelli, eds) pp. 22–42. Aldershot: Avebury.

Thoits, P. A. (1992). On merging identity theory and stress research. *Social Psychology Quarterly*, **54**, 101–112.

Todd, S. (1995). Preludes to secrecy: handling the transition of young people from a special school. In: *Qualitative Studies in Education*, (S. Salisbury and S. Delamont, eds) pp. 6–29. Aldershot: Avebury.

Todd, S., Evans, G. and Beyer, S. (1990). More recognised than known: the social visibility and attachment of people with developmental disabilities. *Australia and New Zealand Journal of Developmental Disabilities*, **16**, 207–218.

Todd, S. and Shearn, J. (1996a). Time and the person: the impact of support services on the lives of parents of adults with learning disabilities. *Journal of Applied Research in Intellectual Disabilities*, **9**, 40–60.

Todd, S. and Shearn, J. (1996b). Struggles with time: the careers of parents of adult sons and daughters with learning disabilities. *Disability and Society*, **11**, 379–402.

Todd, S. and Shearn, J. (1997). Family secrets and dilemmas of status: parental management of the disclosure of learning disability. *Disability and Society*, **12**, 341–366.

Todd, S., Shearn, J., Beyer, S. and Felce, D. (1993a). Careers in caring: the changing situations of parents caring for an offspring with learning difficulties. *Irish Journal of Psychology*, **14**, 130–153.

Todd, S., Shearn, J., Beyer, S. and Felce, D. (1993b). Reflecting on change: consumers' views of the impact of the All-Wales Strategy. *Mental Handicap*, **21**, 128–136.

Traustadottir, R. (1988). Mothers who care: gender, disability and family life. *Journal of Family Issues*, **12**, 211–228.

Twigg, J. and Atkin, K. (1994). *Carers Perceived: Policy and Practice in Informal Care*. Buckingham: Open University Press.

Ungerson, C. (1987). *Policy is Personal: Sex, Gender and Informal Care*. London: Tavistock.

van Gennep, A. (1960). *The Rites of Passage*. London: Routledge and Kegan Paul.

Voysey, M. (1975). *A Constant Burden*. London: Routledge and Kegan Paul.

Welsh Office (1983). *The All Wales Strategy for the Development of Services for Mentally Handicapped People*. Cardiff: Welsh Office.

Zerubavel, E. (1981). *Hidden Rhythms: Schedules and Calendars in Social Life*. Chicago: University of Chicago Press.

Chapter 8

Developing day opportunities

As part of its commitments to an ordinary life in the community, oppor-tunities for all to develop their full potential and to full integration, the AWS looked for a greater diversification of activities which people with learning disabilities undertook during the day. The touchstones of more progressive day services were to be an individual focus, access to a more typical range of opportunities that most other members of the community enjoyed, and appropriate support to help people take advantage of these. In 1983, the predominant form of activity during the day for people with learning disabilities was the local authority day centre. In reviewing this situation, the AWS noted that 'adult training centres (ATCs) are the only significant day care facilities. Not only is this too narrow a range of provi-sion, but many are run so as to provide an all-purpose service which is not conducive to the promotion of independence or responsive to individual needs' (Welsh Office, 1983, p. 7). The AWS also noted that considerable time and resources were being consumed in transporting people to attend day centres, sometimes over considerable distances. It favoured the devel-opment of more local alternatives to help forge better links between the people served and their home communities.

The AWS intended to broaden choice by promoting a wider range of activities. It was particularly concerned that the options should reflect those commonly available to other people. Possibilities included further education, work-preparation, paid employment and the use of general community facilities, such as leisure centres, shops, cinemas, sports facili-ties and other ordinary amenities in the local area. No distinction was made between people with more or less substantial disabilities, all being seen as having a right to a wider choice of day activity. While the AWS looked for choice, it set no strategic priorities. For example, paid employ-ment was not viewed as any more desirable an alternative to attending a day centre than doing a leisure activity or undertaking a college course.

Prior to reaching agreement about the content of county plans, the Welsh Office offered a series of one-off grants to counties to pump prime service development. These were mainly used to establish the infrastruc-ture needed successfully to develop plans, but were also used to encour-age the early creation of alternatives to traditional services. Despite this, the early years of the AWS saw slow growth in alternatives. Certainly, change over and above that created by specific proposals was limited, and so were innovations in the wider culture of day centre operation. Research at the time suggested that morale was low in day centres. Staff felt detached from the AWS. They felt that their work was under-valued and under attack because of the early prioritization of alternative develop-ments and the fact that further investment in day centres was excluded from AWS funding (Evans et al., 1986).

In retrospect, the early pump-priming grants for day opportunities lacked a coherent rationale. However, they did represent, de facto, a model of day service reform whereby the development of parallel provi-sion would logically take people out of the day centres and lead to a lessening of their role in the total service infrastructure. Notwithstanding this, no measure was taken of the likely investment required across employment, social care and education to enable such a strategy to be successful. As we have commented in relation to other areas, AWS spend-ing was not conceptualized within a total resource framework to bring about wholesale service reform.

The projects which evolved as a result of this early funding made a relatively modest impact on service users. They generally involved small numbers of individuals and, with some notable exceptions, had a narrow activity focus. For example, Wales saw the emergence of the horticultural project as a common new day opportunity (Beyer et al., 1986). Some such schemes were characterized as work experience with a view to equip people with core work skills and enable them to move on to further employment. In other cases, schemes were characterized as an end in themselves, capable of providing meaningful occupation and a better quality of life for the individuals involved. The emphasis on horticulture as work experience seldom reflected real opportunities available in the local job market.

From 1986, all counties had access to some level of AWS funding. This encouraged a second wave of day service development both of projects linked to day centres and stand-alone alternatives. Ironically, day centres increased in number and in the number of people they served in this initial period. This was mainly achieved through the introduction of some smaller, more local centres and the beginnings of sessional attendance. Undoubtedly, changes took place as the Strategy progressed in the balance of activity offered by centres and in their reliance on on-site large group activities. The time people spent in their communities increased and people were referred to other organizations for education, work, and other experiences. More provision was offered to people with higher support needs by the expansion of special needs units attached to centres.

By the 1990s, day centres had become more diversified in their range of activities and were offering more to people on an individual basis. However, it was less clear that the lives of the majority of people receiv-ing day services had changed radically, such that their pattern of activity could be regarded as consistent with an ordinary life. In the rest of this chapter, we review our research on day opportunities which has covered three overlapping areas: day centres, alternative day opportunities between 'traditional' centres and supported employment and finally supported open employment. We highlight factors that impact on quality of outcome and identify options for the continued improvement of the quality of life people have during the day.

The reform of day centres

Day centres in 1983 already reflected a number of policy emphases which had been articulated at different times in the past. Their origins in the occupation centres set up after the First World War had left an inheritance of the sheltered work tradition. Their function changed to the training of people for competitive employment in the late 1960s, a role encapsulated by the renaming of facilities as Adult Training Centres (ATCs). The centre role was further broadened in the early 1970s to include assessment and the provision of daily occupation where no other form of paid employment was available. The respite function for families was also recognized. In the period from 1971 to 1984, the number of ATCs in England and Wales rose from 330 to 496, and the number of places offered from 24 537 to 47 464 (Office of Health Economics, 1986). Disappointment over a lack of throughput of people from ATCs to work and an increasing concern in policy with personal development led to further changes in direction towards a social education model (National Development Group, 1977). More recent trends included greater emphases on further education and recreation, and the provision of a range of advice and advocacy resources (Seed, 1988; Social Services Inspectorate, 1989).

The AWS critique of day centre operation was, therefore, within the tradition of a long line of reforming policy initiatives. Change in guidance, however, does not necessarily have the effect of overturning pre-existing dominant models of operation. Rather, new emphases are grafted onto old, with the result that operational models coexist within provision. The original AWS prescription offered little by way of mechanisms for change above the availability of funding for projects consistent with the Welsh Office's key principles. The Welsh Office chose not to promote day centre change by investing in centre-led initiatives. Rather, its early grant giving activity funded alternative services with the hope that involvement in these new services would change the lives of day centre users. The down side of such an implicit strategy was that few formal connections existed between the development of new capacity and the recycling of existing resources. By 1986, concern was growing that AWS funding was not acting as a catalyst to the reinvestment of existing day centre resources. The Welsh Office began to require information on changes to existing service patterns to spur counties to shift investment accordingly. However, this still did not result in a planned strategy for change in day services. Plans for change were formulated at county level and there were still few examples of wholesale reform of day centres well into the 1990s. Apart from some conspicuous exceptions, the translation of existing resources into new services was a slow process.

The more recent introduction of Care in the Community legislation did not have a major impact on the day centre issue. The imperative to spend Care in the Community Transitional Funding on private and voluntary sector providers was not applied in Wales. Subsequent reining in of AWS expenditure, the concentration of new development money on hospital resettlement, and the financial constraints felt by the new Unitary Authorities have collectively had a more powerful effect in turning the attention of planners to how their own funds are invested than did the AWS. Increasingly, new development can only be funded by recycling existing investment. We have yet to see whether these new forces will accelerate the move towards day centre reform or halt it altogether.

Impact of the AWS on day opportunities

The number of day centre places available increased between 1983 and 1988, rising from 2997 to 3192 (Beyer, Todd and Felce, 1991; Perry *et al.*, 1998). The mean size of centres reduced over the same period from 81 to 76 places. By 1991, 16% of day centre users attended on a part-time basis, the majority for three or four days. Provision of day services for people with special needs had been patchy before 1983. The more routine inclusion of this group within the day centre was a part of the overall growth in numbers of people served. By 1991, people with special needs made up 17% of the total number of people in day centres, with 83% of centres offering some form of provision for them.

The trend of increasing day centre places was reversed after 1988. The total number of people attending centres fell to 2466 by 1995, with the average size of centre decreasing to 70. This decline reflected the creation of smaller 'satellite units' linked to centres but located in local population centres to provide a more convenient and accessible base for people and to stimulate greater access to local interest groups, networks and amenities. By 1990, 39% of centres operated this type of unit. By 1995, 71 satellites had been developed to serve 956 people in settings with an average of 13 places each. Managers reported some positive movement in making the day centre more individual in nature with a greater number of activity arrangements established for just one person. A substantial growth in self-advocacy within centres was also reported, along with greater attention to individual planning and assessment of need. Greater managerial control of resources through devolved budgeting increased flexibility to meet individual requirements.

Investment in alternative day opportunities gained momentum after 1986, and significant trends could be observed by 1988. Work experience and college courses were particular growth areas up to 1988. By 1995, 415 and 857 places were available respectively. Places in small businesses or training enterprises and in paid employment both increased during the second half of the AWS, rising from almost non-existent levels in 1983 to 710 and 550 places respectively by 1995. Use of other settings such as health service rehabilitation centres and elderly person's day centres doubled to provide 473 places. Schemes offering individualized programmes of day opportunities rose from none in 1983 to 290 places in 1995.

While these results are in line with the AWS aim of diversification, the overall impact on the level of service provision is less clear. The results of a survey of 404 people selected at random from four districts, whose situations were surveyed in 1986 and again in 1990, showed an equivocal picture of change (Evans *et al.*, 1994). The proportion of adults attending ATCs or other day centres stayed relatively stable across the four districts over the four-year period, decreasing slightly from 53% to 52%. College attendance expanded from 1% to 6% of the sample. Involvement in sheltered, open or voluntary work changed from 5% to 9% and a variety of other options expanded collectively to serve 11% compared to the previous 7%. However, at the same time, the proportion of people who had no occupation or day placement rose from 16% to 23%, and the number having nothing to do for part of the week also rose from 7% to 14%. The apparent expansion of service opportunity and the number of people without a service are explicable by a growth in sessional attendance whereby individuals have more than one type of placement. The increase in the numbers who had an inadequate service reflected a combination of deficiencies in service coverage and quality, the latter prompting some people to withdraw from services where they were dissatisfied with the quality of what was on offer. Therefore, as some people's opportunities were changing and expanding, other people's were contracting.

The next section explores in more detail what day centres were offering towards the end of the AWS's first 10 years. The remainder of the chapter looks at what has been offered by some of the alternative day services developed under the AWS and the development and impact of supported employment. It ends with a consideration of the findings for future service developments.

Development in the day centre model

Research into the balance of activity offered by Welsh day centres showed that, compared with the situation critiqued at the outset of the AWS, day centres had broadened the range of activities they offered. ATCs became more outward looking and increasingly made arrangements for activities to occur in the wider community (Beyer, Kilsby and Lowe, 1994). For example, sport and leisure activities were offered using the resources of sports and leisure centres and people were helped to access further education in colleges and adult education classes. Work was another outlet for integration, mainly in the form of work experience placements in local firms. It represented 15% of the total person-hours offered in day centre timetables. Activities involving use of community amenities such as shopping were also well represented, stemming from a focus on personal development and independent living.

These developments had not fundamentally changed day centre activities. Over two-thirds of person-hours were still being spent within the centres. Arts and crafts activities and contract work accounted for nearly half of day centre programmes (25% and 20% of person-hours respectively). These activities involved relatively large groups (average 7 and 17 people respectively) and overwhelmingly occurred in the centres. Although many people attended colleges of further education, 63% of the person-hours allocated to education in centre timetables still took place within the centres.

It may have been hoped that the creation of smaller satellite units would achieve more individualization of activity. However, the majority of individuals were still required to attend daily registration at the main day centre prior to undertaking their scheduled daily activities. While there had been an increase in the amount of activity occurring in outside locations, these were still mostly coordinated by the day centre. Furthermore, the balance of activity offered through satellite units was similar to that occurring in the main day centres.

Differences in the balance of activities offered to individuals across centres indicated that they differed in their aims. Four models of day centre operation were identified in a survey of Wales (Beyer, Kilsby and Lowe, 1994), the differences between them echoing the changing emphasis in past policy. Five day centres followed a centre-based *occupational model*, characterized by high levels of contract work combined with high levels of arts and crafts activity. These reflected the sheltered work/occupation model which was predominant prior to the policy reformulations of the 1960s. The largest group of centres, 12 in all, operated a *recreation and personal development model*, characterized by equally high levels of these two groups of activities. These centres reflected the social education model advocated by the 1977 National Development Group policy guidelines. Nine day centres followed a *recreation model*, characterized by high levels of arts and crafts organized in large group activities within the centres coupled with sports activities occurring mostly out in the community. The emphasis on recreational activities may have grown as a response to criticism of the unstimulating nature of contract work (Whelan and Speake, 1977). It also provides an easily arranged source of activity as a backdrop to other activities, such as work and community living experience, which, although minority pursuits, may have been seen as the centres' main purpose. Finally, three day centres operated an *employment model*, delivering work experience and opportunities for paid work as majority pursuits. Their emphasis had most in common with the training model introduced in the late 1960s and throughout the 70s, but updated to incorporate the use of external placements rather than the more traditional arrangement of work activities within the centres. However, even though these activities usually took place away from the centres, a number of barriers still prevented individuals moving into proper jobs. In 1991, less than 5% of those attending day centres had obtained paid work.

The diversity of aims across day centres was consistent with the fact that AWS policy did not set clear preferences for day service development. In some counties, different models operated simultaneously implying that the relative worth of particular activities was left for local determination rather than established by county policy. Some of the associations which underlay variation are now discussed. Centres in the occupation cluster tended to be larger than those operating the three other models. Although no tendency was found for particular kinds of centres to have above or below average staffing ratios or per capita costs, the pattern of staff organization and supervision adopted did appear to influence the balance of activity offered. Day centres offering a recreation or occupation model were more likely to have traditional tiered hierarchical management structures, whereas employment or recreation and personal development centres adopted flatter, team management styles. Comments on change by centre managers identified a series of additional factors which influenced the activities and style of service on offer. The extent to which they were able to control their own budgets was a factor. Many centres within each model had some such budgetary control, but employment and recreation and personal development centres had control over higher proportions of their budgets than the other types. This gave them greater control over transport, sessional workers and meeting the costs of outside activities. Although differences in staff:user ratios did not relate to the balance of activities offered, the overall numbers of staff available seemed to be associated with the extent to which activity could be organized away from the centre and individual activity supported. The location of centres in relation to community facilities such as leisure and shopping amenities also had an impact on what day centres felt able to offer.

Follow-up research has also looked at a sample of typical activities in four centres, each exemplifying one of the models of provision. A representative sample of activities in each exemplar was taken and what staff and people with learning disabilities did in them was observed. Engagement in activity and social interaction was found to be higher in employment activities, most favourably in paid work or work experience in outside settings. The trend across the four centres was for higher levels of engagement to occur in individual activities or activities arranged in small groups. However, engagement in activity varied considerably even across groups of the same size. Level of disability was a factor and sessions involving people with high support needs generally had lower levels of service user engagement. How staff organized themselves within activity sessions was another factor. Where more than one staff member was involved and the session lacked prior organization, discussion over roles within the session and organization of materials by staff tended to have an adverse effect on their interaction with service users, leading to lower levels of engagement in the activity. This tended to have an effect irrespective of type of activity and, therefore, of model type. Generally the employment and the recreation and personal development models were shown to be preferable because of smaller group sizes, higher proportions of individual activity and more activity in external settings. These advantages may also have been reinforced by the availability of staff other than day centre staff to run activities. Our findings suggest that activities outside the centre run by outside staff, such as teachers in adult education classes, seemed to be run in more intensive ways which held people's attention longer and produced higher levels of engagement.

In summary, day centres in Wales had not generally undergone a revolution, although some had developed very different menus of activity to others. Change appeared to reflect the original aspiration of the AWS. Although some centres had clearly evolved more than others, all were to some extent a melting pot of past and recent policy emphases. Variation was such that the precise nature of the service individuals received was arbitrary, dependent on where they lived and the particular orientation followed by the centre which served their area. These differences are not without real life consequences. The balance of activities and how they are organized have important implications for the pursuits individuals can engage in, who they are likely to meet, how much of their time is gainfully occupied, and their personal and career development.

Alternative day opportunities

By 1993, 90 schemes could be identified which were different to traditional day centres without being supported employment initiatives (McGrath, 1994). They provided day opportunities for a total of about 1200 service users. Two broad types existed – *community-focused schemes* (34) with a local base or identity and an emphasis on individual activity programmes and *employment-focused schemes* (56) with an emphasis on specific vocational training or employment. Variants of these two approaches and scheme managers' perceptions of achievements are outlined below (McGrath, 1994, 1996a, b).

Community-focused schemes (CFSs)

Three models of CFSs existed. Two, both with a local base, targeted either people living in a defined area or a specific user group. Examples of the latter included eleven for people with special needs, two for elderly service users and two for people resettled from hospital. The third model utilized community facilities for all user activities, restricting the use of a base to administration. CFSs offered a wide range of activities covering leisure, work and personal needs and emphasized social skills training and community integration. With an average size of twelve places, CFSs usually operated for five days a week with over half the users (55%) attending four or five days per week. Over 90% of CFSs were managed by the statutory sector which provided virtually all of their funding.

Employment-focused schemes (EFSs)

There were four models of EFSs distinguished by their main objectives – training, training and employment, community businesses and supported volunteering (McGrath, 1996a). Social skills training was a valued component of EFSs, but the focus of activities was mainly employment preparation, vocational training and work experience. Reflecting the rural nature of much of Wales, nearly half the EFSs were based on horticulture, agriculture or conservation work. Almost a quarter involved cafes and/or food production. Included in the remainder were the manufacture of ironwork, concrete slab production, a computer workshop, aromatherapy, a bike shop, a recycling business, children's nurseries and volunteer shopping for elderly people. EFSs were smaller than CFSs with a median number of six places, and fewer, particularly those in the voluntary sector, operated five days per week. Only 38% of service users attended for four or five days per week. Less than half of EFSs were managed by statutory agencies. Nearly 40% had been initiated by voluntary organizations, parents, local strategy planning groups or one or two committed individuals. Nearly a fifth had received European Social Fund help and a similar proportion had obtained other grants. A majority of EFSs, including all the training/employment schemes and community businesses, generated income from their activities.

There were marked differences between the four EFS models. Training schemes had the highest turnover of attenders. They tended to cater for younger users (25 years or under), were larger than other models (an average of 19 attenders compared with 9–12 for the other models) and had a lower ratio of staff to attenders. Community businesses had a commercial work ethic and encouraged a 'normal' work environment and a stable workforce. Two-thirds of users in community businesses worked full-time in contrast to a similar majority of those in training or supported volunteering schemes who attended for only one or two days. Whereas pay would not be expected in a training or volunteer situation, 10 of the 14 community businesses paid workers at least up to the earnings disregard limit.

Schemes providing both training and employment were sometimes designed to fulfil both of these roles but, in others, the dual roles had arisen by default when it had not proved possible to move attenders on to more independent settings. In general, training/employment schemes had less clear-cut aims and policies than training schemes or community businesses. Training/employment schemes were both relatively unsuccessful in moving attenders on to employment and far less likely than community businesses to pay attenders. Supported volunteering schemes, which by definition did not offer any payment, tended to cater for older service users (53% of attenders were 35 years or older) and to operate for one or two days a week only.

Achievements

Four areas of achievements were described by scheme managers in the audit undertaken of alternative day opportunities.

First, there were changes in the personal competencies of attenders. Managers of both CFSs and EFSs noted general improvements in attenders' self-confidence and social skills. In addition, EFS managers pointed to attenders' acquisition of vocational skills and their sense of achievement. Identification with a small workgroup was seen to be another source of satisfaction for some individuals.

Secondly, improved community integration was cited as an achievement by nearly a quarter of managers. Although CFS attenders used many community facilities, it was not possible to judge how meaningful any community integration was in practice. Work experience placements provided opportunities to meet people without a disability and the work of most EFSs brought attenders into contact with the public. There were, however, a small number of EFSs which offered little integration either because they were still based in a day centre or because they were situated in remote rural areas.

Thirdly, there were achievements concerning employment. Both the work experience arranged by CFSs and, in particular, the activities of EFSs provided work preparation and a form of employment for attenders. As noted above, community businesses were the most successful in this respect and were the most likely to offer some remuneration. The schemes also assisted attenders to move on to either open or supported employment. However, only an average of 7% of EFS attenders and 2% of CFS attenders moved to more independent settings each year, usually on a part-time basis only.

Lastly, there were achievements relating to the scheme itself. Given the difficulties of securing adequate funding for suitable facilities, often the establishment, maintenance or expansion of the scheme was seen as an important achievement. A number had achieved some form of public recognition or award acknowledging the quality of the service provided. The impact of such recognition on the self-esteem of attenders was difficult to assess though we suspect that it was an important means of helping individuals to feel a respected part of the community.

Supported employment

Development of supported employment as a day service

Although the diversity of aims within day centres may have reflected the vagueness of the service prescription offered by the AWS, there has been an emerging consensus on the outcomes which should guide service development (National Development Group, 1977; King's Fund, 1984; Mencap, 1985). Developing personal skills that lead to social competence, personal self-sufficiency, domestic independence and vocational potential are important. A concern for social networks and friendships to grow is also important. Among possible activities, open employment may be seen as an attractive option for people with learning disabilities, with the potential to yield many personal benefits. These include having a role which is societally valued, naturally high levels of engagement due to the imperatives of working life, access to a community of colleagues, contact with members of the public, income, a sense of productivity and an impression of being part of the majority culture. Work remains the main form of day time occupation for the adult population in this country and gaining employment has been reported as a common aspiration among people with learning disabilities. Supported employment is one means of helping those with disabilities and other difficulties access the world of work (Rusch, 1986; Nisbet and Callahan, 1987) and its development is very much in line with the general thrust of policy in Britain which stresses community integration and normal patterns of life as key objectives (DHSS, 1971; Welsh Office, 1983).

Given this perspective, one could reasonably argue that the growth in work experience within day centres is to be welcomed. However, by 1990, only 5% of day centre users had managed to make the transition into paid employment (Beyer, Kilsby and Lowe, 1994). Furthermore, the individuals who gained paid work following work experience were among the most able individuals, people who were highly socially adaptive and could learn without resort to specialized training techniques (McGrath, 1994). Three potential problems have been identified in the use of work preparation as a route to paid employment. First, unless a special effort is made to arrange placements which match the employment profile of the area, work experience is unlikely to be an effective preparation for the jobs available. Second, the environments in which work experience takes place are often different from those which will be encountered in real jobs. By way of illustration, as many as 23% of work experience placements in Wales in 1990 took place within day centres (Beyer, Kilsby and Lowe, 1994). Even where work experience took place elsewhere, supervision and training was typically provided by care workers, rather than experienced employees or supervisors. Placements were often separated in some way from the real work setting and could involve groups of disabled workers who rarely had opportunities to work with non-disabled co-workers individually. Third, many individuals with a learning disability find it difficult to generalize the skills they learn in one environment to another. Therefore, given the difficulties involved in constructing training settings which are sufficiently similar to real work environments, individuals still cannot move into proper jobs without additional training specific to the tasks to be performed and wider workplace culture.

Growth in supported employment in Wales

Supported employment originated in the USA in response to the problems outlined above. Supported employment uses structured ways to find individuals suitable jobs, systematic training techniques derived from applied behaviour analysis to teach the person the job during the initial period of employment, and strategies for maintaining the supported employee's performance once on-the-job assistance has been withdrawn (Rusch, 1986). The supported employment model, popularly referred to as the 'place, train and maintain' approach, revolutionized the way that services enabled individuals to access and maintain paid work. Through this approach, individuals acquired their work skills 'on-the-job'. Reliance on work preparation approaches ceased, along with all their associated shortcomings. With supported employment, throughput into jobs was immediate.

Supported employment agencies have contributed to a growth of paid work in Wales. Social Services departments have provided the majority of funding for these agencies, accounting for 80% of their income compared to a national figure of 58% for Britain as a whole. The impact of AWS allocations on stimulating supported employment is clear. However, it also shows the extent to which Welsh agencies have been less active in securing financial help from other sources. A national survey of supported employment agencies carried out at the end of 1995 identified 210 agencies offering a supported employment service in England, Wales and Scotland, of which 19 were Welsh (Beyer, Goodere and Kilsby, 1996). All had been developed since the inception of the AWS. Half of the agencies in Wales had been in operation for less than three years, a quarter for between three and six years and a quarter for over six years. One hundred and one agencies completed the survey questionnaire, 12 of which were from Wales. Nine Welsh agencies were independent organizations, set up specifically as supported employment services, the remainder being linked to other services such as day centres.

The 101 agencies in Britain were supporting 2446 employees (an average of 24 workers per agency), while the 12 Welsh agencies supported 253 people (an average of 21). If responding agencies were representative of the total identified, one can estimate that there were 5086 supported employees in Britain and 401 in Wales and that more people per head of population were being served in Wales than in Britain as a whole (138 compared to 90 per million total population).

Outcomes of supported employment in Wales

Hours worked

Welsh agencies supported a substantial number of full-time jobs. Forty per cent of jobs offered over 30 hours per week, a proportion which compared favourably to the 25% for Britain as a whole. Nearly two-thirds of those currently employed in Wales work for more than the 16 hours per week which is the Department of Employment's definition of full-time work. Research has shown the advantage of full-time working for the social integration, financial independence and career development of the supported employee and for the cost:benefit ratio of supported employment as an alternative to other forms of day service. It is difficult to justify extensive part-time working among people with mild and moderate disabilities in terms of any problems inherent in training such people to be competent workers. However, other factors have an influence. Job availability has changed in recent years, causing a shift in the balance between full-time and part-time working for the workforce as a whole. In addition, the desire to retain benefit income encourages part-time working (see below).

The impact of full-time or part-time work

While full-time working remains a minority pursuit, supported employment for many people with learning disabilities can only be a part-time alternative to other day services. This has implications for both the economics and process of day centre reform. There are a number of barriers to obtaining full-time employment, many of which are unrelated to the nature of people's disabilities. The local availability of full-time work is one issue. Many of the entry level jobs for poorly qualified people in today's economy are part-time. Traditional expectations are a second issue. Many parents, professionals and service users may question whether paid work of any kind, let alone full-time employment, is a realistic aspiration. The workplace culture is new to many disabled people and concerns are often raised about whether the person is capable of working to a standard commensurate with payment at the going rate, or whether individuals will suffer rejection at the hands of work colleagues. Obtaining part-time employment may be seen as a means of dipping a toe in the water while keeping the obligation to the employer in terms of productivity limited. This caution is reinforced by the benefits system. Many prospective workers with disabilities have a special benefit status due to being considered unemployable. They may also be eligible for a number of benefits which makes their total unearned income equivalent to that offered in low wage employment. This is particularly true for people who are living in supported houses. People often choose to retain their benefit status, therefore, and only earn within allowed limits. Moreover, many individuals, families and service agencies have been cautious about the decision to undertake full-time work because there is the risk that people will not be able to return to the same benefit status should they subsequently lose their jobs. Government moves to tighten the eligibility criteria for Incapacity Benefits and to lengthen periods before benefits can be reclaimed serve to heighten these fears. Retaining benefits, therefore, provides a relative certainty of income which working does not.

Despite the many barriers, there are still people who feel able to make the transition to work and some have made their way into full-time jobs. Gwent Pathway, for example, obtained 64 jobs in the first 18 months of operation. These were representative of the Welsh average of about two-thirds of jobs being above 16 hours per week and about two-fifths above 30 hours per week. Most of the supported employees obtaining work through the Pathway scheme were reported to have mild or moderate learning disabilities at the time of the evaluation, which means the Pathway client group was much the same as that found for Wales as a whole.

Our findings show that a significant number of people benefited financially from working full-time, specifically those who lived in family homes and were in receipt of basic Income Support or Severe Disability Allowance. These benefit levels seldom exceeded £280 a month at 1994/5 prices. The extent to which people increased their income was related to the hours worked. Working full-time could lead to greater financial independence; working part-time rarely did. Employees working less than 16 hours a week received an average monthly gross pay of £77, while those working over 16 hours a week received average gross incomes of £427 per month. These figures compare to average monthly incomes of £740 and £1288 for unskilled and all full-time workers respectively, again at 1994/5 prices.

A number of aspects of the work situation can hinder the extent to which a worker with a disability is integrated into the workplace. The presence of job coaches, for example, can be a barrier between the disabled worker and their colleagues. However, whether the worker is in part-time or full-time employment is a powerful determinant of integration. Various aspects of part-time work separate the worker from the rest of the workforce. Information collected on an integration monitoring tool filled in by staff of Gwent Pathway showed that full-time working yielded higher levels of integration. Compared to those in full-time employment, part-time workers were more likely to work different hours, wear different clothes, perform different tasks and arrive at and leave the work site at different times than their non-disabled counterparts. Full-time workers were more likely to be involved in the internal staff supervision systems of companies, which provide a clear mechanism for resolving problems in the workplace and for identifying possibilities for increasing job responsibility and career progression. Full-time workers also had more contact with their work colleagues than part-time employees, being more likely to interact with co-workers during break-times and outside of working hours. With 58% of employment services in the national survey expressing the view that integration was the most important employment outcome for their clients, the significance of the difference in social and financial outcomes between full and part-time working is obvious.

Income of supported employees

About half (53%) of all Welsh workers earned between £3.00 and £3.99 an hour, while a further quarter (25%) earned hourly rates between £2.00 and £2.99. Both of these proportions were slightly higher than those found for Britain as a whole (48% and 17% respectively). About a tenth did not receive any pay for their work (Wales 9%, Britain 13%). Net wage levels in Wales were, however, similar to those received in Britain. The highest proportion of workers earned between £1.00 and £15.00 per week (Wales 35%, Britain 32%), reflecting the fact that a third of supported employees have therapeutic earnings status which allows them to earn only up to £15.00 without earned income affecting their welfare benefits. The majority of workers increased their income through working although this was less strongly evident in Wales (Wales 62%, Britain 79%). However, where gains were made in Wales, they were more substantial than in Britain as a whole; 22% of Welsh workers increased their net income by between 80% and 400% compared to only 7% of British workers.

Levels of integration

Managers were asked to rate worker integration in terms of whether disabled workers mixed with other workers and joined in conversations. Welsh agencies reported that 55% of their employees achieved 'excellent' levels of integration compared to 40% in Britain. This difference may reflect the higher proportion of Welsh jobs which were for 30 hours a week or more. A few workers were reported to be completely segregated (Wales <1%, Britain 2%) and some only experienced 'fair' levels of integration (Wales 10%, Britain 19%). The remaining employees were reported as experiencing 'good' integration (Wales 35%, Britain 38%).

Service cost:benefit

Cost:benefit analysis is a useful way to look at the utility of spending resources in one way or another. In the USA, cost:benefit studies of supported employment programmes have shown positive net benefits for workers and the taxpayer. In our study of two Welsh agencies, we found that workers with disabilities generally benefited financially from employment. However, there was a net cost to the taxpayer. Cost:benefit ratios were well below unity, indicating that expenditure on providing supported employment services was considerably greater than tax receipts on the employees' earned incomes together with savings from the alternative services foregone. However, there were significant differences between the two agencies. One agency achieved a benefit:cost ratio of 0.50 meaning that it generated savings equal to half its costs over the two-year period, while the other agency achieved a much lower return with a ratio of only 0.07. This was primarily due to a difference in the proportion of jobs which were full-time, with the former having a much higher representation of full-time working than the latter. This led to the former generating higher rates of financial savings through tax paid by and reduced welfare benefit payments to workers, and reduced expenditure on other day services.

Quality of life outcomes

Research carried out in the USA paints a favourable picture of supported employment in terms of integration in the workplace and increased self-esteem and greater financial independence. In Wales, our research has indicated that supported workers experienced significantly higher levels of occupation at work compared to their previous day placements and compared to similar adults attending ATCs. Supported workers were on average engaged in activity for 86% of the time. By contrast, individuals in ATCs spent between 60–70% of their time occupied. Encouragingly, the engagement levels of supported workers were similar to those of workers without disabilities (Beyer, Kilsby and Willson, 1995).

Individuals in day centres spent more of their time in social interaction than those at work. The main reason for this was the extent of direction from staff which people in day centres received compared to supported workers. This implies that individual participation within day centres was more reliant on staff supervision and that those involved acted less independently. There may be a number of reasons for this, including the fact that ATC activities are frequently justified by their developmental or recreational value. As a consequence, they tend to be more diverse and changeable throughout the day and more frequently involve some aspect of novelty. Work routines on the other hand tend to be more consistent and repetitious. Once they are learned, supported workers appear to rely little on directions from supervisors to carry them out.

Over 70% of interactions occurring within ATCs were with care staff and only a small proportion were with non-disabled people. The majority of interactions supported workers had were with non-disabled co-workers and a considerable proportion involved members of the public. This suggests that supported employment promoted interactions with a wider range of people who were less directly associated with services.

Building a new pattern of day opportunities: strengths, weaknesses and the potential of different forms of provision

Counties varied greatly in their approach to day services and to the priority given to developing different alternatives to traditional day centres. Two counties, for example, provided major grants to enable the voluntary sector to build up supported employment. One county focused on developing community businesses, as well as offering supported employment. Another had established small local resource units and yet another CFSs which catered for specific groups of users (McGrath, 1994).

A comprehensive day opportunity service will include opportunities for work experience, social skills and vocational training and support in open employment. It will need to cater for the whole range of abilities. In addition, the leisure and family needs of service users need to be addressed either as part of the same or a separate service. How far the alternative models of day occupation described above provide a contribution to the overall pattern of day services needs to be assessed.

Supported open employment gradually increased over the life of the Strategy. In principle, and particularly with regard to the principles of the AWS, it is against this model that the other alternative day opportunities should be judged. In providing work in typical settings, supported employment has the potential to offer as wide a range of opportunities as exist in the community as a whole. This potential provides considerable flexibility to match employment to individual needs and aspirations. This breadth is greater than in the other employment focused schemes because the latter tend to concentrate on enterprises with a high proportion of entry-level jobs within them. For example, there is a heavy preponderance of horticultural or related activities, and cafes and other concerns involving food production among EFSs. This was particularly true of training or training and employment schemes, especially those in rural areas. Community businesses, found more commonly in urban areas, presented a far wider range of work possibilities and are more comparable to supported employment in this respect, although they too will tend to concentrate on activities requiring only entry-level skills.

However, supported employment schemes have in general been no more successful than the EFSs in catering for people with special needs or in providing remuneration above the earnings disregard limit. Furthermore, unlike many of the EFSs, particularly community businesses, supported open employment has usually provided only part-time jobs.

One of the major strengths of the CFSs was the provision of a service to people with special needs, often excluded from EFSs, although attenders with special needs were more likely to be individuals with profound or multiple disabilities than those with challenging behaviour. The CFSs service was likely to be for five days a week. It was, therefore, one which took account of the respite needs of carers. The best demonstrated a potential for improving the community integration of this group of users. The needs of older service users, targeted in one county, may be more appropriately met by seeking placements in community social activities for older people (Grant, McGrath and Ramcharan, 1995).

CFSs provided a framework for responding to the educational, leisure and work experience needs of service users within the context of a small group and local community. Whether this range of needs should be met by one service or, as in the wider community, by separate services is open to debate. The main problem facing many CFSs was how to provide a quality service with inadequate accommodation, poor facilities and insufficient staff for accompanying attenders in the community while maintaining acceptable staff:attender ratios in the base (McGrath, 1994).

The role of training schemes has been questioned by those advocating a 'place and train' model, particularly for service users with high dependency levels. However, training schemes can provide valuable work experience and specific training for service users with mild or moderate levels of disability who are more able to transfer learned skills to different situations. In addition, training schemes can be designed to meet the local job market. The 'ideal' training scheme prioritized vocational training and work preparation, emphasized social skills training, tended to operate a fixed period of attendance and enabled attenders to move either to some form of employment or to further education. The best schemes had found some way of continuing to offer some service to attenders for whom a further placement had not been found.

Community businesses have the potential to provide long-term sheltered employment for individuals who would have difficulty finding or surviving in open employment. There are a small number of individuals with intractable behaviour or personal problems for whom a small structured scheme may be the only available possibility. Community businesses also offered an alternative to people waiting for open employment. Vulnerability to closure was a drawback of some of the smaller schemes with only one or two staff. The relatively narrow range of activities available in rural areas was a problem in establishing a viable small business niche.

The community business model could be exploited more fully than has occurred to date. To do so requires an understanding of not only learning disability but also commerce and business development. Some schemes were virtually self-financing, although the level of subsidy they received was thought to be essential. There were indications that the most financially successful appeared to be those where the ratio of workers without disabilities to those with disability was high. Issues of size and vulnerability can be overcome where an overall management organization develops and coordinates several businesses. This can offer the additional advantage of shared training of staff and volunteers.

The potential conflict between training and employment was often raised by managers of the training/employment schemes and has been noted by other commentators (e.g. Van Calster, 1992). Either clearer operational policies were required with a definite split between the two roles or these hybrid schemes needed to focus more fully on one role. In some cases the development of a supported employment service would enable the training role to become predominant. In others, an easing of local authority regulations would enable scheme managers to adopt a more entrepreneurial approach.

Supported volunteering schemes can provide useful experience but are not an appropriate long-term solution for people looking for employment. In addition, they usually only offer a one or two day placement a week. However, community integration and offering a service to the community are seen as strengths and, although not remunerated, the schemes give users the status of making a worthwhile contribution to others.

The Community Care legislation has led social services departments to split their purchaser and provider roles and to put more efforts into supporting independent sector services. The voluntary sector has played a vital and important part in developing EFSs but this sector has faced great difficulties in securing adequate and long-term funding. There is scope to enhance these developments in the context of a comprehensive day service plan. Contracts between social services departments and independent sector schemes were established as block contracts to provide a specified number of places. Placements associated with hospital resettlement have been funded on an individual basis. The establishment of care management principles building on the individual planning structures of the Strategy should enable more detailed and flexible plans and funding to be arranged.

Many of the outcomes from employment are constrained by the effects of the welfare benefit system. Realistically, liberalization of the welfare benefit system will not come soon. If the opportunity of employment is to be extended to those for whom constraints make full-time employment unrealistic at present, then agencies need to strike a balance between the extent of full-time and part-time working they support. They need also to be better able to respond to the needs of people with higher levels of disability. Funders need to be clear about the people they want to see supported, and the level of cost:benefit they expect as a result of their decisions.

References

Beyer, S., Goodere, L. and Kilsby, M. (1996). *The Costs and Benefits of Supported Employment Agencies*. London: The Stationary Office.

Beyer, S., Kilsby, M. and Lowe, K. (1994). What do ATCs offer? A survey of Welsh day services. *Mental Handicap Research*, **7**, 16–40.

Beyer, S., Kilsby, M. and Willson, C. (1995). Interaction and engagement of workers in supported employment: a British comparison between workers with and without learning disabilities. *Mental Handicap Research*, **8**, 137–155.

Beyer, S., Todd, S. and Felce, D. (1991). The Implementation of the All Wales Mental Handicap Strategy. *Mental Handicap Research*, **42**, 115–140.

Beyer, S., Evans, G., Todd, S. and Blunden, R. (1986). *Planning for the All-Wales Strategy: a Review of Issues Arising in Welsh Counties*. Cardiff: Mental Handicap in Wales Applied Research Unit, University of Wales College of Medicine.

Department of Health and Social Security (DHSS) (1971). *Better Services for the Mentally Handicapped*. London: HMSO.

Evans, G., Beyer, S., Todd, S. and Blunden, R. (1986). Planning for the All-Wales Strategy. *Mental Handicap*, **14**, 108–110.

Evans, G., Todd, S., Beyer, S. *et al.* (1994). Assessing the impact of the All-Wales Mental Handicap Strategy: a survey of four districts. *Journal of Intellectual Disability Research*, **38**, 109–133.

Grant, G., McGrath, M. and Ramcharan, P. (1995). Community inclusion of older people with learning disabilities. *Care in Place: The International Journal of Networks and Community*, **2**, 28–44.

King's Fund (1984). *An Ordinary Working Life*. London: King's Fund Centre.

McGrath, M. (1994). *Alternative Day Opportunities for People with a Learning Disability: a Welsh Audit*. Bangor: Centre for Social Policy Research and Development, University of Wales Bangor.

McGrath, M. (1996a). *Employment Focused Day Services for People with a Learning Disability in Wales: an Overview of Provision*. Bangor: Centre for Social Policy Research and Development, University of Wales Bangor.

McGrath, M. (1996b). *Employment Focused Day Services for People with a Learning Disability in Wales: Problems, Achievements and Potential*. Bangor: Centre for Social Policy Research and Development, University of Wales Bangor.

Mencap (1985). *Day Services Today and Tomorrow: Mencap's Vision of Daytime Services for People with a Mental Handicap.* London: Royal Society for Mentally Handicapped Children and Adults.

National Development Group (1977). *Pamphlet no. 5: Day Services for Mentally Handicapped Adults.* London: HMSO.

Nisbet, J. and Callahan, M. J. (1987). Achieving success in integrated workplaces: critical elements in assisting persons with severe disabilities. In: *Community Integration for People with Severe Disabilities*, (S. T. Taylor, D. Biklen and J. Knoll, eds) pp. 184–201. New York: Teachers College Press.

Office of Health Economics (1986). *Mental Handicap: Partnership in the Community?* London: Office of Health Economics/Mencap.

Perry, J., Beyer, S., Felce, D. and Todd, S. (1998). Strategic service change: development of core services in Wales, 1983–95. *Journal of Applied Research in Intellectual Disabilities*, **11**, 15–33.

Rusch, F. R. (1986). *Competitive Employment: Issues and Strategies*. Baltimore: Paul H. Brookes.

Seed, P. (1988). *Day Care at the Crossroads*. Tunbridge Wells: Costello.

Social Services Inspectorate (1989). *Inspection of Day Services for People with a Mental Handicap.* London: HMSO.

Van Calster, L. (1992). Transition from school to work. A Belgian experiment dealing with work rehabilitation. In: *Innovations in Employment Training and Work for People with Learning Disabilities*, (R. McConkey and P. McGinley, eds) pp. 63–76. Chorley, Lancs: Lisieux Hall.

Welsh Office (1983). *The All Wales Strategy for the Development of Services for Mentally Handicapped People.* Cardiff: Welsh Office.

Whelan, E. and Speake, B. (1977). *Adult Training Centres in England and Wales.* Manchester: National Association of Teachers of the Mentally Handicapped.

Chapter 9

The impact of the AWS: taking stock and looking to the future

In looking to summarize the strengths and weaknesses of the AWS, there can be no doubt that the AWS reflected a genuine commitment to progressive philosophies and values. Central government backed that commitment by leadership and resources. Arrangements were established in the Health and Social Policy Division of the Welsh Office to manage policy implementation and the promised financial investment was more than delivered. There was a genuine desire to see people with learning disabilities and their carers receive the support necessary to enjoy a better quality of life. Similarly, there can be no doubt that the AWS was founded on the principles, service prescriptions and administrative arrangements that advisory bodies and campaigners for reform wanted to see. It reflected much conventional wisdom in its definition of a comprehensive service, its role for local authorities, its ring-fenced funding arrangements and the acknowledged need to achieve a higher priority for learning disability concerns throughout the political and service system. The AWS established patronage for learning disabilities and sponsored the progressive view against the more traditional.

Prior to the AWS, learning disabilities had been an impoverished service. It had no power and no political voice. The AWS was the key to unlock the political power and the will and attitudes to change things. If there had been no strategy, learning disabilities would have still been competing with the elderly, child and mental health services, and would have been bottom of the order for resources. Without the resources we wouldn't have been able to change anything.

The AWS encouraged commitment to a field. Prior to 1983, all available resources, and there wasn't much, were used in a reactive way. The AWS gave us the scope to change and create. It created a common viewpoint.

The founding principles of the AWS – the rights for all people with learning disabilities to normal patterns of life within the community, to be treated as individuals and to receive additional help from their communities and from professional services – provided a vision of what was to be achieved and fostered a common rationale for service development. Access to generic services was to be promoted with a view that people's needs should be met by services available to the general public whenever possible. Helping people to make decisions was not seen as the sole responsibility of professionals, but was broadened to a range of relevant others and by extension to society as a whole. In this connection, one could see the AWS as moving towards the adoption of a community treatment model (Abrams, 1978) in which the capacity of individuals to become respected members of the community ultimately lies with families, friends and the community. Services have a role to play in helping communities to become more competent in responding to the needs of minority members with disabilities, but they cannot successfully replace the natural contexts and networks which constitute communities, a point we argue in greater detail in the next chapter.

However, it is difficult to say how much the AWS, the 'bold and imaginative proposals for a radical new service in Wales' (Audit Commission, 1987, p. 8), changed the course or pace of learning disability service development. As reported at various stages in this book, progress in developing new community-based services was uneven. It would be easy to adopt the stance that the 'AWS-as-practice' failed to live up to its own rhetoric or the extensiveness of its service reform agenda. However, what policy of widespread organizational change ever can deliver all that the most hopeful or ambitious proponent of change might expect? The AWS has served as the closest expression in UK policy of the leading edge of radical reform, an agenda which has been refined over time. It would be too much to expect those charged with implementing policy to manage change so well that they were able to keep service development in line with the pace of changing ideas while maintaining widespread popular support for evolving courses of action. As views typically diverge, uncertainty and conflict about the nature and correct course of service development are inevitable. It is unrealistic to assess the achievements of the AWS against a naive and apolitical view of social change. For all its implicit ideological intent, the AWS had relatively straightforward objectives to provide networks of professional, individual planning, housing, respite and domiciliary support services in every locality, to diversify the range of day occupation for adults, to support existing educational policies and to do whatever could be done by indirect means to encourage enhanced awareness of learning disability in generic services and communities in general. It also endorsed greater consultation with and involvement of consumers and their representatives. It is by its effectiveness in delivering these more practical aims that it should be judged. Even here, policy implementation cannot be expected to be perfect. There are real tensions between trying to press forward at the leading edge and creating a more general readiness to deliver change within the agencies on whose competence success depends.

Progress under the AWS

One way of attempting to assess whether such a committed strategy had any impact on the nature or pace of change is through comparison of service trends in Wales with those elsewhere. The most significant point of comparison is with the rest of the UK, particularly with England as it shared a common policy framework with Wales up until 1983. However, the lack of available comparative data often prevents a firm conclusion as to the distinctiveness of development in Wales. The following provides a broad summary of the contribution of the AWS:

1 Wales has achieved a more wholehearted transition from health to local authority commissioning of social care services. Many NHS Trusts in England still provide residential care and other services unrelated to health care as core areas of business. Therefore, disappointing though the pace of early reform in Wales may have been and stuttering though its subsequent progress, the frustrations of creating joint agency collaboration may have been worthwhile.

> Positively, it has got us away from the medical model to a more humanistic approach.
> There is a clearer definition now of who's responsible for what and it's really helped clarify that what went on before was not appropriate. ... The people who we work with are people with a learning disability but we're only interested in doing business for them concerning health related problems. Dealing with social care is the job of the lead agency so I don't have any problem with that – it's probably helped firm up how we should move forward. It's helped clarify roles and I'm happier to let people do what they're trained to do rather than to hold onto other people's jobs.

2 The development of MCTs in Wales was rapid. It followed similar development in England and could therefore be construed as catching up, at least initially. It is not known whether the professional infrastructure is now better established or organized in Wales than elsewhere. Individual Planning as a means of service coordination and review grew in Wales, but was only ever available to a minority of service users. Whether it was more or less available in England is not known.

3 Consumer representation in planning at local and county levels was established throughout Wales in a way that probably cannot be said for England as a whole. Consumer involvement in the management and review of service quality has grown. It is not known whether this is more common in Wales than in England. Nor is it known whether the various forms of citizen or self advocacy have become more widespread or firmly established or whether they have had more of an impact on service development or on the quality of life of service users. Citizen advocacy remains at a low level in Wales in any case.

4 Deinstitutionalization progressed more slowly in Wales than in England up to the early 1990s but it has accelerated subsequently. The final stages of deinstitutionalization from all but one hospital in Wales should be achieved in the next five years. Such changes are in keeping with a general pattern of reform in Europe and North America (Hatton, Emerson and Kiernan, 1995; Emerson *et al.*, 1996). The rate of provision of residential services was relatively low in Wales compared to England at the beginning of the 1980s and service coverage did not increase during the AWS (Emerson and Hatton, 1996; Ericsson and Mansell, 1996; Perry *et al.*, 1998).

5 However, reform has been more radical on the whole in Wales than elsewhere in the UK. Wales has made a more uniform commitment to a small ordinary housing model in the wake of deinstitutionalization than, for example, has England. Community settings provided by local

authorities and the independent sector in Wales had average residential groups of just over four and just under three respectively. The character of English services was very different. English local authorities operated 660 staffed homes in 1995, serving 8544 residents in groups of just under 13 on average (Department of Health, 1996). They had no 'small' homes with fewer than four places (Department of Health, 1996). In addition, there were a total of 5172 staffed homes in the independent sector in England in 1995 which served 29 539 people in average residential groups of six (Department of Health, 1996). Such differences may be related to differences in assessed quality. Compared to a random sample of services in England (Raynes *et al.*, 1994), conducted at about the same time as our evaluation of housing services in South Wales, the houses we studied were smaller and more individually-oriented, allowed more choice and promoted greater community integration (see Perry and Felce, 1994). Community integration also compared favourably to that reported by Knapp *et al.* (1992) for the English Care in the Community demonstration projects.

6   The development of family aide and respite services was a high priority of the AWS. The number of individuals and families receiving domiciliary support worker input has grown substantially. It is not known whether comparable growth has occurred in England, but it is perhaps less likely given the strong deinstitutionalization emphasis to English policy. However, developing respite services has been a priority throughout Britain. According to the second national survey of family-based respite care (Beckford and Robinson, 1993; with additional information from Robinson, personal communication), Wales had more family-based respite care services in ratio to population (9.0 per million) than the UK as a whole (5.8 per million), although they were biased more towards children (25 services to 1) than in the UK generally (257 children's services to 74 for adults). The same source estimated that 9821 children and 2960 adults received some family-based respite care in the UK in 1992 (a combined rate of 22.4 per 100 000 total population). The number of Welsh users in 1995 was 739 (a rate of 25.5 per 100 000 total population).

7   Day service reform may also have progressed differentially. Indicators by which to compare how services have changed are not readily available due to the nature of the reform and the proliferation of sessional attendance at a wide range of activities, often organized from the traditional centre base. A few Adult Training Centres or Social Education Centres have been completely reprovided and the old centres closed in both countries. A greater use of colleges of further education and an increased emphasis on work and community-based activity have been general but not universal trends. However, it is clear from national surveys that supported employment in Wales has grown more rapidly than in England in ratio to population.

I think there has been a huge development of services, especially around the late 80s. There are more people living independently, greater home support and respite care. The Parents' Forum has given people not only support but a voice. There has been the development of employment services and link courses with FE colleges.

The above shows that there were some areas where progress in Wales seems to have been more extensive or more surely founded than elsewhere in the UK. As a strategy of service reform, it has had a measure of success. In principle, the AWS extended the right to normal patterns of life in the community to all people with learning disabilities. Reform of specialist services and the provision of new forms of specialist support were the main means for achieving such an outcome; 'the concept of new patterns of comprehensive services lies at the heart of the strategy' (Welsh Office, 1983, para. 4.1). While few would dispute the importance of specialist services, many would now see families, friends and the community itself as equally important and essential players in any strategy which sought to help individuals become respected members of their communities. Despite the effort to direct resources to family support, the strategic targeting of friends, neighbours, community groups or other communities of interest under the AWS was less in evidence. At the individual casework level, attention was of course given by MCT workers to ways of linking individuals to people from such interest groups, but there has been and remains a heavy dependence on service supports. The absence of any systematic strategy for enlisting more general community support to broaden people's social networks may be seen as a missed opportunity to increase community participation. Social networks perform many functions for people: the provision of physical and emotional support; a buffer against stress; protection of interests; and the transmission and shaping of values, attitudes and social norms (Gourash, 1978). If people with learning disabilities continue to remain devoid of friends and isolated from community groups, they will be deprived of these advantages of community living and be less able to *be* part of the community. This issue raises questions about the fundamental definition of community care and the proper purview of services to enhance the community's capacity to provide a typical quality of life for its most disabled members rather than inventing parallel worlds and substitute communities. We return to this in the next chapter.

Access to the generic world was recognized as an important goal of the AWS and the use of generic services was to be promoted. However, it is probably true to say that the specialist/generic debate has never been satisfactorily concluded. On the one hand, one might question how people can be integrated into the community if they are largely dependent on specialist services which are segregated by nature. On the other hand, there is reasonable doubt as to whether generic services and agencies possess the expertise and commitment necessary to help people in the best possible way. Specialist services may become obstacles to the very outcomes that they are trying to achieve and yet they can also provide protection from the devaluation, neglect and abuse which might otherwise be a more common part of people's experience. A compromise which seeks to provide specialism, but in the least special way possible, might provide the best solution to an apparent paradox.

For example, Chapter 6 illustrated the strides made in creating the opportunity for adults with learning disabilities to be householders and order their domestic lives. However, access to genuinely normal patterns of living remains difficult to achieve. Property ownership is the most common option for the general population and marriage or cohabitation with a similarly aged peer the typical state. Both of these options are extremely rare for people with learning disabilities, although both can occur. Despite the significant shift in the scale of communal living to household units approximating those of the general population, a genuine achievement in itself, segregated living is still the norm and likely to continue. The active participation of people with severe learning disabilities in local community life and the broadening of their social networks to include many age peers without disabilities have not commonly been achieved. People with learning disabilities may choose to live with one or two other people with learning disabilities, or to live alone – an arrangement which may enable services to claim falsely that they no longer segregate – but they rarely have the option to live in a peer and reciprocal relationship with people without disabilities. However, specialist services have moved to arranging what they provide in less special ways. Ordinary housing, domestic-scale groupings, locations in ordinary residential areas, the involvement of housing associations, tenancy arrangements and changing staff identities have all contributed to this.

The AWS also extended the right for people to be treated as individuals and, although recognizing that there was no universally applicable formula for addressing the needs and capacities of everyone, it recommended that everyone should have a form of needs assessment and an opportunity to play a full part in decisions intended to help them. In their various forms, individual planning systems represented a key mechanism and considerable time and creativity were invested in Wales in designing and piloting such systems. However, as we have already commented, coverage was limited. Further, the intention was for the individual plan to provide a regular and ongoing opportunity to review progress, reassess needs or preferences, reset directions and set new short-, medium- and long-term goals. Even when individual plans occurred, such consistency was not always achieved. Planning might begin for an individual and then not be sustained. Alternatively, it might be conducted episodically as issues requiring discussion arose in a way similar to the traditional case conference. There have also been inevitable difficulties in fostering meaningful participation of service users in decision-making. One possible strategy for independent representation of the views of those unable to speak for themselves – citizen advocacy – was and remains in restricted supply. The Conservative Government's refusal to implement all the provisions of the Disabled Persons (Services, Consultation and Representation) Act 1986, Sections 1, 2 and 3 in particular, signalled that representation of the needs of disabled people was not high on the political agenda, despite the rhetoric of stated policy and strong and continued lobbying from the disability movement. Knowledge about the best ways to involve people in making plans and taking decisions about their lives was not widespread in 1983, but it is probably true to say that the AWS helped to set an agenda where these issues were taken much more seriously than before. There are now examples of people with learning disabilities being involved in the design and management of services, recruitment and training of staff, quality assurance and service evaluation, even if they remain uncommon in practice.

The third AWS principle – the right to additional help from the community and professional services – was predicated on ideas about helping people to develop their maximum potential as individuals. In pinpointing the impact of services on individuals, the AWS underlined the importance of outcome as the ultimate criterion of the adequacy of their design and operation. The emphasis on achieving typical or valued lifestyles, personal development and roles in society has increased throughout the AWS years, particularly in the widespread adoption within the mission statements of services of the Five Essential Service Accomplishments (O'Brien, 1987): community presence; community participation; competence; choice; and respect. Our research on the outcomes of housing, domiciliary or community support services, day services and supported employment has highlighted the progress made and the ambition of these objectives. The AWS has been a step in reform, but considerable further progress is required before such broad quality of life goals can be considered reasonably achieved. Part of the contribution of the AWS has been to make services open to scrutiny and to break a narrow professional viewpoint that traditional service structures, arrangements and processes were not only the best, but also the only possible means of responding to what were seen as largely intractable problems. The disruption of professional hegemony was a starting point to a greater openness in service planning. Such openness permitted parents and users to play a bigger role in shaping the delivery of support both locally and nationally.

The nature of service support has continued to evolve as knowledge and experience have increased. Realization that the provision of 'an ordinary house, in an ordinary street with ordinary staff' did not guarantee the quality of support which people needed to live a productive home and community life has been a widely appreciated lesson. The investment in changing thinking, attitudes and values in line with AWS principles has been considerable and probably worthwhile. However, experience has shown that changing practice requires more direct and competency-led input. If specialist services do have a unique role in providing help to people with disabilities, then it is because they work with people in special ways, ways which effectively ameliorate the disabling effects of people's impairments. Making sure that the newly provided services have such competencies is an important sequel to the structural change already undertaken. Further, some innovations more widely available in other countries from an earlier time, such as supported employment, gained ground in Wales only towards the end of the AWS. This undoubtedly helps to explain the continued relatively modest access people with learning disabilities have to paid employment. Continued structural reform of outmoded services is still necessary. Moreover, the AWS did not clarify all of the major policy decisions which affect people with learning disabilities. The relative merits and disadvantages of education in specialist or mainstream schools continues to divide teachers, parents and commentators. The AWS did singularly little to resolve this issue.

Whither comprehensiveness?

The AWS embraced the concept of comprehensiveness which had emerged and been elaborated in Britain throughout the previous decade. Comprehensiveness implied an adequate range and supply of services to meet different types of need and an equality of service coverage in ratio to population. Yet, there is clear evidence and a widespread perception that change in service provision has neither been uniform across Wales nor evenly distributed within the former counties. For example, rates of residential provision across the former counties in 1994/5 varied between 60 and 214 places per 100 000 total population, an inequality which has given the recently created 22 unitary authorities very different service inheritances. Our survey of traditional day centres in Wales illustrated the variability in the programmes of activity offered and the extent to which services had become more community or work oriented. The coverage of virtually all services remained below comprehensive levels. Viewed at a national level, there was a diversity of service provision, but people did not have choice. Indeed, what and whether services were available for the individual remained a lottery determined by place of residence.

That the AWS had not resulted in a comprehensive pattern of services by this stage is not in itself surprising. A total resource framework for the AWS was given in the original Working Party report (Welsh Office, 1982). The Working Party recognized that nothing other than marginal growth could come from local authorities and central funding was identified as the only realistic option. The target of reaching an additional annually recurring investment of £26 million (at 1983 prices) by the end of the first ten years was to bring expenditure on learning disability services up to only half the level which the Working Party estimated as necessary to see their plan realized. In other words, further investment of twice that amount would be required to finish the job. The constraint on additional central resourcing after 1993 and its narrow focus on achieving hospital closure did not appear to stem either from an openly stated reappraisal of the original AWS goals or from a rational assessment of how much of the envisaged service reform had been achieved. Rather, it seemed to stem from changed political priorities – a sense, in the face of restrictions on the public purse, that learning disability had had a privileged status long enough. It is interesting in this connection that regional strategies in England have had similar shelf lives: from the mid-1960s to the late 1970s in Wessex and from the early 1980s into the 1990s in the North West and South East Thames. Key personnel change, organizational memories are short, knowledge and strategy are imperfectly communicated across changing personnel, and direction and commitment become more vague.

Although we have explored why it became necessary, the late policy and funding focus on resettlement was seen by some as evidence of such diluted commitment to the full vision of the AWS. The attempt to achieve widescale reform quickly was also seen as giving rise to a lack of further development or refinement of service models. The scale of investment in resettlement implied less development for people living in the community. To some, the needs of carers and their relatives were going largely unrecognized and unmet.

I think hospital closure has hi-jacked the AWS.

It would have been helpful to have models of good practice and . . . (more) ideas . . . after about four or five years somebody, somewhere managed to set up a production line for group homes and they started to drop off the conveyor belt at a rapid rate. There was no more about individual needs than in the old style of solution. It was just that the production process had been amended slightly.

All people should have the right to ordinary housing. What will happen to our son when we die?

One failure of the Strategy was that there was not enough long-term planning to consider the needs of people who were born in the community and stayed in the community and so we had an imbalance of services.

An absence of strategic service planning and total resource management contributed to the sense that the AWS had been characterized by shifting priorities and opening and closing windows of opportunity for individuals and their families. Potentially, local strategic plans could have been initially based on the AWS Working Party projections and updated year by year. The use of the finance available could have been related to a progressive implementation of elements of these plans in a way which could have preserved equity between competing priorities and territories, and constrained the costs of new service elements within limits set by the overall resource framework. However, the AWS became dominated by discrete project or service proposals. Some commentators have suggested that its financing assumptions and allocation procedures were not conducive to strategic planning, but encouraged haste. Difficulties of coordinating large, multiagency joint planning groups were also identified as contributing to poor strategic planning and the absence of a comprehensive view. Failure to estimate need at the population level or to aggregate assessed individual need meant that AWS proposals were developed expediently, particularly in the initial years. Those counties whose initial project proposals were perceived to be more closely aligned to AWS principles were given a greater share of funding. Later, funding became linked to total population. Therefore, although allocations were lower in the first years than later, the influx of early funding and its uneven distribution throughout Wales contributed towards an imbalance in service provision which was not corrected. Sufficient funding to sustain service development at the trajectory set was not forthcoming. Evidence of escalating costs within proposals put to the Welsh Office towards the end of the first phase of the AWS contributed to the restriction of its future scope.

What we seem to have is a patchwork of uncoordinated schemes . . . does it result in providing the services the community needs?

I think the way the planning group was seen as the custodian of the plan probably had an impact. There were about 40–50 people on it and it's very hard to talk sensibly about strategic direction and resolve complex issues in a group that large, with individuals putting forward their own priority and a sort of 'horse trading' occurring . . . plans were assembled from the bids that came forward (according to) the pressure that individuals or . . . groups were applying rather than from a planning group actually saying 'This is the strategy – this is the level of services that we require to cover say respite care or to deal with pressures of people with mental health problems'.

When someone comes to our planning group with a proposal there's nothing in their proposals about how services might be integrated in a coherent package.

There's nothing about how they will (affect) mainstream funding. . . . The AWS has always been treated as something separate in social services and we've never developed an account of how all this money fits together into a comprehensive coherent pattern of local services. . . . If the AWS has failed in anything, it's failed in its strategic functions. Everyone sees it as a bit of extra cash. The intentions were there. We had the money, the plans and the commitment, but it all went wrong in terms of a strategy. . . . It's been a great pity that the huge surge of goodwill in the early days has been dissipated and a lot of good work and effort is being undone because we never had the skills or the motivation for strategic planning. The money we had might not have been enough to take us to the end, but I think we could've done a lot better.

The best way I can describe it is that it is like having the rug pulled from under you, one minute you are being told that the aim is to provide better services, the next you are being told that there is not enough money.

Financial rationing has added uncertainty to how things will work out in the future.

The early years of the AWS saw the funding of schemes for children in the expansion of pre-school home teaching, family-based respite, domiciliary support services and locally-available short-term care. However, as policies to prevent the admission of children to traditional residential services predated the AWS, the reprovision of hospitals and hostels mainly concerned adults. The growing concentration on resettlement, together with the increased emphasis on reforming adult day services meant that the AWS became seen as an adult strategy in its later years. Such a perception was strengthened by the failure to develop a comprehensive perspective on children caused by the consistently marginal role which education authorities played within the AWS. Consideration of the future of special school provision was no greater than would have occurred anyway as a result of the 1981 Education Act and more general shifts in thinking. The needs of children during their years of schooling tended to be overlooked as if relevant concerns were being dealt with by educational services. Therapeutic and support services and housing adaptations for this age group fared less well at times under the AWS than might have been expected.

I'd have to say that education should've been dragged in a lot earlier. We sat on the fence for a long time, but I suppose that's all you could've expected. We thought the AWS wasn't our ball park and that there was no real money to attract us into it. The main emphasis went on adults. The situation of children got lost somewhere I think. The education side of things didn't get a look in. . . . So it was a chance lost in terms of the AWS being a comprehensive strategy. If the AWS was about cradle to grave services, somebody made a mistake leaving us out.

The therapeutic needs of adults came first. . . . Getting adaptations in the home is a really big thing for children. . . . Their equipment needs change every year because they're growing. But their needs should be dealt with when they are younger not when they're adults.

This sense of incomplete and patchy development has an obvious corollary that some individuals and families benefited from the AWS and others did not. Precisely who benefited and in what ways they benefited varied from county to county. Our research has not been specific enough to trace these effects in detail. During the first half of the AWS, individuals and families living in the community felt that their opportunities were expanding. Individuals were offered support in the home and a greater chance than before of residential support outside of the family home. Those already living in community residential services had more chance to move to smaller ordinary housing services. Individuals also began to see their daytime opportunities grow and become more varied. However, those who remained in hospital received little benefit from the AWS; there is even some evidence that their activities and social worlds contracted (Evans *et al.*, 1994).

The diversification of daytime opportunities was sustained in the second half of the AWS but, in other respects, the window of opportunity for people living in the community closed again. It was clearly necessary for the AWS to affect the lives of people living in traditional institutions, arguably the most deprived and in need of change. However, the sustained switch in priorities has created a widely reported build-up of need in the community from school-leavers and adults requiring day services and the opportunity to leave home. The balance between institutional and community-based 'gainers' and 'non-gainers' from the AWS seems to have tilted one way and then the other. Moreover, while some people's circumstances have clearly improved greatly during the years of the AWS, others will have barely been touched at all. Included in the latter are the 700 or so people who have lived in institutional care throughout the period, many of whom have the greatest difficulties and disabilities, as well as people living with their families with little support and either not receiving day services or attending traditional centres. Overall, family carers receive more support now, but little has occurred to alter the prospective length of time for which they will care for their offspring with disabilities, four decades on average and five or six decades for a substantial minority. The dilemma facing parents of what will happen to their offspring when they are unable to continue caring is likely to remain as acute as ever.

Strategic implications

If the strategic implementation of the AWS failed to match its comprehensive intent, why was this so? Probably the reasons lie in that set of factors which we discussed in Chapter 3. The visionary nature of the AWS may have been overstated, but it set a radical reform agenda nonetheless. Building support for radical change in local service agencies and among consumers, their representatives and communities at large takes time, particularly in an area that historically has had a low public and political profile. Large scale reform also takes preparation and competent execution. The local authorities were given responsibilities that they had not undertaken before. Although ideologically sympathetic to change, they had neither a strong track record nor in-depth experience in providing the type of services which the AWS heralded. Indeed, such was the initial planning and operational competence gap that some authorities had only just begun to respond to the scale of the task at an appropriate rate when the AWS was given a more restricted focus. As we have discussed, the establishment of a joint agency approach also took time.

With the benefit of hindsight, there was a clear need for a reasonably extended preparation period to allow local agencies to get ready for implementing the changes which were to come. This would have involved garnering local consumer and political support, creating relevant competency (particularly within the lead agency), establishing planning arrangements, establishing the prerequisites for local comprehensive service specification, and setting out strategic service development milestones and costings to indicate the build-up of different types of service in constituent localities. There was an awareness in the Welsh Office that preparation and a lead-in time were necessary. The Vanguard Area proposal reflected the realization that nothing less than a national experiment was being initiated and the proposed phasing of the AWS finance recognized that investment demands in the first years would be lower. However, the extent to which the available funding began to drive the implementation of ill-prepared plans was not foreseen. It is clearly difficult to announce a political initiative without backing it with funding. Any equivocation over investment is interpreted as a lack of commitment. Yet, it is arguable that better use would have been made of AWS resources had there been a planned delay until local authorities were in a proper state of readiness to implement agreed reform. This would have allowed the Welsh Office to have monitored progress against strategic intent as well as conformity to the AWS values base. That the Vanguard Area proposal did not work only adds strength to this proposition.

Looking ahead: the long-term influence of the community care legislation and the impact of local government reorganization

Although the AWS started life as a distinctive policy, it was not isolated from other policy developments which affected England and Wales, or Britain as a whole. Most significant were the global changes in the organization of health and social care embodied in the NHS and Community Care Act. Although interpretable as echoing AWS values in its rhetoric of promoting individual choice and independence, its stress on individualized service arrangements and the granting of lead agency status with regard to social care to local authorities, it brought with it other changes and contributed to the erosion of learning disabilities as a separate policy focus. The new organizational arrangements resulting from the Act were a disruptive influence upon planning groups and the working relationships within them. In turn, this threatened the voice which consumers had developed in planning and changed the role of voluntary organizations from partners to potential contractors in a competitive market. The balance of power in future planning was shifted. Care assessment was resource-led in comparison to the needs orientation of earlier individual planning and professionally dominated.

The power of an assessment is held by a care manager. They decide, they can assess needs, they can decide whether you are eligible for a community care assessment.

In Shared Individual Planning, the way we'd always worked, eligibility wasn't an issue, people received services who needed them.

Parents and carers have said to me that at the end of the day the care manager goes away saying 'Now we know what you want but you can't have it'.

The impact of the Community Care changes was initially qualified by the traditions and breadth of resource investment of the AWS. These seemed to provide a buffer to the implementation of learning disability policy coming into line with more general community care policies. However, such a buffer was only temporary. The slimmed down and more tightly focused second phase of the AWS restricted the special status of learning disabilities to resettlement. Other developments had to come through community care arrangements. Moreover, local government reorganization also contributed to a loss of distinctiveness for learning disabilities and a break-up of experienced planning and officer teams, just at the time when it was evident that the Welsh Office had withdrawn from leading the AWS from the centre. With local politicians in new authorities and structures ill-prepared to assume leadership, the AWS moved into a political void where recent gains are vulnerable.

Local government reorganization created 22 unitary authorities in the place of the previous eight counties. In a country of under three million people, many of these have a small population base. They inherited disparities in services, not only in learning disabilities but across the community care concerns. Whereas most previous counties had learning disabilities represented within Social Services Departments at Assistant Director level as a separate specialism, new authority structures combined community care groups and specialism in learning disabilities was carried forward only at more junior levels. Even then, reorganization fragmented the previous specialist personnel infrastructure. There are considerable fears that initial service imbalances and budget pressures will combine with the fact that learning disabilities is again subject to prioritization within a more generic assessment framework to result in an end to development or even a reversal of fortune. The special status of learning disabilities under the AWS has resulted in it being seen as resource rich, as an area that has received considerable investment in recent years. The ring-fencing of AWS investment is due to end very shortly and advocates of the other community care concerns could well seek some level of budget adjustment in their favour, a virement which may not be defended as strongly as it would have been if specialist senior officers had continued to exist.

There are particular concerns regarding the continuation of participative structures and the status of self-advocacy and parental groups. While the development of joint planning and consumer representation may have been one of the acknowledged achievements of the AWS, they could also be among some of the most short-lived. Other implications stem from the loss of coterminosity between local and health authorities, previously enjoyed by seven of the eight Welsh counties (even in the eighth, two health authority areas were located within the boundaries of one county council). This adds complexity to the task of maintaining joint strategic planning arrangements. Moreover, since the new unitary authorities are now smaller than existing health authorities (which were combined in any case to just five), there is a view that health could possibly regain a prominence in learning disability services that had been lost under the AWS. The health authorities will naturally seek policy consistency within their own boundaries and, therefore, may play a greater lead in coordinating the constituent unitary authorities. In addition, the new unitary authorities will be less able to respond to changing demand from very high cost service users. The AWS planning principles and values may prove insufficiently robust against the emerging pressures for expediency, particularly as officer commitment has been fragmented and political support is uncertain.

There will be a loss of learning disabilities as a distinct sector and multi-user groups will be inevitable.

There is a huge risk here. If it goes to a very localized level, trying to get a strategic avenue for the next 15–20 years will be very difficult. Smaller scale will make it more difficult to manage large revenue demands.

It will depend on the make-up of politicians, whether there are votes in it and whether there is pressure on their internal budgets.

I hope that enough of the principles are now embedded within the individual professional mind set and amongst service users and parents to survive the end of ring-fencing, the withdrawal of Welsh Office involvement and LGR and the Community Care Act. There is still a lot of commitment to the AWS principles on the statutory side. People currently involved will be as committed as ever. But new players (e.g. councillors and chief officers) will be starting from scratch and will need to be educated about the values.

The one thing the AWS hasn't done is to build up a level of political investment. Now that local planning groups will lose their executive functions, councillors aren't going to listen to us when we talk about the thousands something or other will cost.

Learning disabilities is seen as insular by many other disability groups because they kept themselves separate during the AWS. And since the AWS has been officer-led not member-led we might be lacking in political support for the things we'd like to keep carrying out. ... We've never had councillors on our committees or on our planning group, so they've no insight into the AWS. ... I think our members are pretty sympathetic and care, but the whole thing's been officer-led. If it comes down to it and if something has to close, it won't be an entity, a building, or a centre or a school. That would create political controversy. ... It's easier to chip away from a community oriented budget, they're easier targets. ... So if you lost a few family aides there would be limited complaints.

There are people out there who think the AWS was deluxe treatment. Once ring-fencing has gone, we'll go back to the old system which doesn't bode well for people with learning disabilities. It'll mean we'll end up fighting within our own agencies for funds again.

I think many of the developments will be maintained, but I don't think that there is much chance of developing on from there, with people with learning disabilities reverting to the bottom of people's priority lists.

Moving beyond presence to participation

Considerable changes in where people live and what they do during the day, in the support families receive and in consumer consultation have all occurred under the AWS. Chapters 4–8 provide a picture of people with learning disabilities having a more visible place in our society's life.

Supported community housing has given adults the opportunity to live independently of their families in typical residential circumstances. Most people previously living in hospitals and hostels have had the opportunity to regain typical community presence. Day services are breaking out from the enclosed, segregated centres that were the norm throughout the 1960s and 1970s. Family support services are giving parents a greater chance to sustain expectations about achieving a typical lifestyle and people with learning disabilities individual support to access community amenities and activities. Individual planning, self-advocacy and consumer representation in planning are giving people with learning disabilities a place in meetings which discuss their future or their service provision needs. Opportunities for involvement and the pursuit of valued roles within society are beginning to become available. The reforms under the AWS have done much to extend these opportunities throughout Wales.

However, Chapters 4–8 also show where presence in the community and opportunity for greater involvement do not automatically translate into genuine participation and accomplishment. User self-determination is still a less powerful force than professional assessment. Self-advocacy has grown in strength and people with learning disabilities are involved in planning, but there is doubt over the extent to which self-advocacy has changed the course of service development. People may live in typical housing but they typically do not receive the support that they require to be typical householders, seeing to their own personal and household needs themselves. Rather, particularly those with more substantial disabilities have little to do while others 'care' for them. People may get out and about in the community much more but the extent to which they are joining other citizens as equal partners remains limited. People with learning disabilities still have limited social lives and few people without disabilities, particularly age peers, among their friends. Their pursuits may not take place in segregated settings so much any more, but functional segregation may still apply in the way that arrangements for their use of typical facilities such as colleges of further education or sports centres are made. Parental carers may have greater support and some 'free' time but their lack of control over its timing and its limitations in terms of extent and flexibility may mean that they are no nearer to sharing the lifestyles of their age peers than before.

The AWS has certainly created some of the conditions necessary for substantial quality of life changes for people with learning disabilities and their carers. However, such conditions have not proved sufficient for the full participation in normal life envisaged by its architects to be realized. Reform to date has inevitably been broad brush. We return to a finer grain analysis of what is required to promote genuine participation in the next chapter.

References

Abrams, P. (1978). Community care: some research problems and priorities. In: *Social Care Research*, (J. Barnes and N. Connelly, eds). pp. 78–99. London: Bedford Square Press.

Audit Commission (1987). *Community Care: Developing Services for People with a Mental Handicap. Occasional papers no. 4.* London: HMSO.

Beckford, V. and Robinson, C. (1993). *Consolidation or Change? A Second Survey of Family Based Respite Care Services in the United Kingdom.* Bristol: Norah Fry Research Centre, University of Bristol.

Department of Health (1996). *Residential Accommodation. Detailed Statistics on Residential Care Homes and Local Authority Supported Residents. England 1995.* London: HMSO.

Emerson, E. and Hatton, C. (1996). *Residential Provision for People with Learning Disabilities: an Analysis of the 1991 Census.* Manchester: Hester Adrian Research Centre, University of Manchester.

Emerson, E., Hatton, C., Bauer, I. *et al.* (1996). Patterns of institutionalisation in 15 European Countries. *European Journal on Mental Disability*, **3**, 11, 29–32.

Ericsson, K. and Mansell, J. (1996). Towards deinstitutionalization. In: *Deinstitutionalization and Community Living. Intellectual Disability Services in Britain, Scandinavia and the USA*, (J. Mansell and K. Ericsson, eds) pp. 1–16. London: Chapman and Hall.

Evans, G., Todd, S., Beyer, S. *et al.* (1994). Assessing the impact of the All-Wales Mental Handicap Strategy: a survey of four districts. *Journal of Intellectual Disability Research*, **38**, 109–133.

Gourash, N. (1978). Help seeking: a review of the literature. *American Journal of Community Psychology*, **6**, 413–423.

Hatton, C., Emerson, E. and Kiernan, C. (1995). People in institutions in Europe. *Mental Retardation*, **33**, 132.

Knapp, M., Cambridge, P., Thomason, C. *et al.* (1992). *Care in the Community: Challenge and Demonstration.* Aldershot: Ashgate.

O'Brien, J. (1987). A guide to lifestyle planning: Using the Activities Catalog to integrate services and natural support systems. In: *A Comprehensive Guide to the Activities Catalog: an Alternative Curriculum for Youth and Adults with Severe Disabilities*, (B. Wilcox and G. T. Bellamy, eds) pp. 175–189. Baltimore: Brookes.

Perry, J. and Felce, D. (1994). Outcomes of ordinary housing services in Wales: objective indicators. *Mental Handicap Research*, **7**, 286–311.

Perry, J., Beyer, S., Felce, D. and Todd, S. (1998). Strategic service change: development of core services in Wales, 1983–95. *Journal of Applied Research in Intellectual Disabilities*, **11**, 15–33.

Raynes, N., Wright, K., Shiell, A. and Pettipher, C. (1994). *The Cost and Quality of Community Residential Care.* London: David Fulton Publishers.

Welsh Office (1982). *Report of the All Wales Working Party on Services for Mentally Handicapped People.* Cardiff: Welsh Office.

Welsh Office (1983). *All Wales Strategy for the Development of Services for Mentally Handicapped People.* Cardiff: Welsh Office.

Chapter 10

Moving beyond the AWS: strengthening reform and policy

There may be those who already see the AWS as consigned to history, subsumed within a wider community care policy and currently of limited or no relevance to people's lives. Certainly, it is difficult to see a distinctive edge still being given to learning disability policy in Wales by the AWS. Indeed, policy now has only one specific goal, to see the final closure of the hospitals as residential institutions. Otherwise, there is a policy vacuum on a wide range of important questions: whether the full scope of service provision intended by the architects of the AWS is still to be achieved; how effective family support is to be delivered and how widely it is to be made available; what is the preferred nature of schooling; how is transition from school to adult occupation best achieved; how is self-determination to be fostered; what options for adult occupation are to be pursued; how available is the opportunity to be made for adults to set up homes of their own with support; and what policies need to be brought forward in the light of the increased lifespan of people with learning disabilities? In spite of the apparently ambitious and comprehensive objectives stated in recent policy guidance (Welsh Office, 1996), there is little consideration in this guidance about how to realize these.

However, it would be unwise to dismiss the continued relevance of the AWS as we believe that it provides important lessons about how to design service supports which have a profound impact on the quality of people's contemporary everyday lives. In our view, these operational issues transcend policy imperatives and therefore deserve some reflection in their own right. Below we offer an interpretation of our findings from earlier chapters based on an adapted structure-process-outcome model (Donabedian, 1988; Felce and Beyer, 1996). The model allows us to make some connections about the various ways in which both service structures and processes can be seen to mediate service outcomes. In effect, we outline a 'technical competency' model for services.

The scope of the questions which remain and the financial implications of the expansion of provision to a genuinely comprehensive pattern of local support continue to require some form of strategy. The first ten-year period of the AWS was always seen as the first stage of a longer reform. It is therefore timely to reflect upon how to improve service design so that there is a greater likelihood that people with learning disabilities might become genuine participants within their families, in their own homes, at work and in the community. Accordingly, we describe below what we think needs to be done to complete the transition from segregation to community inclusion, outline a technical competency model for services as the means to achieve this transition, and then, anchored by our research findings, offer some prescriptions about the required service competencies by drawing on illustrations from different spheres of people's lives.

Completing the transition from segregation to inclusion

Although there is still undoubtedly a gap between the vision of the AWS and what has been achieved on the ground, the proper province of service involvement in people's lives is now much more clear if a typical, culturally valued lifestyle is the aim. It is not the role of services to supplant people's natural environments and settings, to ignore the human and other resources which surround them or to provide a set of parallel environments and communities, an imitative existence, in short, a virtual reality. Rather, the real service contribution is one construed in forms of support, treatment and technical assistance related to the nature and consequences of people's intellectual disabilities. The application of such specialism is in helping people derive the most from the communities and cultures of which they are or should legitimately be a part (Felce and Beyer, 1996). In this way, services act as a bridge between people's natural or typical conditions of life and the quality of life they experience. This mediating role for services in enhancing the quality of life of people with disabilities in their naturally varying circumstances is depicted in Figure 10.1.

The model suggested here is based on achieving a mix of natural environment and specialist support as the means to achieving valued outcomes, specifically: 'the achievement of development and experience typical of the wider culture in which family life, social relationships, competence and independence, involvement in activity, community participation, individual choice and control, status and self-esteem are important elements' (Felce and Beyer, 1996, p. 53). Increasingly, the emphasis is on services enhancing the support and expertise people already have around them. This involves being very clear about the kinds of technical competencies services will need to have to do the job properly.

Service specialism: competence in responding to the particular difficulties which arise from intellectual disability

Figure 10.1 sets out the nature and place of the service contribution in relation to the outcomes integral to a decent quality of life described above. These outcomes rarely arise naturally for people with learning disabilities to the same degree as they do for people without disabilities, and the more severe their intellectual impairment, the less likely they are to occur. Much of the research and development in learning disabilities

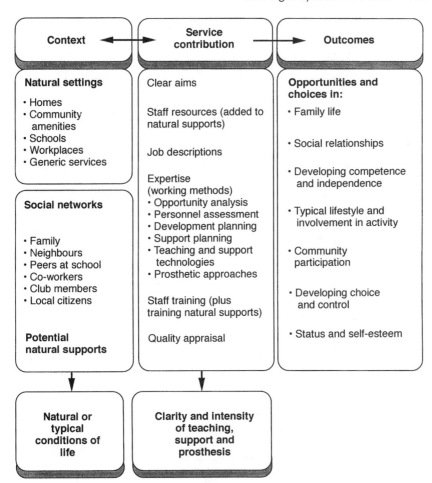

Context	Service contribution	Outcomes
Natural settings • Homes • Community amenities • Schools • Workplaces • Generic services **Social networks** • Family • Neighbours • Peers at school • Co-workers • Club members • Local citizens **Potential natural supports**	Clear aims Staff resources (added to natural supports) Job descriptions Expertise (working methods) • Opportunity analysis • Personnel assessment • Development planning • Support planning • Teaching and support technologies • Prosthetic approaches Staff training (plus training natural supports) Quality appraisal	**Opportunities and choices in:** • Family life • Social relationships • Developing competence and independence • Typical lifestyle and involvement in activity • Community participation • Developing choice and control • Status and self-esteem

Natural or typical conditions of life	Clarity and intensity of teaching, support and prosthesis

Figure 10.1 Services and the promotion of typical lifestyles

can be seen as directed towards finding out how to develop opportunities for people and help them succeed in areas which, although unremarkable for most other community citizens, are difficult for people whose capacity to learn and resulting independence are diminished. How to arrange for successful and meaningful participation despite intellectual impairment may be regarded as the defining feature of a service specialism specific to learning disabilities. Such specialist competencies have developed markedly in recent decades as services have risen to the challenge of a quality of life agenda. Increasingly, the focus of service competence is on how services generate opportunities, analyse the person-environment fit, adjust environmental demands, develop specific aspects of the person's independence and enhance the support they have to participate effectively while remaining less than fully independent. In general terms, services need the competencies to:

1 analyse the nature of the opportunities or demands that a person has before them, and, if necessary, break them into component steps or otherwise simplify them
2 assess people's independent abilities given various forms of assistance, their preferences, motivation, learning strategies and potential to develop in the short, medium and longer term
3 match opportunities and demands to people's capacities, building on strengths and exploiting the potential to adapt the natural environment to suit individual requirements
4 adopt systematic, evidence-based approaches to teaching which aid the development of people's independence in meeting environmental demands
5 adopt systematic, evidence-based approaches to providing prosthetic supports which promote people's independence in meeting environmental demands, and
6 adopt systematic, evidence-based approaches to providing assistance which enable people to meet environmental demands.

Service developments, such as supported living and supported employment, exemplify the application of specialist approaches to the achievement of ordinary goals – arranging one's homelife and going to work – in ordinary settings. These and other conceptualizations of family and community living support services are illustrated in the following pages. Consistent with the framework in Figure 10.1, the illustrations which follow acknowledge the natural context in which the service operates, express the service contribution in terms of clear outcomes and procedures, and make explicit the resultant service/service recipient interface, which is a prerequisite to meeting these outcomes. Below, we take examples from different life spheres: family life; running one's own home; going to work; and having an active life in the community. These can be regarded as a set of service prescriptions based on our research findings. For convenience, we have boxed the key findings as we do not wish to elaborate them further at this stage though we think their inclusion at various points helps to give substance to our lines of argument.

Supporting family life

Figure 10.2 illustrates support for family life. Family life is the most complex of the models we put forward because it involves the welfare of two distinct groups – parents or other family members as carers and their offspring or relatives with disabilities. However, we have not separated their two perspectives at this point because of the importance of approaching the family as a whole unit. A family-centred approach is central to the interpersonal harmony and the assumed or negotiated ties and obligations between family members.

The left-hand column of Figure 10.2 depicts key dimensions of ordinary family contexts which merit some comment. The family in all its forms continues to provide the bulk of care and support to vulnerable individuals. The variety of family forms in which people, including those with

An ordinary context	Getting organized	Delivering quality
Chosen family form and composition parent(s) child sibling(s) other relatives	**Clear outcomes** rewarding mutual relationships and ties personal growth and development balance of care with employment and social obligations	**Access to activities and opportunities fitting to age and stage of family life cycle** parents offspring other relatives
Support networks, ties and obligations structure relationships functions	**Lifespan perspective** **Staff/resources in ratio to needs (added to informal supports)**	**Choice of activity/ career development** **Quality support** mutual relationships outside relationships
Housing	**Staff selection**	balance of activities choice
Income	**Job descriptions**	
Possessions	**Working methods** Needs assessment	**Effective teaching/ behaviour change** personal growth as
Neighbourhood	Family centred care management (family as partner and expert)	family carers personal growth for offspring
Community resources	Information/advice Family development and support planning	
Household autonomy	Practical and psychological support Family-family links Monitoring success	**Staff:user interface**
Structure embedded in natural environment	**Staff (plus natural supports) training** **Quality appraisal**	
	Service orientation and procedures	

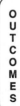

O U T C O M E S

Figure 10.2 An ordinary life and service design: family life

learning disabilities, grow up are affected by prevailing rates of divorce and remarriage, cohabitation, patterns of fertility, and women's labour force participation. These, coupled with intra-family conflicts about values concerning inheritance, care, gifts, and inter-generational obligations within families (Thomas Patterson, 1997) suggest that diversity of family forms and lifestyles is likely to be a constant backdrop to the operation of family support services.

Families are also defined by the mutual emotional ties and obligations between family members. The support available to individuals both within the family and in terms of wider informal support has been shown to vary according to the structure of people's support networks. Their size, density and membership provide an initial indication of potential support. Stability of support networks is too often assumed when, in fact, life events often intercede, causing considerable change in the availability and supply of support. Further, the theoretical availability of such support does not guarantee that help or care from such sources is sufficient, consistent or valued (Grant, 1993; Grant and Wenger, 1993). The qualities of relationships between support network members is therefore of crucial concern. This refers to things like the frequency of contact, reciprocity, multiplicity of ties and affinities between people. Such factors denote aspects of familiarity and intimacy within human relationships which are so often vital ingredients in ensuring that potentially vulnerable people are well supported.

Nevertheless, people linked by kinship or otherwise by affinities based on shared identities and interests may not necessarily direct their support in ways likely to foster personal development, autonomy and community inclusion. Our research has shown the need to develop a better, theoretically rooted understanding of the means and ends of caregiving. This is a key developmental challenge which entails linking the tasks and responsibilities of caregiving to what is achieved, judged if possible from the perspectives of both family carers and the person with learning disabilities (Nocon and Qureshi, 1996; Nolan, Grant and Keady, 1996).

Key research findings: family life

- Stability of family support is often assumed rather than real
- Most families find caregiving simultaneously stressful and rewarding
- Over time families develop unique competencies and expertise in caregiving yet disclosing details about the individual with learning disabilities can continue to be a painful experience
- Families perceive caregiving as much more than the sum of a series of discrete instrumental tasks
- There are many kinds of reciprocities and obligations involved in caregiving
- Much caregiving is invisible to outsiders
- Families want to be able to balance employment and caregiving demands
- Caregiving often involves social and economic restrictions
- Family support networks can act as both a bridge to or a barrier from the community for the person with learning disabilities
- Tailored family support services are too often in limited supply

---

Besides social support, the welfare of all family members will be affected by their housing, income, possessions and the characteristics and resources of the neighbourhood. Ecological and structural factors therefore need to be part of a family assessment. This suggests the importance of examining what kinds of gatekeeping roles families play in mediating community inclusion since gatekeeping is affected by such factors as well as by the personal skills and resourcefulness of family members. It also indicates concern about the changing balance of independence and control between family members as individuals mature, a difficult area given the traditional idea of autonomy that parents have within their own households.

Expectations of family self-sufficiency and the competing obligations of family members to be gainfully employed as well as provide a nurturing environment for their offspring can place enormous demands on individuals as Chapter 7 illustrated. Inflexible employment practices often give families little scope to negotiate terms which allow better dovetailing of domestic and work considerations. With increasing numbers of people, especially women, in full- or part-time work, and with many dependent upon a single household income, the relationship between the demands of care and employment need to be carefully monitored. Moreover, the legitimacy of the goals of family carers as service recipients needs to be made explicit. Whether carer support is made available only to help carers extend their caring, as opposed to their other interests in life, such as their work or social pursuits, requires policy clarification.

Effective family support services have their basis in an understanding of the family and the family home as an environment. A clear idea of the outcomes to which support is directed is, of course, vital as are approaches to family assessment and support planning which will deliver support which matches family members' needs. A specification of the goals of family support services is outlined in the second column. Social systems (Dunst, Trivette and Deal, 1994 among others) and stress-coping models (Nolan, Grant and Keady, 1996) have been influential in clarifying outcomes related to work with families. Hence, there are outcomes related to the position of individual family members – rewards of care, stress reduction, reduction of social restrictions, personal growth, relationships outside the home, caring and non-caring careers, and balance between obligatory and chosen activities for example – as well as those which affect the family as a unit like family harmony and reciprocities between members. In summary, the objectives of family support may be seen in terms of fostering rewarding mutual relationships and ties/obligations between family members (rewards outweighing stresses), personal growth and development of a sufficiently multi-faceted life consistent with one's age and responsibilities, fostering of a variety of relationships outside the family home for all family members, a balance of activity in line with people's preferences, ambitions and mutual obligations, and due exercise of personal choice.

Services clearly need staff and resources to deliver support, but the main emphasis on service specialism is concerned with the working methods which are most likely to be effective. Job descriptions should reflect these working methods as should staff selection criteria. Our research evidence points in the direction of services recruiting and training staff into roles which require them to be proactive, though not intrusive, in their work with families. The evidence builds upon ideas of empowerment where the object of services is to strengthen family resources and expertise (Dunst and Trivette, 1988; Barnes, 1997). Families are assumed to have a position as active partners in these processes, a position which enables them to dictate the speed at which things will happen and the form in which support will be provided to achieve identified goals (see Chapter 4). A lifespan approach to family support works particularly well in this connection.

Families are autonomous in our society within the framework of the law. Working methods recognize this autonomy when they help families to develop a sense of control over the management of events over the life course. Dunst *et al.* (1994, pp. 178–179) outline eight basic principles for effective work in supporting families:

1 active and reflective listening skills are used as a basis for understanding the needs and concerns of families
2 families are helped to identify, clarify and prioritize aspirations as well as needs
3 help is offered on a proactive basis rather than merely as a response to requests
4 help is compatible with the family's own culture
5 help offered is congruent with the family's own appraisal of problems and needs
6 help leads to the acquisition of competencies that promote independence, thus reducing dependency on formal support systems
7 help is carried out in a spirit of cooperation and partnership for meeting needs and solving problems with families, and
8 the locus of decision-making clearly rests with the family, including decisions about the need or goal, the options for carrying out interventions, and whether or not to accept help that is offered.

Dunst and Trivette (1994) go on to illustrate how these general principles can be applied to family-centred case management practices which involve needs assessment and subsequent planning for family development and support. With the impetus given by the Carers (Recognition and Services) Act 1995 to a proper assessment of the needs and perspectives of family carers, these principles would seem to offer a useful basis for a closer examination of best practices. In addition, the more invisible aspects of 'caring about' an individual – the planning, the anticipating, the less tangible aspects of care related to promoting the supported person's self esteem and so on (Nolan, Grant and Keady, 1996) which are often found to be very stressful as well as potentially rewarding – need to be acknowledged as vital components of caregiving.

On a practical level, these perspectives can help to inform decisions about how best to provide quality support. This may include information sharing, instrumental and psychological help, respite, and skill sharing directed towards helping families to maintain effective coping strategies which reflect their expertise and resources. Direct professional advice or intervention may help members of either generation develop relevant skills. Alternatively, helping families to network one another can be an extremely effective way of enabling them to develop a good understanding of what works. In this regard, families may serve as visible 'demonstration projects' to one another. However, the importance of matching the intervention to the circumstances and ambitions of respective family members should never be overlooked in an eagerness to provide input and relief. As examples in Chapter 7 illustrated, support and respite are transactional entities. They are achieved when input results in what is sought; they are not properties of the input per se.

Staff need to be able to work to clear, achievable targets with individual families in order to be able to deliver these kinds of support, something that frequently involves being able to accommodate short- and long-term family aspirations at the same time. Families so often seem to lack written case documentation either because it has never been made available or because it has been so long since a case review that documentation has been misplaced in the home. Unless this is put right, it will be extremely difficult to develop the lifespan perspective of family functioning and to demonstrate the success of the support process with sufficient transparency. Without access to such documentation, families will be less able to raise pertinent questions about what is supposed to be happening. Hence, backing needs assessment, goal setting and planning with a means of monitoring and appraising the quality of what has been done and achieved – access to activities and opportunities for family members which fit their age and stage in life, extended choice of activity and career development, the support for relationships, activities and choice made available and the effectiveness of counselling and teaching on the personal growth of family members – is essential.

Running one's own home (with support)

Service reform has done much to return residential services to their natural context. The changes which we have seen in recent years in Wales are shown in Figure 10.3 by the emphases on ordinary housing, small scale, domestic standards, community location and household control over budgeting, purchasing and the rhythms and routines of household life. As we have already indicated, it is not good enough to think about these issues in simple terms. Living in the community does not simply equate to living in any ordinary house in any street in any residential area. There has to be detailed consideration given to the question of why an individual or group are suited by living at a precise address. Criteria for exploring the advantages or disadvantages of the location vis à vis community resources and access issues, for example transport, are also important.

Greater consideration of why and how individuals come to live with each other is in itself also being urged (e.g. Kinsella, 1993). A great deal of effort in the process of deinstitutionalization has been given to the issue of finding residential groupings which make sense in terms of friendship and other relevant matters. However, there is still a suspicion that individuals have been made to fit the model of small group home provided rather than provision being made according to the best interests of individuals. The idea that people with and without learning disabilities might live together has found some expression in a limited number of 'life-sharing' schemes (Harper, 1989). These might become more common if services sought to promote them more. In addition, there has been an extension of tenancy rights to people with learning disabilities and some examples

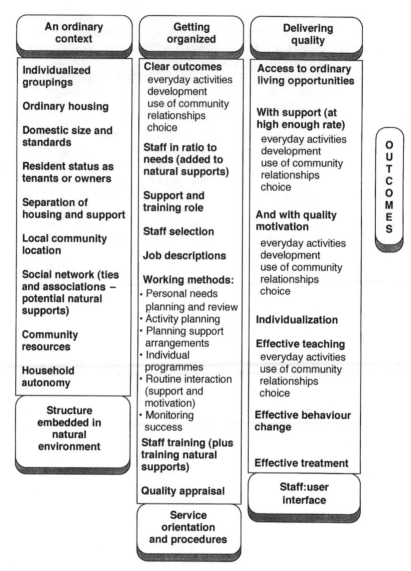

Figure 10.3 An ordinary life and service design: home

where individuals have been helped to become owner-occupiers. However, there is still concern that one or other of these two arrangements have not become universal and that the arrangements for the support that people require have not been disentangled from their accommodation arrangements. In particular, it is perhaps more common for private proprietor-managed services to perpetuate this disadvantage. However, voluntary and statutory sector providers may also not have done all that is possible to separate housing and support.

Many services have a view about the outcomes that they intend to achieve although they may be expressed in rather abstract terms and sometimes poorly communicated to staff. Figure 10.3 considers outcomes in terms of participation or engagement in a broad range of everyday activities, personal development over time, use of the community, relationships with the community and other people (family, friends, acquaintances, neighbours, associates with similar interests) and self-determination. As outcomes, they are interdependent. For example, use of the community and a person's relationships with others are usually transacted through engagement in typical everyday activities and influenced by personal development. Personal development can only come through participation in activities, but aspects of that development and experience may subsequently determine choice of activity.

Key research findings: running one's own home

- No-one resettled in the community expressed a wish to return to hospital
- None of the individuals in any of our research samples owned their own home though increasing numbers enjoy tenancy rights
- Locating people in ordinary housing does not, by itself, guarantee community participation
- Within ordinary housing, more severely disabled residents tended to live in less home-like settings
- People living in smaller community-based homes, especially those developed since 1985, were generally more involved in controlling their own lives than those living in other residential facilities
- Interventions within homes were only exceptionally oriented towards promoting personal development
- Provision of a well-staffed, community housing service does not, by itself, guarantee personal development
- Involvement in the running of one's own home tended to reflect individual ability rather than staffing input
- Staff are not geared up to providing effective support, particularly to people with more severe disabilities
- An 'active support' model shows promise in demonstrating how residents can receive opportunities and support consistent with their needs and preferences

---

Staff are required in ratio to needs but, as our research (Chapter 6) and that of others (Hatton *et al.*, 1995; Stancliffe, 1997) shows, a balance needs to be struck. Too few staff may repeat the lack of stimulation and unacceptable circumstances which characterized institutional care in the past. However, too many staff may erode choice and autonomy and take away opportunities for individuals to participate in the daily activities that need to be done, particularly if staff take an intuitive approach to providing care. Although staff may spend much of their time interacting with residential service users, the extent to which they assist and teach people has been found to be limited (Repp, Barton and Brulle, 1981, 1982; Hewson and Walker, 1992; Felce and Perry, 1995). This means that only those with many relevant skills have the opportunity to participate in the breadth of household life and staff themselves do much of the household activity for people with more severe disabilities. The organization of staff resources and the clarity of job assignment for staff may be as, if not more, important to the quality of care as the staff input itself. Clear allocation of staff to duties and arranging the setting so that staff work alone with as few residents as possible, as opposed to being with other staff and responsible for supporting larger numbers of people, has been shown to result in more staff interaction with residents than increasing the number of staff (Harris *et al.* 1974; Mansell *et al.*, 1982; Duker *et al.*, 1991; Felce *et al.*, 1991). Thus, the working methods, job descriptions and staff training are the keys to service specialism. Staff selection criteria may also be derived from a detailed understanding of the nature of the job. Other selection criteria will stem from the need to have characteristics in common with the person to be supported – interests, tastes, age and gender – or a good appreciation of such characteristics and their implications for the person's self-image, how he or she might be perceived and their relationships with and integration in wider society.

Individual planning and needs review are a part of required working methods. There are many models for how this can be done, but the key is making sure that the breadth and ambition of the process is maintained, especially on behalf of people whose self-advocacy might be limited. Research has shown that services often do not prioritize areas for action, even though people's needs may be long-standing and obvious, for example in relation to challenging behaviour and language development (de Kock *et al.*, 1988; Emerson *et al.*, 1997). This may plausibly be because services avoid setting goals in areas where they lack either the resources or the expertise to achieve them. Structures which make sure that different potential lifestyle issues are always considered and which prevent issues being dropped when the service is not up to the mark can help to retain the focus on the person's needs. Involvement and representation of the person are also important. In this respect, the slow development of citizen advocacy is a continuing problem.

The three elements – activity planning, planning support arrangements and training staff (or natural supports) how to support and motivate participation in a routine way – have come to be called 'active support' (Emerson and Hatton, 1994; McGill and Toogood, 1994). Emphasis on taking a proactive approach is consistent with the conceptualization that choice for people with severely constrained independence is dependent on the level of opportunity and support extended. At least for people with severe learning disabilities, one could argue that opportunity only exists under the conditions that all three factors – an activity, a source of support, and effective assistance – are available. A circumstantial case for the importance of active support can be made by reference to a number of comparative and analytic studies (Felce, de Kock and Repp, 1986; Hatton *et al.*, 1995; Felce, 1996). Moreover, a recent experimental demonstration of the impact of active support on staff activity, resident activity and the relationship between the two (Jones *et al.*, 1997) has shown definitively that, without increasing staff resources, active support:

1 significantly increased the level of assistance residents received
2 significantly increased resident engagement in domestic activities around the house
3 significantly increased total resident engagement in activity
4 changed the prevailing tendency for staff to interact more with and give more support to behaviourally more able residents, and
5 allowed behaviourally less able residents to gain a more equal access to opportunity, without adversely affecting the extent of participation of their more able fellow residents.

Although we have discussed active support in relation to staff organization and performance, it can be argued to apply equally to the involvement of natural supports. Whether opportunity and assistance are provided by a paid or unpaid person, a member of a formal or informal support network, matters little compared to whether they are given or not. There may be a bias towards time being spent with ordinary members of the community from an integration perspective but, unless the person with learning disabilities is positively supported in the prevailing activity, their experience will be impoverished and their appearance will perpetuate traditional images of disability. Moreover, at an organizational level, it is difficult to see how the best use can be made of natural supports unless the service is proactive in creating and sustaining reliable arrangements.

Developmental progress as a goal of services is, of course, closely related to the defining characteristic of learning disabilities. Skill acquisition reverses the tangible consequences of intellectual disability. To this end, emphasis has been placed on the need for individual, structured programmes which develop new or change existing patterns of behaviour. The level of structure may range from the mere programming of opportunities to practice targeted skills through to formal written teaching programmes. Specific functional areas such as motor skills or communication and language may be the concern of professionals such as physiotherapists and speech therapists. Medical and nursing involvement with people, even the simple drug prescription, also constitute a form of individual programme. A well organized setting which is able to follow individual programmes consistently is a conducive environment for the effective use of specialist professional expertise.

Concern for accountability and the maintenance of quality over time means that some systematic approach to quality assurance is required. Establishing a quality circle or quality action group (IDC, 1986) which represents various stakeholders – users, their representatives, direct carers, managers, commissioners, inspectors – is one approach. It is greatly aided if the working methods followed by the service contain a means of recording what has been achieved so that success can be recognized and problems solved. Monitoring should relate to quality of life goals, as should, of course, the working methods. Therefore, one would look to see monitoring systems which reflected quality at the service-service user interface:

1 the level of opportunity to be involved in the activities of ordinary living (in the home, in the community and with family and friends)
2 the frequency and nature of support and encouragement
3 the extent to which individuality is recognized; the breadth, number and achievement of individual plan goals
4 the implementation and success of teaching
5 the implementation and success of approaches to develop alternatives to challenging behaviour, and
6 the breadth and effectiveness of other specialist treatments.

Adult occupation: going to work

Figure 10.4 illustrates the interaction between the natural environment and service specialism in assisting people with learning disabilities to obtain and retain paid employment. Those familiar with the model of supported employment will recognize these elements (Beyer, 1995). Helping adults with disabilities to have meaningful and gainful employment has been a long-standing goal of policy (King's Fund, 1984). Initially, it was implemented through the provision of sheltered workshops which typically subcontracted jobs from other manufacturers or firms. Concern about the repetitive nature of the work, low productivity, low wages and the segregation of people with disabilities as workers led to a reappraisal of adult day services (Whelan and Speake, 1977). Training for work rather than providing a substitute workplace became the aim. However, the attempt to train people in non-work settings to be competent in an unspecified future job without ongoing support – the 'train, place and hope' model – was unsuccessful except for people whose learning disabilities were so slight that it was unlikely that they differed greatly in ability from many other people who found work in the ordinary way (Bellamy *et al.*, 1986). Supported employment repositions service training and support so that it comes after the person has entered a job placement. In teaching people to meet the specific demands of specific jobs, it has been much more successful in aiding people with more severe learning disabilities to become employed.

The context for work is a real job in a real business. In entering the commercial world where productivity is exchanged for wages, there is an obvious concern for realistic working standards. As first-time workers without advanced academic or vocational qualifications, people with learning disabilities will generally be seeking entry level jobs. Part of the service expertise is to analyse the required job performance and help people select jobs to which they are suited (see below). Non-disabled co-workers and the supervisory and training structures of the workplace are a source of natural support. The balance between direct service input, with a job coach working with the person to teach them the job and the social requirements of the workplace, and reliance on the context of natural support, albeit shaped by service input, are now a particular focus in the search for the most effective methods (Callahan, 1992). This applies equally well to employment-focused schemes as well as to supported employment. A greater involvement of the workforce in general in the

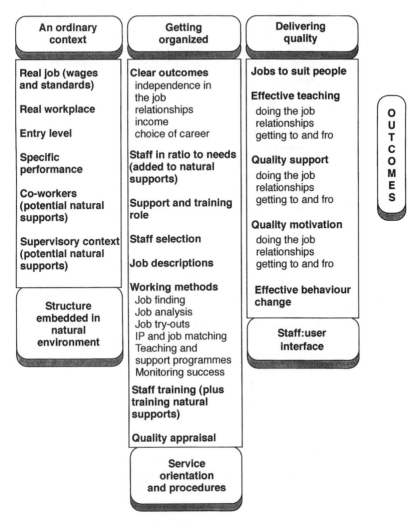

Figure 10.4 An ordinary life and service design: work

person's induction may be related to better subsequent social integration and job retention.

The focus on real employment makes the outcomes for service intervention clear. One is independence in the job. Ideally, the training phase is seen as temporary. The additional input the person requires during this phase is gradually withdrawn to leave the worker fully competent within the context of ongoing natural support. However, the severity of some people's learning disabilities may be such that total independence is not envisaged in the short or medium term, in which case the service may provide continuing support to ensure that productivity criteria are reached. Nevertheless, progress towards independence is still a goal. Greater dependency on a support worker than is necessary not only detracts from cultural understandings about the nature of working, but is a potential barrier to social integration.

Key research findings: going to work

- Day activity and supported employment options were limited and choice for the individual restricted
- Segregated day activity within the confines of traditional day centres still predominates
- People with more severe learning disabilities are over-represented within traditional day centres
- Increasing numbers of people now enjoy activities at satellite units, FE colleges, community-based work projects and supported employment schemes
- Activities organized outside traditional day centres tend to keep people more purposefully engaged
- Acquisition of personal competencies and self-confidence and signs of social integration were more evident among individuals attending supported employment or alternative day activity schemes
- Present social security rules about the 'earnings disregard limit' prevent people from pursuing full-time supported employment
- The conditions and parameters of part-time work reinforced status differentials and acted as a significant impediment to social integration within the workplace

---

Social integration, a person's relationships with his or her co-workers within the workplace and potentially outside of work, is an important outcome for many workers, a key part of overall job satisfaction. Research has also shown that supported employees have often lost their jobs, not because they could not do the job but because they failed to fit into the social culture of the workplace (Greenspan and Shoultz, 1981; Hanley-Maxwell *et al.*, 1986). Teaching and supporting appropriate social behaviours are, therefore, important to gain the full benefits of working and to retain employment over the longer term.

Receiving an income at the going rate for the job and exercising choice over career to the extent that one's qualifications and experience permit are other normally expected aspects of working. There are many advantages to full-time working from the perspective of earnings, learning the job and social integration. The extent to which people work full-time is also a factor in the cost:benefit ratio of service provision (Beyer, Goodere and Kilsby, 1996). However, the welfare benefit income which many people with learning disabilities receive and the regulations which surround benefit entitlement and which determine loss of benefit as earnings rise complicate the situation in practice. These constraints are not helpful as they encourage a culture of part-time working which lowers the intensity of job training and the extent to which people may be seen as an integral part of the workforce. Support for people to exercise a choice over their career paths relates to a variety of working methods which promote such self-determination.

As in other life areas, staff are required in ratio to people's needs. Moreover, staff selection, roles, job descriptions and training are important aspects of the quality of the service. Again, these must relate to effective working methods. Helping people find a job to suit them may be approached systematically. Job finding entails creating an employment profile for the locality of concern and an inventory of the range of entry level jobs available. Potential employers need to be informed and recruited to make job opportunities available to people with learning disabilities. Two forms of opportunity are needed: work experience and permanent jobs. People who have not worked before may have a limited appreciation either of the range of potential jobs available or what jobs entail or feel like to do. Creating opportunities for people to go through a series of job try-outs to gain this experience greatly helps informed decision-making. In this connection people may benefit from having access to a range of employment-focused day opportunity schemes as we described in Chapter 8. Once a person can form a preference, then potential jobs in that area can be identified. Job finding is concluded through a process of matching a job to the abilities and views of the person.

Job matching involves analysing the job to be done, assessing the strengths and abilities of the potential employee and concluding that there is a sufficient degree of overlap for the placement to prove feasible. Achieving the goal of independence in the job can be made much easier if good job matching has been done in the first place. The job analysis is derived through observing a competent worker and completing an inventory of the tasks involved. Assessment of the person can then focus on such tasks and the prerequisite skills which are involved. Consistent with the research on the importance of social behaviour in the workplace, the job analysis should take an holistic view of job performance. It should take account of the social culture and may, for example, include issues to do with getting to and from work. Moreover, job analysis may involve restructuring the distribution of job tasks among workers in order to create a new job capable of being done by the worker with disabilities. The new job would comprise a combination of the simpler elements of a number of people's jobs. This approach has particular application when looking to give people with more severe disabilities the opportunity to work.

Once placement in the job has happened, the focus is on teaching the job and supporting productivity. An efficient teaching technology is essential but consideration also has to be given to how choice of teaching method relates to eventual withdrawal of on-the-job support. There has been a reappraisal of the traditional approach of placing a job coach with the trainee worker who teaches him or her the job by using methods based on systematic instruction, initially prompting performance and subsequently fading prompts. One line of development is to work more with the natural supports in the environment and to adapt existing training practices to make them effective (Callahan, 1992). Another is to use techniques of self-instruction and problem-solving to teach the person to regulate their own performance on the job and to be more adaptable to changing working conditions (Wehmeyer, Kelchner and Richards, 1996). Whatever approach is followed, teaching and support programmes of some degree of sophistication need to be devised and implemented consistently.

As in the previous models, quality appraisal and monitoring go hand in hand and relate to the interface between service and service user. In this case, monitoring would be concerned with the range of jobs found, the placement of people into jobs, indicators of choice and the degree of self-determination which people have exercised, the quality of teaching (input, rate of fading prompts, rate of fading input etc.), the quality of support and motivation concerned with doing the job (productivity and employer appraisals of satisfaction), relationships (integrative potential of the job, nature and frequency of interactions with co-workers, how break time is spent, carryover to out-of-work association with co-workers) and travelling to and from work. Equally effective behaviour change may well be relevant to a person with a tendency to show challenging behaviour.

Developing a social and leisure life

Figure 10.5 sets out a directly analogous model for supporting people to participate in activities in the community, particularly leisure pursuits alongside community peers without disabilities. It could be used as a guide to develop a technology for the community support aspect of domiciliary support services and for community-oriented day services, both of which have expanded under the AWS (see Chapters 7 and 8). However, unlike supported employment, the model is not founded in widespread experience but in a logical analysis underpinned by the premise that there is no difference between effective participation at work and effective participation in leisure activities. Indeed, the apparent assumption in day and community support services that leisure is a less demanding context than work is at the heart of why we believe that individuals often only achieve the most minimal level of integration, some form of parallel presence in the community but not true participation.

The types of one-to-one domiciliary support services which attempted to promote community integration which we observed in the course of our research (Evans et al., 1992; see also Chapter 7) were unsophisticated. The individual was allocated a support worker. There did not seem to be any match between the characteristics of the support worker, the individual and the community activity which was the focus of support: for example, a middle-aged woman accompanying a young man to a youth club, a hearing man with little knowledge of sign language accompanying a deaf man to a club for deaf, signing people. Importantly, supporters were not part of the social context themselves and could not provide any privileged entry for the person into a ready made social grouping. Indeed, selection of the support worker clearly came before development of the activity. Generating something to do, setting developmental goals, working out how to provide support and trying to balance the tension between leaving

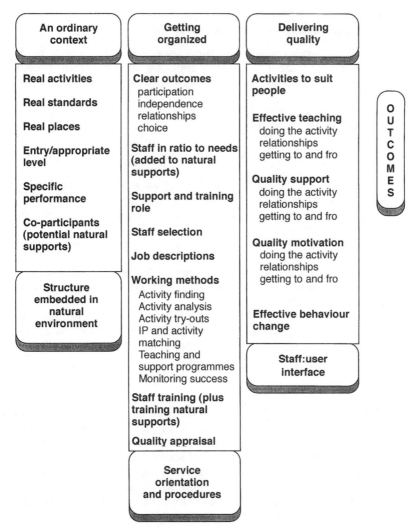

Figure 10.5 An ordinary life and service design: community life

the person unsupported and getting in the way of their potential involvement with other people in the setting were left mainly to the initiative of the support workers.

One reason why leisure may be viewed as easier than work is that there may be a convenient disregard for the true standards of activities as performed by citizens without disabilities. Independence in the activity at a reasonable standard is rarely seen as a goal. Rather, the continued presence of the support worker is assumed. Leisure does not have the productivity/wage contract which in work makes performance standards obvious. Ignoring informal standards is easier but it is a pretence nonetheless. Of course, not everyone who gets involved in competitive games, art

---

Key research findings: social and leisure life

- Significant strides towards community presence have been made
- Strategies for identifying and enlisting support from friends, neighbours and other communities of interest were generally lacking
- Generic services were too often propelled by policies insensitive to the needs of people with learning disabilities, hindering access and use
- Individuals lacked non-disabled confidantes in their personal networks
- Individuals with more severe disabilities were more dependent upon families as gatekeepers to social and leisure activities
- People in long-stay hospitals continued to lead more socially restricted lives
- Ordinary citizens were typically not involved in strategic or service planning
- Achievement of community participation by individuals often depended upon others acting as mediators, benefactors or personal supporters
- Widespread community participation is yet to be accomplished
- Citizen advocacy schemes which might promote both leisure and community integrated lifestyles were few and far between

---

and culture, interest groups and the like is an expert, but that does not mean that standards are unimportant. Many clubs and associations set threshold standards for membership and many others achieve them informally by the extension or withdrawal of social acceptance. Particularly in adulthood, people gravitate to the activities which they can do reasonably well and give up those at which they are not good enough. Therefore, if people are being involved in activities where real standards apparently do not apply, it is likely that they are not real activities. Real integration is, therefore, unlikely to be achieved.

For example, in the course of the research referred to above, we observed a young man attend a youth club where the activities were pool, table tennis, a disco and 'watching television' in a darkened side room, all conducted against a backdrop of male:female adolescent relationships. The person with learning disability spent some time playing table tennis with the much younger daughter of the youth club organizer. Neither could play well and both were content to retrieve the ball from around the hall with the frequency that it was hit, missing the table altogether. It was difficult to see how the standard of performance could be reconciled with peer group norms. Later, he spent some time playing pool with another man with learning disabilities also attending the club with a different support worker. Neither could reliably hit the coloured balls with the cue ball let alone pot the coloured balls or play according to the competitive rules and strategies of the game. They stopped playing when other boys came to have a go, seemingly intimidated. The nature of the game that followed with the boys being watched by male and female friends alike was utterly different.

Once reaching threshold competence is seen as a relevant issue, the importance of analysing activities for the demands they make becomes clear as does systematically generating as long a list of alternative 'entry level' activities as possible. Realistic assessment of individual skills and preferences is a complementary process. Therefore, the working methods of activity finding, activity analysis, activity try-outs, individual planning and activity matching are the essential starting points of service expertise. Once an activity has been identified, one can select a support worker with advantages in terms of supporting the introduction of the person with disability to the specific setting in question. There is the potential to recruit and train people already involved in the activity to provide support, that is to use a natural supports approach which capitalizes on the integration potential of that arrangement. There will need to be a means of establishing efficient and effective teaching – techniques of systematic instruction and self-instruction for example – and a means of monitoring success.

In directly similar fashion to supported employment, monitoring would be concerned with the range of activities found, the placement of people into activities, indicators of choice and the degree of self-determination which people have exercised, the quality of teaching (input, rate of fading prompts, rate of fading input etc.), the quality of support and motivation concerned with doing the activity (participation and peer appraisals of satisfaction), relationships (integrative potential of the activity, nature and frequency of interactions with peers, carryover association with peers outside of the activity) and travelling to and from the activity. Equally, effective behaviour change may well be relevant to a person with a tendency to show challenging behaviour.

The complexity of service design

What we have tried to illustrate is that the 'devil is in the detail'. For example, the poverty of institutional care was not explained by the metaphor of institutionalization any more than the neglect was experienced in reality as a conceptual abstraction. What occurred within the institutions was due to the complex interaction of many factors; some resulting from intentional design, others by omission. The institutions were not poor simply because they were large, poorly equipped and isolated. They were poor for many other reasons as well: the absence of relevant goals; the absence of effort put into planning and providing people with opportunities and support; the absence of staff expertise in behavioural development; the absence of managerial attention to performance indicators related to quality of life and so on. Behaviourally, institutions were extremely permissive environments, seeking rarely to encourage or discourage any particular form of activity among people (Felce, de Kock and Repp, 1986). Reversing the reality as opposed to the metaphor of institutionalization requires the kind of conditions to be put in place which we have described in the preceding section. No levers have been found which, when pulled, start a chain reaction so that everything else falls into place. No variables have been identified which when manipulated have had such a powerful effect on the quality of life of the people served that guidance on how to provide a high quality service can be simplified. Policy makers and the professional world have often acted as if there were just a few key decisions to be taken or parameters to be determined. Experience has shown that the truth is far more complicated.

The prescriptions we have outlined are only a start in fleshing out what is to be done. For the most part, we have assumed that the person with the learning disability, and his or her family, are the most important figures in all this. We have not considered what is to be done when there are differences or clashes of perspective between them since this raises issues about relationships of power which are considered in the concluding chapter. We also wish to stress that it would be wrong to lay the responsibility for change and adaptation principally at the feet of service users and their families, even with the help of technically competent services. The responsibility lies with the whole community. This takes us back to the realms of policy and to ideas about community and citizenship.

References

Barnes, M. (1997). Families and empowerment. In: *Empowerment in Everyday Life: Learning Disability*, (P. Ramcharan, G. Roberts, G. Grant and J. Borland, eds) pp. 70–87. London: Jessica Kingsley.

Bellamy, G. T., Rhodes, L. E., Bourbeau, P. E. and Mank, D. M. (1986). Mental retardation services in sheltered workshops and day activity programs: consumer benefits and policy alternatives. In: *Competitive Employment: Issues and Strategies*, (F. R. Rusch, ed.) pp. 257–271. Baltimore: Paul H. Brookes.

Beyer, S. (1995). Real jobs and supported employment. In: *Values and Visions: Changing Ideas in Services for People with Learning Disabilities*, (T. Philpot and L. Ward, eds) pp. 55–72. London: Butterworth Heinemann.

Beyer, S., Goodere, L. and Kilsby, M. (1996). *The Costs and Benefits of Supported Employment Agencies*. London: The Stationary Office.

Callahan, M. (1992). Job site training and natural supports. In: *Natural Supports in Schools, at Work and in the Community for People with Severe Disabilities*, (J. Nisbet, ed.) pp. 257–276. Baltimore: Paul H. Brookes.

de Kock, U., Saxby, H., Felce, D. *et al.* (1988). Individual planning for severely and profoundly mentally handicapped adults in a community-based service. *Mental Handicap*, **16**, 152–155.

Donabedian, A. (1988). The quality of care: how can it be assessed? *Journal of the American Medical Association*, **260**, 1743–1748.

Duker, P., Seys, D., Leeuwe, J. V. and Prins, L. W. (1991). Occupational conditions of ward staff and quality of residential care for individuals with mental retardation. *American Journal on Mental Retardation*, **95**, 388–396.

Dunst, C. J. and Trivette, C. M. (1988). Toward experimental evaluation of the family, infant and preschool program. In: *Evaluating Family Programs*, (H. B. Weiss and F. H. Jacobs, eds) pp. 315–346. New York: Aldine de Gruyter.

Dunst, C. J. and Trivette, C. M. (1994). Empowering case management practices: a family-centred perspective. In: *Supporting and Strengthening Families: Volume 1 Methods, Strate-*

gies and Practices, (C. J. Dunst, C. M. Trivette and A. G. Deal, eds) pp. 187–196. Cambridge MA: Brookline Books.

Dunst, C. J., Trivette, C. M., Davis, M. and Cornwell, J. C. (1994). Characteristics of effective help-giving practices. In: *Supporting and Strengthening Families: Volume 1 Methods, Strategies and Practices*, (C. J. Dunst, C. M. Trivette and A. G. Deal, eds) pp. 171–186. Cambridge MA: Brookline Books.

Dunst, C. J., Trivette, C. M. and Deal, A. G. (1994). *Supporting and Strengthening Families: Volume 1 Methods, Strategies and Practices.* Cambridge MA: Brookline Books.

Emerson, E. and Hatton, C. (1994). *Moving Out: Relocation from Hospital to Community.* London: HMSO.

Emerson, E., Alborz, A., Kiernan, C. *et al.* (1997). *The HARC Challenging Behaviour Project Report 5: Treatment, Management and Service Utilisation.* Manchester: Hester Adrian Research Centre, University of Manchester.

Evans, G., Felce, D., de Paiva, S. and Todd, S. (1992). Observing the delivery of a domiciliary support service. *Disability, Handicap and Society*, **7**, 19–34.

Felce, D. (1996). The quality of support for ordinary living: staff:resident interactions and resident activity. In: *Deinstitutionalization and Community Living: Intellectual Disability Services in Britain, Scandinavia and the USA*, (J. Mansell and K. Ericcson, eds) pp. 117–133. London: Chapman and Hall.

Felce, D. and Beyer, S. (1996). Making progress together: the interplay between research and services. In: *Innovations in Evaluating Services for People with Intellectual Disabilities*, (R. McConkey, ed.) pp. 41–60. Whittle-le-Woods, Lancashire: Lisieux Hall Publications.

Felce, D. and Perry, J. (1995). The extent of support for ordinary living provided in staffed housing: the relationship between staffing levels, resident dependency, staff:resident interactions and resident activity patterns. *Social Science and Medicine*, **40**, 799–810.

Felce, D., de Kock, U. and Repp, A. (1986). An eco-behavioural analysis of small community-based houses and traditional large hospitals for severely and profoundly mentally handicapped adults. *Applied Research in Mental Retardation*, **7**, 393–408.

Felce, D., Repp, A. C., Thomas, M. *et al.* (1991). The relationship of staff:client ratios, interactions and residential placement. *Research in Developmental Disabilities*, **12**, 315–331.

Grant, G. (1993). Support networks and transitions over two years among adults with a mental handicap, *Mental Handicap Research*, **6**, 36–55.

Grant, G. and Wenger, G. C. (1993). Dynamics of support networks: differences and similarities between vulnerable groups. *Irish Journal of Psychology*, **14**, 79–98.

Greenspan, S. and Shoultz, B. (1981). Why mentally retarded adults lose their jobs: social competence in work adjustments. *Mental Retardation*, **19**, 103–106.

Hanley-Maxwell, C., Rusch, F. R., Chadsey-Rusch, J. and Renzaglia, A. (1986). Factors contributing to job terminations. *Journal of the Association for Persons with Severe Handicaps*, **11**, 45–52.

Harper, G. (1989). Life sharing. *Community Living*, **2**, 6–7.

Harris, J. M., Veit, S. W., Allen, G. J. and Chinsky, J. M. (1974). Aide-resident ratio and ward population density as mediators of social interaction. *American Journal of Mental Deficiency*, **79**, 320–326.

Hatton, C., Emerson, E., Robertson, J. *et al.* (1995). *An Evaluation of the Quality and Costs of Services for Adults with Severe Learning Disabilities and Sensory Impairments.* Manchester: Hester Adrian Research Centre, Manchester University.

Hewson, S. and Walker, J. (1992). The use of evaluation in the development of a staffed residential service for adults with mental handicap. *Mental Handicap Research*, **5**, 188–203.

Independent Development Council for People with Mental Handicap (IDC) (1986). *Pursuing Quality.* London: King's Fund Centre.

Jones, E., Perry, J., Lowe, K. *et al.* (1997). *Opportunity and the Promotion of Activity Among Adults with Severe Learning Disabilities Living in Community Housing: the Impact of Training Staff in Active Support.* Cardiff: Welsh Centre for Learning Disabilities Applied Research Unit, University of Wales College of Medicine.

King's Fund (1984). *An Ordinary Working Life*. London: King's Fund Centre.

Kinsella, P. (1993). *Supported Living: a New Paradigm*. Manchester: National Development Team.

McGill, P. and Toogood, A. (1994). Organising community placements. In: *Severe Learning Disabilities and Challenging Behaviours: Designing High Quality Services*, (E. Emerson, P. McGill and J. Mansell, eds) pp. 232–259. London: Chapman and Hall.

Mansell, J., Felce, D., Jenkins, J. and de Kock, U. (1982). Increasing staff ratios in an activity with severely mentally handicapped people. *British Journal of Mental Subnormality*, **28**, 97–99.

Nocon, A. and Qureshi, H. (1996). *Outcomes of Community Care for Users and Carers: a Social Services Perspective*. Buckingham: Open University Press.

Nolan, M., Grant, G. and Keady, J. (1996). *Understanding Family Care: a Multidimensional Model of Caring and Coping*. Buckingham: Open University Press.

Repp, A. C., Barton, L. E. and Brulle, A. R. (1981). Correspondence between effectiveness and staff use of instructions for severely retarded persons. *Applied Research in Mental Retardation*, **2**, 237–245.

Repp, A. C., Barton, L. E. and Brulle, A. R. (1982). Naturalistic studies of mentally retarded persons V: the effects of staff instructions on student responding. *Applied Research in Mental Retardation*, **3**, 55–65.

Stancliffe, R. J. (1997). Community living-unit size, staff presence and residents' choice-making. *Mental Retardation*, **35**, 1–9.

Thomas Patterson, N. (1997). Conflicting norms in modern British kinship: case studies of domestic violence and competition for care in North Wales 1920–1996. *The History of the Family; an International Quarterly*, **2**, 1, 1–29.

Wehmeyer, M. L., Kelchner, K. and Richards, S. (1996). Individual and environmental factors related to the self-determination of adults with mental retardation. *Vocational Rehabilitation*, **5**, 291–306.

Welsh Office (1996). *The Welsh Mental Handicap Strategy: Guidance 1994*. Cardiff: Welsh Office.

Whelan, E. and Speake, B. (1977). *Adult Training Centres in England and Wales*. Manchester: National Association of Teachers of the Mentally Handicapped.

Chapter 11

The policy context: ashes in search of a phoenix

Our concern in this final chapter is to explore how optimistic we can be about the future development of learning disability services. The focus remains Wales but much of the analysis is relevant to the UK and beyond. What is the likelihood that the extension of services required to make them genuinely comprehensive at the local level will occur? To what extent can we expect further refinements in service design in line with our discussion in the previous chapter? As both questions relate to the initial scope and underlying principles of the AWS, we end by addressing the policy and operational context of learning disability services in Wales as it now stands.

Even though 'relaunched' as recently as 1994, the AWS has largely and effectively been superseded by the NHS and Community Care Act 1990 (NHSCCA), the Carers (Recognition and Services) Act 1995 and the Community Care (Direct Payments) Act 1996. We have already commented on the hollow aspirational nature of the current guidance specifically relating to the AWS (Welsh Office, 1996). It contains virtually no consideration of the precise service infrastructure required to meet its far ranging recommendations, sets no planning targets and is mute about the financial implications of what it urges local authorities to do. Indeed, in some respects, the new guidance replaces the previous distinctive clarity of the AWS over the nature of services to be developed with a return to more traditional non-prescription. For example, guidance on residential accommodation, once clearly recommending ordinary housing, now endorses the provision of 'other forms of accommodation, especially for those who want a more protected environment or who have special needs' (Welsh Office, 1996, p. 11). If the AWS is still considered to exist, it is in many respects devoid of strategy.

As embodied in the document which launched it, the AWS was regarded as a detailed and prescriptive policy. It was backed by a Working Party report which had set out a costed model of local services and it made clear statements about what it wanted to see developed, for example, in relation to individual planning, community teams, housing, user consultation and involvement in planning and inter-agency working. That it can still be criticized for being too general and for leaving much latitude for uncontrolled local variation in practice shows how loosely framed traditional British policy has been. There have been exceptions where the government itself has taken the policy initiative, such as in some of the educational reforms of recent years, but policy often remains broad brush when government is responsive to a changing professional tide. If a prescriptive policy like the original AWS only went part way to meeting its goals, what can be expected from the more generally framed current policy? Now that the AWS is a policy in ashes, will the NHSCCA rise like a phoenix and finish the job?

We discuss this question by comparing community care policy as a successor to the AWS and examine whether it represents a more or less conducive framework for providing the range and quality of service support required. In doing so, we explore five issues:

1 the basis for deciding the scope of services in response to individual need
2 the power relationship between service commissioners and service recipients in determining the scope and nature of services
3 the extent to which service provision guidance is evidence-based
4 the attention given to learning disability specialism, and
5 the idea of community care and the emphasis given to embedding services in the complex ecologies of local communities.

The scope of service support: Appealing to individual needs and rights

There is no incompatibility between setting indicative provision targets for populations as whole, for example provision norms, and individual assessment of the precise nature of service input different people require or want. The two operate at a different level. Variation at the population level is always less than that at the individual level as variation decreases with aggregation. Browne (1996) has argued that 'initially population needs assessment came second to individual needs assessment in the implementation of community care, but now it needs to move centre stage' (pp. 63–4). However, service provision norms have been seen as a symbol of the 'menu-driven' service allocation approach criticized by reformers keen to see a move to individualized 'needs-led' service design. At the same time, it also suited those wanting to constrain the welfare commitments of the state to avoid guaranteeing a certain level of provision and to devolve responsibility for determining response to need to the local level. Assessment of individual needs and the notion of services being responsive to local variation in need has been part of recent government ideology. Since the AWS and community care policy share a similar rhetoric, one might have expected a smooth transition from one to the other. However, their emphasis on individual determination of needed services may stem from different motivations.

Need has been seen as a key justification for the existence of public services since the formation of the welfare state. However, there is a debate about the usefulness, validity and acceptability of the concept (Percy-Smith, 1996; Sanderson, 1996). There is also a distinction to be made between normative (professionally assessed) need and felt or expressed need (Bradshaw, 1972). Thus, which concept of need is being employed is critically important to the scope of service provision. The notion of 'wants' may be more inclusive and imply greater entitlement to support than that of 'needs' (Barnes and Wistow, 1992; Dowson, 1997). Moreover, there can be an appeal to civil 'rights' and 'well-being' as necessary outcomes (Oliver, 1991; Coote, 1993; Rioux, 1994). Additionally, one can distinguish 'procedural' rights, that is a right to participate in a process of identifying needs or wants, from 'substantive' rights, that is the right to stated outcomes. A further contemporary distinction in the needs literature is that between individual needs as expressed in the market, and collectivist needs arising from a consideration of the general welfare of communities. Policy is not explicit about the terminology it uses so that any link between expressed need and a duty to respond to need is not clear.

Although community care policy is generally more vague on questions of individual needs and rights than was the AWS, where there is clarity, it is in a return to professionally regulated and rationed procedures. Perhaps the most substantial difference between the AWS and the NHSCCA is in the extent to which individual planning should become a regular feature of people's interface with services. If service provision is to be based on an individual assessment of need, then one might conclude that any policy which sought comprehensive implementation of individual review was directed towards opening up the availability of support to those in need, while any policy which sought to restrict needs assessment was directed towards limiting demand for services. The AWS proposed that the vast majority of people and their families would be involved in an individual assessment of need, an aim which came close to legitimizing comprehensive cradle-to-grave coverage, although it was never achieved in practice. Need was expressed as an absolute concept and there was an expectation that service provision would be organized and funded in response. In contrast, the NHSCCA describes much more restricted criteria akin to establishing whether threshold criteria for certain service inputs are met. Need under these circumstances is a relative concept, framed within service availability and budgetary considerations (Ellis, 1993; Roberts, 1997).

One could argue that the NHSCCA learned from the apparent inability under the AWS to organize comprehensive individual planning and that a means had to be found to slim down the amount of professional time spent coordinating need assessment by prioritizing only those most in need. However, the service gatekeeping role of needs assessment is only one of its functions. Detailed individual planning is inextricably bound up in the quality of service delivery as we have portrayed it in the previous chapter, whether one is seeking to provide support to families or to individuals in their own homes, in the workplace or in the community. The burden placed on professional resources by individual planning as it is often conducted may well need to be reduced, but an alternative to reducing the scope and function of individual planning is to devolve it away from professional control to those more intimately concerned, such as support workers or other carers. Another alternative is to make sure that what is essentially a new service process is funded properly. The NHSCCA has made no moves in this direction. Rather, extensiveness of care assessment seems to have been targeted at the expense of detail and recent evidence indicates that the professionals involved feel that the burden of administration it entails is heavy (McGrath *et al.*, 1997; Parry-Jones *et al.*, in press).

One of the failings of the AWS was in not foreseeing that individual planning was a resource intensive process. The development of community infrastructure was an early AWS priority through the creation of multidisciplinary community teams. However, individual planning sets challenges for services by unpeeling successive layers of needed action and by rendering the expertise of the service accountable to its users. Good assessment and proper review take time. They work best when there is a quality of empathy perceived between the keyworker and service user or family (Grant, McGrath and Ramcharan, 1994; Grant, 1997). Moreover, if assessment is to be the basis of an enhanced quality of life, it is important that the process is empowering, involving service users fully, treating their opinions with respect and creating a sense of their equal ownership of the process and resulting assessment. Added to this is the need to establish a comprehensive perspective of the interlocking relationships between family, home, school, work, community and professional agencies and therapists. This needs to be undertaken in ways which generate clearly recorded goals and which help render the service accountable for its action. As a consequence, there is no sense in which individual planning can be conducted other than as integral to the long-term working of the service system. A comparison of these characteristics of needs assessment with the exhortations of the Community Care White Paper (Secretaries of State, 1989), policy guidance (Department of Health, 1990) and practice guidance on care assessment (Social Services Inspectorate, 1991a, b) reveals some sharp contrasts in assumptions and expectations.

Perhaps the most obvious is the impact of the purchaser-provider split in community care. The episodic nature of care review as conceived by the NHSCCA and the separation of needs assessment (part of the purchasing function), from the ongoing business of service provision, undermines the culture of participation between different service elements and service users that had begun to form under the aegis of the AWS. These changes were contrary to what many practitioners in learning disability services in Wales felt constituted good practice. Reservations are being expressed about the application of an administrative model of care management to services rather than one which genuinely seeks to understand the service and community support which individuals need in order to enjoy a typical quality of life.

Who decides the level of service support?

Ultimately, decisions about the level of service support must rest with those required to match the resource implications of service support to available expenditure. However, there are many different shades in how negotiated arrangements may be and in the structures which are developed to link identification of need to the provision of services. Care assessment, like statementing in relation to special educational needs, locates the assessment of need and the recommendation of services to meet need within the agencies responsible for commissioning those services. In contrast, systems of service brokerage invest the assessment of need in an independent third party and view the development of a service package to meet need as a negotiation between parties. The AWS envisaged this negotiation as being conducted within a wholly collaborative partnership centred on the process of individual planning in which all stakeholders were equally involved. 'The individual plan is a means of enabling . . . people to form a collaborative partnership with the client and their family in order to plan and deliver the services required by the client . . . The importance of (their) full involvement . . . cannot be overstated. Plans must not at any stage be the product of professional assessment alone' (Welsh Office, 1983, para. 6.4.4).

The rather weaker statements in present policy do not match the force of the AWS, e.g. 'Assessments should take account of the wishes of the individual and his/her carer' (Secretaries of State, 1989, para. 3.2.6). Moreover, whereas need construed in terms of a quality of life improvement created scope for service users and their representatives to determine the specific directions or goals to be set, need more narrowly defined as a need for services or need for treatment reinforces traditional professional hegemony over resource decisions. There are relatively few enforceable legal rights in this area (Roberts, 1997) and the precedent has now been established by the courts that individuals do not have the right to services simply on the basis of an assessment of need if authorities do not have the resources to provide the recommended service input. However, there are indications that unit costs of services, even when available, are not linked to service outcomes (Cambridge and Knapp, 1997). Perhaps not surprisingly, social care plans have not emphasized mechanisms to strengthen user or carer involvement (Ramcharan, 1994). Nor can carers look too hopefully at the Carers (Recognition and Services) Act 1995. Eligibility for an assessment is restricted and some have argued that the criteria overemphasize a task-based view of caring (Nolan, Grant and Keady, 1996).

Although Meethan (1995, p. 133) has seen recent legislation as prompting 'substantial changes in the pattern of power relations . . .(in which) users were no longer to be considered as passive recipients, but as active participants in the assessment of their needs', our analysis sees the NHSCCA and other recent legislation as extending procedural rights but not substantive rights and, then, only to some. Admittedly, the principles of the AWS were worded in only general terms, but they did provide a vision of what people might expect as a minimum outcome from the provision of services. Any notion of substantive rights is undermined by the absence of a policy commitment to outcome. Such an absence also raises questions about the veracity of a concept of need in the social policy arena and support for user empowerment. While, as we have seen in the experience of the AWS, user or more particularly carer influence over planning did not necessarily result in proposals seen as compatible with AWS values, the NHSCCA has done nothing to resolve this tension except by being less concerned about outcome.

Consumer control over the nature and quality of services can be established by individualized funding (Roeher Institute, 1991, 1993) through direct payment or voucher systems or something similar to the Independent Living Fund (Morris, 1993). The Community Care (Direct Payments) Act, 1996 takes a tentative step in this direction by enabling local authority social services departments to make direct payments to some people whom it has assessed as needing care services. There remain, however, some problems with access to such funds for many people with learning disabilities because the Policy and Practice Guidance (Welsh Office, 1997) states that 'everyone to whom direct payments are made must be willing and able to manage them (alone or with assistance)' (para. 11, p. 4). Further requirements are that the person must understand the nature of direct payments, be able to make a decision between services for him or herself and understand the legal responsibilities of becoming an employer. Most importantly, the whole system of direct payments still requires a needs assessment under current community care legislation and is not related to outcome criteria such as personal well-being, citizenship or integration.

Developing evidence-based social care

A characteristic of well formulated policy is that the service structures and processes recommended are consistent with the outcomes which the policy espouses. For example, we commented earlier that the policy *Better Services for the Mentally Handicapped* (DHSS, 1971) can be criticized for continuing to recommend institutional service models which had already been demonstrated not to deliver the outcomes contained within its statement of general principles. The AWS on the other hand was seen as taking account of research and development in the decade which preceded it and advocating the development of services which were consistent with its goals. Currently, particularly within the NHS, there is much discussion of the need to adopt evidence-based practice. The effectiveness of services or procedures needs to be taken into account and must qualify professional autonomy. There is a less strong culture of empiricism within social care, but the principle that services should reflect knowledge about the link between service design and outcome is difficult to contest.

The AWS set out a number of outcomes for the lifestyles of people with learning disabilities and their families and made recommendations about the nature of services to achieve these outcomes. Some recommendations were clearly ideological or based only on professional wisdom or prediction; for example, the change in agency roles between health and social services, the establishment of multidisciplinary community teams and the restructuring of day services. Others, such as the emphasis given to community-based ordinary housing as the basis of residential services and the respite function of domiciliary support services, were based on emerging evidence. The AWS and similar reforms throughout Britain have promoted further research which has strengthened the basis of evidence. Much of this has been described in the course of this book. The British literature on the replacement of institutional residential services by community housing provides one particularly clear example as it has recently been reviewed (Emerson and Hatton, 1994; Hatton and Emerson, 1996). Hatton and Emerson concluded that people in community housing services live in more pleasant and enriched surroundings, are more satisfied, have greater privacy and choice over everyday aspects of their lives, may make some modest gains in skills, and have more opportunities for activity at home and in the community. Generally, their parents and relatives express greater satisfaction with community services than institutions. The recent change in the AWS guidance lessening emphasis on the provision of housing models is clearly not evidence-based.

Nor has the NHSCCA furthered the idea of evidence-based policy. It has not taken from and built on a further decade of research and development in the field. The opportunity to get to grips with the necessary level of detail generated by research evidence – the refinements which could now be made to the processes of service delivery and the better understanding of the relationships between the independent variables of service design and dependent outcomes – has been missed. Rather, there has been a retreat from prescription save in the setting up of apparent market dynamics which are supposed to drive up standards, an innovation which itself was not empirically tested.

Many commentators have indicated that the community care market differs in character from a free or commercial market (LeGrand, 1990; Hoyes and Means, 1993; Wistow *et al.*, 1994). The consumer is not the customer and is not presented with a range of substitute 'goods'. Rather the commissioner acts as customer. However, the commissioner may value outcomes differently to the consumer and has a separate self-interest which may not be consistent with consumer welfare. Competition is mediated by a contracting process which may meet the commissioner's problem-resolution and financial interests but may have little to do with consumer outcomes. There may be too few providers to ensure effective competition in any case. There is an arm's-length inspection process to review contract compliance but, apart from the suspicion that there is inadequate independence of the inspection machinery from the commissioning agency, there are serious questions to be asked about the extent to which quality of outcome is specified in contracts and whether the inspectorate have the technology and resources at their disposal to measure it. The efficiency of a market to regulate quality of outcome is, therefore, compromised. As Cambridge and Knapp (1997) conclude in their analysis of learning disability services, information about the relationship between the costs of individual services, service packages and their outcomes is often missing. The adoption of the market separation between purchasers and providers does not remove the need for specialist knowledge related to specifying service structures, processes and outcomes. Rather, such knowledge needs to drive purchasing and the specification of contracts and inform quality inspection.

Learning disability as a specialism

There is an obvious fundamental difference between the specific nature of the AWS as a policy concerned with learning disabilities and the more general NHSCCA. The planning focus at local authority level engendered by the AWS was considerable and the common cause created around learning disabilities was, with time, able to break down long-standing inter-agency barriers. Learning disabilities emerged from its traditional Cinderella status alongside other more powerful lobbies and commanded a concentration of planning effort which led to an accumulating expertise. A review of the social care plans (1993–6) for the then eight Welsh counties (Ramcharan, 1994) indicated that most proposed to maintain the county and local planning structures of the AWS years. However, in creating 22 unitary authorities in Wales, local government reorganization has altered arrangements. The reduced size of authorities has meant that new planning and management structures have typically adopted a multi-user group focus, a move to genericism in line with the NHSCCA. The AWS had underscored the priority of learning disability developments by ring-fenced funding. With the withdrawal of this arrangement, learning disabilities has been returned to a competition for funding with other specialisms, in which it is unlikely to fare well, particularly in the short-term. The level of seniority of social services officers wholly specializing in learning disabilities is now lower, the previous specialist Assistant Directors being replaced by those with a multiple remit. Moreover, local government reorganization caused a break-up of previously experienced specialist planning and development teams as personnel found or failed to find jobs in the new structures throughout Wales.

This destabilization within professional ranks has been matched by disarray in the carer and self-advocacy movements which had been aligned to the previous county boundaries and drew financial support from the old authorities. Without the safeguards of population needs assessment (see Browne, 1996, for arguments to support the need for demographic and epidemiological information to complement individual needs assessment) and strong consumer representation, there is a distinct likelihood that AWS principles, service provision targets and planning mechanisms will quickly dissipate. Learning disabilities has seen a concern for quality of life and a willingness to restructure the characteristics of services which have not been matched in some other community care groups. For example, the residential care received by elderly people in both its hospital and local authority forms has changed little in comparison with the deinstitutionalization effort in learning disabilities. It is possible that a more generic approach across the community care groups will broaden the application of the types of development seen in learning disabilities. It is equally possible that learning disability thinking will be subordinated and the emphasis on quality of outcome lost.

Moreover, while there may be some value in the idea that there is much common ground in principle in the issues concerning the different community care groups, the particular nature of the group's disabilities or difficulties varies as do the means by which people can be helped. One of the central lessons from experience in the last decade is that desired outcomes are not fully realized if macro-organizational change is not accompanied by micro-organizational change. The latter is dependent on specialist expertise and this is an issue of the particular client group. The greater genericism of organization of the lead social care agency does not augur well in this respect. Social services were not experienced at the outset of the AWS at providing the type of services which it recommended, but it was building expertise out of the focus which the AWS demanded. Increasingly, the importance of the micro-organization of service support was becoming realized. It is less clear now whether the acknowledgement of the need for technical competency will be sustained.

The place of community

Bulmer's (1987) reworking of Abram's (1978) conceptualizations of support identified four different applications of the term 'community care'. In its original use, it meant care outside of institutions. Then again, it can be applied to all professional services which operate outside of institutions. In its third sense, it can be used to define care by the community, principally through the family or not-for-profit collectives. Finally, it can be used to describe provision which is as close to ordinary living as possible. We can locate change under the AWS along this continuum. There has been a major shift to community care as defined by the first two of these criteria, although there is a lingering presence of institutional residential, day care, and professional inpatient and outpatient services. There has been an injection of resources to support family care and the contribution of not-for-profit voluntary agencies in planning and delivering services has expanded. One could conclude that there has been a strengthening of care and support by the community. However, the ways by which services have sought to maintain family care may not have broadened their community involvement to any great extent. Service input has been directed at providing the most obvious instrumental relief but there is a potential still to reinforce the family's ties to the community by strengthening or expanding informal support networks. Moreover, many of the voluntary agencies have originated from the service world rather than by collective community action and peopled by local citizens. So there is scope to use the resources of the community more in promoting the goal of inclusive communities.

In terms of the fourth definition, attempts to re-work services so that they build on typical community contexts in line with the model we illustrated in Chapter 10, have been particularly evident in integrated school and pre-school provision, ordinary housing, supported employment and attempts to provide people with individualized community support. That these were not always successful in moving beyond community presence to community participation prompted our analysis of the needed specialist competence upon which outcome depends. However, even this analysis is incomplete in that, consistent with the emphasis on individualized service design, it assumes that all necessary solutions to people's needs and problems can be resolved at the individual level. Although much can undoubtedly be done, it is not an acceptable generalization. As Smale *et al.* (1994, p. 72) urge, 'we have to confront the tendency to regress to the individualization of social problems'. Social models of disability explore how people's identities are shaped by structures, processes and understandings which give rise to society's political, administrative and welfare institutions. Remedial action which changes the nature and practice of society's institutions will not fully solve the problem. The community itself has to be involved in reconfiguring disability and its response to it. This leads to a further interpretation of community care to those detailed above by Bulmer, namely care for the community in which the positive resolution of the difficulties faced by people with disabilities enhances the collective well-being of the community.

Lessons for the new community care can be summarized in these connections. First, a concentration on assessment and care management risks perpetuating the individualization of social problems. It therefore runs the risk of placing too much responsibility for change and adaptation on the shoulders of the individual with learning disabilities, and allows government and society to abdicate responsibility for change. Assessment and service support for individuals is important and it is equally important that it is done competently, but the community needs to be part of the process and party to the outcome if people with learning disabilities are to be seen as contributors and not just as dependent. Secondly, the experience of the AWS and the new community care suggest to us that neither government nor local agencies are too interested in cataloguing and publicly reporting unmet needs. Reports of service deficiencies within the service world are a weak force for change. Hence, the very system of individualized assessment is vulnerable to failure in one of its primary functions. Local political and social support for the concerns of community members affected by disability has to be engendered. Thirdly, a more concerted approach is required to deal with those environmental and social factors which accentuate disability. In particular, a community development approach needs to be seen as integral to service design (Henderson and Armstrong, 1993). Community work and community development were lacking within the AWS and there is little sign that they have emerged with any force within the new community care arrangements. Consequently, there continue to be dangers that latent human resources in the community will lie untapped, opportunities to help people be and feel part of the community will be overlooked and systematic approaches to appreciate and bolster people's networks of support will be underutilized. Fourth, people with life-long disabilities need reassurance that their entitlements to support will not be jeopardized by instabilities created by a competitive welfare market. A framework of agreed population-based provision norms provides a safeguard against local neglect.

A new AWS

The trajectory set by the AWS foresaw development reaching the half-way point at the end of the first ten years. Since then, it has continued to exist in only diminished form, superseded by a policy which does not compensate for what has been lost. Not surprisingly, there is still much to do to make service availability comprehensive and service operation sophisticated enough to attain the ambitious goals of the Strategy. Although unlikely to occur in the short to medium term, nothing less than a new central government initiative on the scale of the AWS is needed to take forward the developments which we have discussed in the last two chapters. In the absence of political protection and any further concerted attention being given to learning disability concerns, there is a danger that it will return to its Cinderella, backwater status. Professional and officer influence is likely to be reasserted in a period of retrenchment and the balance between more and less progressive views may change. The AWS sponsored the progressive, reforming professional viewpoint. Its demise might see a return to more traditional perspectives, a re-emergence of the idea that one can serve people by segregating them coupled with a willingness to economize on resource expenditure and the ambition of the outcomes to be achieved.

We finish by considering the remit which a new Strategy would fulfil. It would:

1 update the Working Party specification of needed service support in the light of contemporary epidemiological and service evaluation research
2 establish a locality, neighbourhood understanding of community as a planning backdrop
3 take stock of existing service distribution, the inheritance of the new unitary authorities, and set goals towards equality of provision between authorities and across localities
4 invest in a cradle-to-grave, multiagency system of person-centred planning to bring together needs assessment and service support across the different arenas of people's lives – home, school, work, leisure, community involvement – and plan and manage life-stage transitions and transitions between service systems
5 involve departments other than health and social care, notably education, employment and housing, as equal partners, centrally and locally, in a way which was never achieved by the AWS
6 redevelop a focus on children which became lost as the AWS became increasingly concerned with deinstitutionalization and the reform of adult day services
7 develop an evidence-based policy on pre-school, primary and secondary educational provision to raise a focus comparable to that on other services
8 clarify the goals of family support and bring a new focus to the means by which support in practice is differentiated according to the goals and development of the family
9 integrate social care and employment policies in relation to the career ambitions both of family carers and people with learning disabilities
10 expand the opportunities for adults with learning disabilities to have homes of their own with support in line with past service provision targets, progressively moving beyond these to promote access to typical lifestyle development

11 develop the technical sophistication of services to ameliorate the impact of learning disabilities, and

12 establish service development mechanisms which involve service recipients and the population of the localities to be served.

If the 'devil is in the detail' as we have suggested, then those charged with framing and implementing policy must either become personally informed of the complexity of required knowledge or use those with such knowledge in strategic roles. Central government arguably did the latter given the influence which the Working Party report had on the policy which launched the AWS. What was much less successful was the use of such a 'technical assistance' model to help field authorities implement the policy. There is now a recognition that broad-brush reform will not result in the quality of outcome that is sought. Local determination of service delivery needs to be balanced by a systematic approach to making sure that services are structurally and operationally well designed, wherever they occur throughout the country. The problem is no different to issues in other areas such as improving academic attainment, literacy, numeracy and teaching standards. Here, the new government has shown a willingness to back policy objectives with expert teams to advise local authorities and particular establishments. A similar commitment to backing the wide-ranging policy objectives in learning disabilities with an advisory structure that gives those with expertise a role to help authorities implement best practice is long overdue.

References

Abrams, P. (1978). Community care: some research problems and priorities. In: *Social Care Research*, (J. Barnes and N. Connelly, eds) pp. 78–99. London: Bedford Square Press.

Barnes, M. and Wistow, G. (1992). *Researching User Involvement*. Leeds: Nuffield Institute for Health Services Studies, University of Leeds.

Bradshaw, J. (1972). The concept of need. *New Society*, 30 March, pp. 640–643.

Browne, M. (1996). Needs assessment and community care. In: *Needs Assessment in Public Policy*, (J. Percy-Smith, ed.) pp. 49–65. Buckingham: Open University Press.

Bulmer, M. (1987). *The Social Basis of Community Care*. London: Allen and Unwin.

Cambridge, P. and Knapp, M. (1997). At what cost? Using cost information for purchasing and providing community care for people with learning disabilities. *British Journal of Learning Disabilities*, **25**, 7–12.

Coote, A. (1993). *Bridging the Gap between 'Them' and 'Us': Developing New Social Rights*. London: Institute of Public Policy Research Rivers Oram Press.

Department of Health (1990). *Community Care in the Next Decade and Beyond: Policy Guidance*. London: HMSO.

Department of Health and Social Security (DHSS) (1971). *Better Services for the Mentally Handicapped*. London: HMSO.

Dowson, S. (1997). Empowerment within services: a comfortable delusion. In: *Empowerment in Everyday Life: Learning Disability*, (P. Ramcharan, G. Roberts, G. Grant, and J. Borland, eds) pp. 101–120. London: Jessica Kingsley.

Ellis, K. (1993). *Squaring the Circle: User and Carer Participation in Needs Assessment*. London: Joseph Rowntree.

Emerson, E. and Hatton, C. (1994). *Moving Out: Relocation from Hospital to Community*. London: HMSO.

Grant, G. (1997). Consulting to involve or consulting to empower? In: *Empowerment in Everyday Life: Learning Disability*, (P. Ramcharan, G. Roberts, G. Grant and J. Borland, eds) pp. 121–143. London: Jessica Kingsley.

Grant, G., McGrath, M. and Ramcharan, P. (1994). How family and informal supporters appraise service quality. *International Journal of Disability, Development and Education*, **41**, 127–141.

Hatton, C. and Emerson, E. (1996). *Residential Provision for People with Learning Disabilities: a Research Review*. Manchester: Hester Adrian Research Centre, University of Manchester.

Henderson, P. and Armstrong, J. (1993). Community development and community care: a strategic approach. In: *Community Care: a Reader*, (J. Bornat, J. Pereira, D. Pilgrim and F. Williams, eds) pp. 327–334. London: Macmillan/Open University Press.

Hoyes, L. and Means, R. (1993). Markets, contracts and social care services: prospects and problems. In: *Community Care: a Reader*, (J. Bornat, J. Pereira, D. Pilgrim and F. Williams, eds) pp. 287–295. London: Macmillan/Open University Press.

LeGrand, J. (1990). Quasi-markets and social policy. *The Economic Journal*, **101**, 1256–1267.

McGrath, M., Ramcharan, P., Grant, G. *et al.* (1997). Care management in Wales: perceptions of front-line workers. *Community Care Management and Review*, **5**, 5–13.

Meethan, K. F. (1995). Empowerment and community care for older people. In: *Power and Participatory Development*, (N. Nelson and S. Wright, eds) p. 133. London: Intermediate Technology Publications.

Morris, J. (1993). *Independent Lives: Community Care and Disabled People*. London: Macmillan.

Nolan, M., Grant, G. and Keady, J. (1996). *Understanding Family Care: a Multidimensional Model of Caring and Coping*. Buckingham: Open University Press.

Oliver, M. (1991). *Understanding Disability: from Theory to Practice*. London: Macmillan.

Parry-Jones, B., Grant, G., McGrath, M. *et al.* (in press). Stress and job satisfaction among social workers, community nurses and community psychiatric nurses: implications for the care management model. *Health and Social Care in the Community*.

Percy-Smith, J. (1996). Conclusion: themes and issues. In: *Needs Assessment in Public Policy*, (J. Percy-Smith, ed.) pp. 143–145. Buckingham: Open University Press.

Ramcharan, P. (1994). *A Review of Social Care Plans 1993–6 in Wales*. Bangor, Centre for Social Policy Research and Development, University of Wales Bangor.

Rioux, M. (1994). Towards a concept of well-being: overcoming the social and legal construction of inequality. In: *Disability is Not Measles: New Research Paradigms in Disability*, (M. Rioux and M. Bach, eds) pp. 67–108. North York, Ontario: Roeher Institute.

Roberts, G. (1997). Empowerment and community care: some of the legal issues. In: *Empowerment in Everyday Life: Learning Disability*, (P. Ramcharan, G. Roberts, G. Grant and J. Borland, eds) pp. 156–171. London: Jessica Kingsley.

Roeher Institute (1991). *The Power to Choose: an Examination of Service Brokerage and Individualized Funding as Implemented by the Community Living Society*. Toronto: The Roeher Institute.

Roeher Institute (1993). *Direct Dollars: a Study of Individualized Funding in Canada*. Toronto: The Roeher Institute.

Sanderson, I. (1996). Needs and public services. In: *Needs Assessment in Public Policy*. (J. Percy-Smith, ed.) pp. 11–31. Buckingham: Open University Press.

Secretaries of State for Health, Social Security, Wales and Scotland (1989). *Caring for People: Community Care in the Next Decade and Beyond*. London: HMSO.

Smale, G., Tuson, G., Ahmad, B. *et al.* (1994). *Negotiating Care in the Community: the Implications of Research Findings on Community Based Practice for the Implementation of the Community Care and Children Acts*. London: HMSO.

Social Services Inspectorate (1991a). *Care Management and Assessment: Practitioners' Guide*. London: HMSO.

Social Services Inspectorate (1991b). *Care Management and Assessment: Managers' Guide*. London: HMSO.

Welsh Office (1983). *All Wales Strategy for the Development of Services for Mentally Handicapped People*. Cardiff: Welsh Office.

Welsh Office (1996). *The Welsh Mental Handicap Strategy: Guidance 1994*. Cardiff: Welsh Office.

Welsh Office (1997). *Community Care (Direct Payments) Act: Policy and Practice Guidance, March 1997*. Cardiff: Welsh Office.

Wistow, G., Knapp, M., Hardy, B. and Allen, C. (1994). *Social Care in a Mixed Economy*. Buckingham: Open University Press.

Author index

Subject index